ROBERT J. JOHNSON
257 WEST 6TH SOUTH
LOGAN, UTAH

MORMON FORTUNE BUILDERS

AND HOW THEY DID IT.

MORMON FORTUNE BUILDERS

AND HOW THEY DID IT.

BY LEE NELSON

Council Press

Dedication

Dedicated to those who made this book possible by sharing with me the success stories that appear on the following pages.

Published by Council Press
209 North 400 West
Provo, Utah 84601

ISBN 0-936860-08-1

Printed in the United States of America
First printing November 1981

Contents

Foreword

The purpose of this book is to give the reader a better understanding of what it takes to be successful, financially and otherwise, by allowing the reader to look into the lives of 11 individuals who have achieved remarkable successes.

All of the individuals featured in the Mormon Fortune Builders are self-made millionaires, having started with little or no money of their own. All are active members of the Church of Jesus Christ of Latter-day Saints, and were active while achieving their business successes.

The Mormon Fortune Builders is a book about success, not in a general sense, but specifically as success relates to the entrepreneur, the individual who risks time, talent and money with the expectation of earning a profit.

Although each story is different in its content (names, dates, places, types of businesses), the same basic elements of success appear again and again. The careful reader will recognize a repeating pattern of success, a reoccurrence of applied principles or secrets which enabled the individuals in this book to succeed.

What is an entrepreneur?

I first remember hearing the word, entrepreneur, during

a study group meeting at the beginning of my first year in the Master of Business Administration (MBA) program at Brigham Young University. It was the fall of 1967 and members of my study group were expressing career aspirations, mostly dreams of scooting quickly up corporate ladders to top levels of management, and receiving the accompanying top salaries.

One classmate said he wasn't interested in the corporate ladder. He said, "I want to be an entrepreneur, not a corporate monkey." I remember wondering what an entrepreneur was. I guessed that it probably had a common root with the word enterprise, but that little insight didn't help me to understand what my classmate was talking about.

I went to the nearest dictionary. It defined an entrepreneur as a person who organizes and manages a business undertaking, assuming the risk for the sake of profit. Now I knew what my friend was talking about. An entrepreneur is the person who starts and runs businesses, the one all the rest of us work for—the one who takes the risk in the hope that he will earn a profit.

I remembered several times in my life when I had been an entrepreneur, but not on the grand scale my classmate was talking about—like the time when our family visited Yellowstone National Park. Firecrackers were cheap, plentiful and legal in Wyoming. In my home state of California they were illegal and scarce. I was only 11 years old, but quickly recognized the profit potential of smuggling Wyoming firecrackers back to California in the trunk of my parents' car. I doubled my investment in a few short weeks while holding back enough inventory to last through several New Year's Eve and July 4th celebrations.

At age 18, while in basic training in the U.S. Marine Corps, I again became an entrepreneur. During the frequent inspections I noticed that even though my comrades and I had glossy boots, carefully starched and pressed clothing, immaculate rifles, polished buckles and clean-shaven faces, our helmet liners were a scuffy dull grey. There didn't seem to be any way to clean up and polish a tarnished aluminum helmet.

During the first furlough to Washington, D.C., I purchased several aerosol cans of silver paint. At the next inspection my helmet looked brand new. As soon as we were dismissed, the other soldiers in my platoon began lining up at my bunk to get their helmets painted, too. I charged 50 cents each and could paint two or three a minute. I painted about 15 helmets with one 79-cent can of paint, almost a 1,000 percent return on my investment!

Soon everyone in the platoon had a shiny helmet, and we looked so sharp on the parade ground, that men from other platoons began lining up at my bunk until I ran out of paint. One nice thing about the business was that the helmets became scuffed and dingy after several days of use and needed to be painted again. I had dreams of becoming financially independent by the time basic training was over.

My dreams were short-lived. The next time we had furlough, about ten other guys went into nearby towns and loaded up on spray paint. My monopoly disappeared overnight as other soldiers began to offer helmet painting services. The price of a paint job dropped to 25 cents, and there were so many guys doing it that I couldn't maintain enough volume to make it worth my while. I got out of the business.

Two years later I ran into a similar opportunity while serving as a missionary for the Mormon Church in Germany. I discovered that one of the things American missionaries missed most, with the exception of girlfriends, was peanut butter. The Germans ate very little of this, so it was generally not available on store shelves. The fortunate missionary who received a jar of Skippy from home, shipped airmail across the Atlantic Ocean, was the envy of the other missionaries. I decided to do something about the peanut butter shortage.

I approached the manager of the largest grocery store in town, suspecting he might not even know the meaning of the word, "Erdnus Butter." I was wrong. Not only did he know what peanut butter was, but said he could order it from his distributor if I wanted some. I ordered a whole case.

As soon as word got out that Elder Nelson had an entire case of peanut butter stashed under his bed, the orders started pouring in, and I had the beginnings of a nice little business. When the case was about half gone, however, I began to feel guilty about making a profit at the expense of my fellow missionaries. Their friends and relatives back home were sacrificing to keep them in the mission field, and I just couldn't feel good about taking their money.

I liquidated the remaining jars at cost, and spent the rest of my mission selling the product I had come there to sell in the first place, the Gospel of Jesus Christ.

As I explored the meaning of the word entrepreneur through these personal experiences, I began to appreciate my classmate's goal. He was shooting for the top of the business world. He wanted to be the person at the top of the ladder, the one who makes it all happen, the one for whom everyone else is working.

On the surface, the MBA curriculum did not appear to prepare me or my classmates in the art of making money or becoming entrepreneurs, except indirectly through some of the information learned in basic courses in accounting, economics and computer science. The thrust of the program seemed to be preparing us to work for large corporations as employees. There was a feeling that the MBA graduate was destined to become a corporate executive. As I think back on the experience, however, I believe the intense pressure applied by the teachers, combined with the fierce competition among students was an excellent basic training ground for the prospective entrepreneur. Students became tough and self-confident, two essential traits of successful entrepreneurs.

Upon finishing school I followed the lead of my classmates and went to work for a big company, in my case Ford Motor Company in Dearborn, Michigan. I soon noticed that amidst all the struggling for grade advancement and salary increases, no one seemed to be in the business of making money. I suppose the top executives who made the key production and marketing decisions could be called entrepreneurs, but no one else in the company saw enough of the total picture to be in the business of earning a profit. For every top executive with moneymaking responsibilities there were thousands of others in support functions, important and necessary functions, but still support functions for the entrepreneurs upstairs who called the shots and had the fun. I concluded that a big company was not the right place for someone who didn't want to wait 20 years or longer for a possible chance to sit in the driver's seat.

A few years later when I moved to Montana to run a car and truck dealership, I began to meet some real entrepreneur—owners of small businesses; independent people who were their own bosses; people involved in retailing, construction, real estate, and publishing. These small-town entrepreneurs were different from the Ford executives. The little guys dressed as they pleased, kept their own hours, went fishing or elk hunting when they felt like it, and didn't hesitate to express their political or religious opinions without fear of how it might affect their careers.

Many of these small-town entrepreneurs didn't know what an MBA was, and didn't even know the meaning of the word entrepreneur—but many of them made a lot more money than their corporate counterparts. Nobody ever told me *that* in MBA school! I became friends with a car dealer who made over $100,000 a year selling Oldsmobiles and Cadillacs. On the side, he bought and sold cattle ranches, which I think was more profitable for him than the car business. I knew a publisher who made over $7,000 a week on a weekly newspaper-shopper, and that wasn't the most profitable of his publishing ventures. He had a twin-engine airplane to carry him around to his numerous real estate investments. He was a Jewish, born-again Christian law school graduate who was so busy making money that he had never bothered to take the state bar exams to practice law.

I hadn't been in the backwoods of Montana very long before I concluded that successful small-town entrepreneurs lived better than their corporate counterparts. In many cases they made more money, were their own bosses, worked fewer hours and lived where they wanted to live.

Of course, I also noticed plenty of small-town entrepreneurs who didn't make a lot of money, and whose businesses were struggling. I began to wonder what the differences were between the successful ones, the less successful ones, and the failures. I thought that if I could isolate the differences, I would have a better chance of succeeding in my own endeavors. By that time I had decided to focus my career in publishing and writing, and was publisher of a monthly tabloid publication called the *Bitterroot Journal.*

As I observed these small-town businessmen, one of the

first things I discovered was that length of formal schooling seemed to have little bearing on success. Even at Ford I knew a fellow with a PhD who reported to a man who hadn't gone to college. I don't think my rich car dealer friend graduated from high school, whereas the successful publisher had a law degree. The businesses owned by people with doctoral degrees seemed to go broke just as easily as those owned by high school dropouts.

On the other hand, the most successful entrepreneurs seemed to be very knowledgeable in their chosen fields of business. Without exception, they seemed to know more about their business than did their less successful competitors. I concluded that successful entrepreneurs were good learners, eager to study and digest new information. Traditional schooling with its degrees and grades seemed meaningless to the enterprising individual if the schooling had not made him a good learner.

It takes money to make money.

As I began studying small businesses, I often heard the statement, "It takes money to make money." I think many people misunderstand this statement to mean that the successful business person needs a fat inheritance or a rich uncle. This statement simply means that most successful businesses need operating capital, which is generally tough to get—especially for a new, unproven business. Somehow, the determined entrepreneur usually finds a way to get his operating capital—by begging, borrowing, floating checking accounts, or selling stock or partnerships. The majority of individuals I studied, and everyone featured in this book, started out in meager circumstances, with little or no start-up capital of their own.

Once I concluded that the obvious outward "success" symbols, like money and schooling, were not key ingredients to becoming a successful entrepreneur, I began to look at inner qualities—character traits, personal habits, behavioral patterns and personality, in my efforts to discover the secrets of success.

What the scriptures say about success and wealth.

One Saturday afternoon in 1974, during the opening song of an LDS Church stake leadership meeting in Missoula, Montana, a simple idea entered my mind—an idea so clear, so basic, I knew it had to be correct.

I had been pondering several scriptures which seemed to indicate that the Lord did indeed have a formula for success, which applied not only to spiritual salvation, but to worldly undertakings. In Joshua, the Lord makes it clear that the paths of righteousness lead to worldly success. "This book of the law ... thou shalt meditate therein day and night, that thou mayest observe to do according to all that is written therein: for then thou shalt make thy way prosperous, and then thou shalt have good success." (Joshua 1:8)

The same idea, that righteousness results in success and wealth, is mentioned frequently in the Book of Mormon, "And now, because of the steadiness of the church they began to be exceeding rich, having abundance of all things...." (Alma 1:29)

The scriptures contain numerous promises of wealth and success for the righteous, but never is poverty presented as a virtue. Historically, it appears that the "piety of poverty" idea was sold to the masses during the middle ages by the predominant church in an effort to forestall discontent and revolution among the destitute masses. Christ never taught such doctrine, nor did his apostles.

C. Douglas Beardall said of poverty, "Poverty fills prisons with thieves and murderers. It drives men and women to drink, divorce, prostitution, dope addiction and even suicide. It drives potentially fine, talented, intelligent children to delinquency and crime. It makes people do things they otherwise would never dream of doing." (*Latter-day Bondage*, page 4)

Brigham Young said, "My policy is to get rich.... Do I want to become rich in the things of this earth? Yes, if the Lord wishes me to have such riches, and I can use them to good advantage." (*Discourses of Brigham Young*, page 310)

When I mentioned to one of my fellow publishers that I was putting together this book, he tried to discourage me,

saying the masses, particularly Mormons, should not be
encouraged to achieve financial independence, that financial success corrupts, that people are better off in poor,
struggling conditions. He told me these things as he was
about to go to lunch in his new Mercedes Benz. He
mentioned Jesus's statement that, "It is easier for a camel
to go through the eye of a needle, than for a rich man to
enter into the kingdom of God." (Mark 10:25)

We didn't talk about the discovery of the small opening
in the Jerusalem wall which was called the "eye of the
needle." A camel could pass through the "eye of the needle",
but only on its knees.

If Jesus's statement is read in context with preceding
verses, one discovers that he is talking about, "them that
trust in riches." (Mark 10:24) In the Old Testament, King
David talks about those who trust in riches, "Lo, this is the
man that made not God his strength; but trusted in the
abundance of his riches, and strengthened himself in his
wickedness." (Psalms 52:7)

In the New Testament, Paul summed up the problem of
riches in his letter to Timothy. "Charge them that are rich
in this world, that they be not high-minded, nor trust in
uncertain riches, but in the living God, who giveth us richly
all things to enjoy." (I Timothy 6:17)

The conclusion seems obvious. Riches don't corrupt. It is
the love of riches that corrupts. Riches are both permissible
and desirable, if one can keep love of God and service to
fellow men in first place, if one can maintain priorities.

I suppose I should offer a warning at this point. If you,
the reader, think you are the kind of person who would be
corrupted by wealth, then you shouldn't want to be an
entrepreneur. You shouldn't read this book. Successful
entrepreneurs make lots of money. Different professions
have different primary objectives, and success is measured
by the obtaining of those objectives. A successful teacher
educates and molds the lives of his students. A successful
doctor heals people. A successful runner wins races. A
successful cook produces mouth-watering meals. Likewise,
a successful entrepreneur produces profits. There are plenty
of side benefits like providing jobs, and goods and services—but the main incentive for entering a business venture
is the earning of a profit, often at substantial risk. Those

not interested in earning profits make poor entrepreneurs, and should work for someone else as an employee.

As I contemplated the scriptures concerning wealth and success, there was one nagging problem. I knew a lot of pious, good Christians who were poor—people who seemingly lived all the commandments, paid their tithes, said their prayers, attended all their meetings; yet were not blessed with the things of this world.

It occurred to me that perhaps the Lord didn't automatically pour out riches on the heads of those who followed him, that perhaps those followers had to do something on their own to earn the blessings of success. The Lord told Moses, "But thou shalt remember the Lord thy God: for it is he that giveth thee power to get wealth." (Deuteronomy 8:18) The Lord gives the *power* to get the wealth. He doesn't dole it out.

There are good people who exercise this "power" to get wealth, and there are other good people who do not exercise the power. I began to wonder how one obtained and used this power. Perhaps the Lord had a formula for success, possibly the ultimate success formula of the universe. Surely, if anyone understood the secrets of success, God did.

These questions about success had been coming in and out of my conscious mind for years, but as I sat in that leadership meeting in Missoula, Montana, on that Saturday afternoon, suddenly there was an answer—so clear, so simple, so obvious, that I knew it was right. It really wasn't a new idea, but a new way to look at an old, well-established idea.

The thought occurred to me that if the Lord had a success formula that could lead people to eternal salvation—a formula of faith, repentance, baptism and the gift of the Holy Ghost—it seemed only logical that the same basic success formula could be applied to any worthy endeavor, including the business objectives of the entrepreneur.

I compared God's salvation formula, the first four principles of the Gospel, against the successful people I had been observing. There was no question that the first principle, faith, was a key ingredient in the lives of these successful people. Without exception, these individuals had what appeared to be an unshakeable faith in themselves

and their ability to succeed in their chosen fields. Faith is
synonymous with will, and according to Joseph Smith is
the "assurance which men have of the existence of things
which they have not seen, and the principle of action in all
intelligent beings." (*Lectures on Faith*, page 7) Faith is
developed by doing hard things, by overcoming fears, by
constant striving, by fasting and prayer, through preparation.

Applying the principle of repentance to the lives of
successful entrepreneurs required more thought on my part.
But as I realized that repentance was nothing more than a
"churchy" word meaning to change, to learn, to adjust, I
concluded that it, too, was a common trait among successful
people. I had already discovered that successful individuals
knew and understood more about their chosen fields than
did their less successful competitors. They had learned
more, had adjusted more, had *repented* more than did their
competitors.

Even the third principle of salvation, baptism, had a
direct application to success. There are numerous symbols
of commitment in our society, such as the signature on an
agreement, the handshake, the hand over the heart in the
pledge of allegiance. Baptism in water is nothing more than
a symbol of commitment used in joining a Christian church
and promising to keep commandments. Baptism is a
commitment, and I certainly had to agree that the making
of, and sticking to commitments is a characteristic of
successful entrepreneurs—the ability to make a decision,
then stay on course when the going gets tough, not giving
in when things aren't working out right. Successful entrepreneurs are people capable of exercising a high level of
commitment in their lives.

The fourth principle, the gift of the Holy Ghost, didn't at
first seem to fit the pattern as easily as the other three
principles. Most of the successful entrepreneurs I knew at
that time were not members of the LDS Church and had not
been given the gift of the Holy Ghost as a constant
comforter and guide. My first thought was that this portion
of the Lord's success formula would not apply to non-LDS
people.

I thought about the Holy Ghost in terms of some of the
things I had read in success books—references to a sixth

sense, the subconscious mind, the lucky hunch, that general feeling of well-being, of having one's universe in order, that inner feeling that one is on the right track. Many success writers had already recognized the Holy Ghost as an ingredient of success, only they had called it by different names.

To this day I have no idea what was talked about in that leadership meeting. I only know that it was one of the most significant learning experiences of my life. I had discovered the Lord's formula for success—a formula that could be applied to business, athletics, science, parenting and any worthy field of endeavor. I knew I was onto something important, something significant enough to be featured in a book someday. But first I had to gain a better understanding of the formula by testing it in my own life, and observing it at work in the lives of others.

It wasn't until five years later that I began to study successful entrepreneurs in earnest. I had moved to Utah and was writing and publishing books. Council Press wanted to publish the results of my interviews.

Since the successful formula had close parallels with the Gospel of Jesus Christ, I decided to focus my studies on successful Mormon entrepreneurs, individuals who had started without any money, were active in the Church while achieving their successes, and had become financially independent through their own efforts. It didn't take long for me to discover that there were literally hundreds and perhaps thousands of individuals who met these basic requirements. In fact, I could have filled an entire book writing about individuals from my own little community of Mapleton, Utah, with a population of only 3,000 people!

My plan was to interview the subjects in detail about their business successes, then write the stories in the first-person point of view as they were told to me. I wanted readers to feel as if they were hearing the stories first hand, to feel almost like they were in a private, relaxed conversation with a successful entrepreneur who was telling the reader how he had achieved his success.

Getting appointments to interview successful individuals was more difficult than I had expected. Some of them were very busy and could only be reached through secretaries and administrative assistants. Many had unlisted phone numbers, making contact even more difficult.

Some of the people I contacted didn't want their stories published, for various reasons. One man cancelled his appointment to be interviewed at the request of his teenage son who didn't want the kids at school to know he was rich. One of the more well-known individuals I contacted said he didn't qualify as a Mormon entrepreneur because he had recently been excommunicated from the Church.

Another individual, who owned a very profitable business, declined because he felt the story might attract competitors and unwanted public exposure. He died a few months after the interview would have taken place. Now his success story will be lost forever, except for a few miscellaneous entries in family journals.

Those who agreed to have their stories published, did so without any expectation of payment. They talked to me because they agreed with me that their stories would offer enlightenment and encouragement to others attempting to become successful.

I tried to gather a wide variety of success stories. It would have been very easy to fill the book with stories of people who made fortunes in real estate. There are several real estate stories in the book. There are more manufacturing stories covering a wide range of products, from computerized control valves and automatic potato sorters to herbal tablets and plastic catheters. There are publishing, direct sales and advertising success stories, too. There are accounts of agonizing defeats and glorious victories—some bad breaks and some fantastic streaks of good luck.

And through it all, there is a silver thread, a common theme, a pattern of success—faith, repentance (learning and changing), commitment, and an ability to receive guidance from beyond the five senses. In the chapters of this book, every reader will see the Lord's success formula at work in the lives of daring risk takers or entrepreneurs. The serious reader can gain understanding and encouragement that will help him or her achieve comparable, if not greater, successes.

Doug Snarr—a stuttering Idaho farm boy who built a million-dollar billboard advertising business covering nine states. Today he is the majority stock holder, the executive officer, and one of the principal speakers for Positive Thinking Rallies, Inc.

Douglas Snarr

Part I

"Doug, it's in you! I can see it, I can hear it, I can feel it; and when the day comes that you see it, that you hear it, that you feel it, *nothing will stop you!*"

Those words, to this day, still ring in my ears. Coach McHargue (W.H. "Walt" McHargue), my high school boxing coach, gave me confidence. He taught me how to win. Because he taught me how to win with my fists, I later became convinced I could win with my tongue.

My story began with me sitting on the back row in the classroom, hoping beyond hope that I would never be asked to participate in any classroom discussion. The phenomenon of talking was beyond my capability. I was an inveterate stutterer.

I cannot remember when the stuttering began. I only know that I always had the impediment, and as time went on, the stuttering and stammering increased in intensity.

All through school I experienced the same disillusionment—the harder I tried to talk, the stronger the habit gripped me. So I avoided all situations requiring speech and channeled my energies, instead, into using my hands—my fists for boxing and my fingers for painting signs.

We lived on a farm in eastern Idaho, five miles west of Idaho Falls. Our farm was on a hill, and as I looked out across the valley and saw the lights scintillating from the far-off buildings of Idaho Falls, I knew I had to go. I was in the ninth grade.

I walked to the big city. Along with three other boys, I tried for a job as janitor and stockroom boy at J.J. Newberry's local five-and-dime store. I knew I was the best person for the job, but I wasn't going to take any chances. The other kids could talk. So I approached the manager with a bargain. I told him I would do all his sign painting after hours at no extra charge, if he hired me. After showing him my art samples, I got the job. Deep down, I felt that he gave me the job because of the pain and anguish I suffered in attempting to converse and explain my proposition. Nevertheless, Howard Thompson gave me my first break.

At this time I found the prettiest girl in the high school, irresistible. Through a friend, who served as my mouth-piece, a date was arranged. I remember walking up the sidewalk to her home—a beautiful, two-story colonial structure with shutters and imposing columns, on a hill back from the street. It was a long walk to the front porch.

By the time I reached the door, I was petrified. Her father answered the doorbell, and after sizing me up asked,

"And young man, what is your name?"

I struggled and fought for the power to speak, but nothing came out but sweat.

Finally, after what seemed an eternity, my secret love came floating down the staircase in a most elegant dress. With graciousness bordering on sublimity, she casually called out,

"Oh, Dad, meet Doug Snarr."

The unbearable burden was lifted from my shoulders. I smiled and shook hands, but inside I was bleeding.

I think she had a great time. She did all the talking. I did, however, manage to sandwich in a couple of words. I told her I was going to marry her. In one date I had fallen irrevocably in love. I was a sophomore.

I started then and there to decide how I could make enough money to support her. Behind the drawing board I worked incessantly to master the brush. Desire burned deep.

My grandfather Snarr perceived my ambition to succeed and taught me one of my greatest lessons in life.

"Doug, there are two ways to make money: man at work, and money at work. You are a high school student, and you'd better start figuring out right now how you can get money working for you so that you can always be assured of an income. If you play your cards right, by the time you are 40 years old, you can be self-sufficient. But the first thing to remember is, don't eat the 'seed corn.'

"Now there are many ways to earn 'seed corn.' The best way is to start your own business, build up ownership, then take the 'seed corn,' the capital, and plow it into situations that produce income. Always remember, money at work."

So at age 17, while a senior in high school, I went into business for myself. My father loaned me $50.00 which I repaid in two months.

It took about 15 seconds to figure out the name of my new company. I wasn't interested in names like Acme, Apex, Supreme, Triple A. I called my new company "Snarr Sign Company." I painted a big sign with my name on it, stood back, took a long look, and felt good all over.

Next, I painted special selling samples, and using Newberry as a reference, I started up and down Main Street of Idaho Falls looking for customers.

It quickly became apparent that, like Moses, I needed an Aaron, a mouthpiece. I worked out a deal with my best friend, 40 percent for him and 60 percent for me. I had to have the control, and Don Bybee, my sparring partner, became my business partner.

We were a great team. We worked hard and never argued. He brought in the business, and I cranked out the signs. We were making money and our names were fast becoming known in Idaho Falls and the nearby country towns.

But I was not satisfied, not deep inside. More than anything in the world I wanted to be able to stand on the doorstep of my girlfriend's home and say to her father, without stuttering,

"Good evening, sir. My name is Doug Snarr."

The desire to speak became a passion, and then a blinding obsession, until I was consumed day in and day out with a longing, yearning, craving—for the gift of speech.

I remember the fascination I experienced as I watched Don sell signs. I stood back, out of the way, observing and carefully watching his lips move, and marvelling at the magic of the words tumbling effortlessly from his mouth.

I was amazed how the speaking process never crossed his mind. He never talked about talking. Conversely, the phenomenon of speech absorbed my waking moments. I never heard anyone express appreciation for the power of speech. Somehow, that universal taking-for-granted-the-privilege-of-speech bothered me.

Why didn't my partner let his hair down and yell out at the top of his voice,

"Hey, I can talk! I'm the luckiest man in the world!"

I was told a thousand times by well-meaning friends, relatives, teachers, and others,

"You can do anything you want to do in this world. If you want to speak, just make up your mind and go out and speak!"

But I learned that such statements can be a gross oversimplification. I always asked the same question,

"How do I talk without stuttering?"

Never did I receive a constructive answer, but rather,

"Oh, talk real slow."

"Make sure you take a deep breath before you speak."

"Just don't get excited and you'll be all right."

One of my father's hired hands on the farm once advised,

"Stamp your right foot with each word and you will be able to speak."

The summer following my graduation, I investigated various universities and colleges throughout Idaho and Utah, hoping to find a school that could help me with my speech impediment. I decided upon Brigham Young University in Provo, Utah. By the end of the summer, the business had produced enough money for me to go to B.Y.U. to learn to talk.

I enrolled in a special speech class for stutterers only. I also enrolled in a scripture class, a requirement for all students.

I'll never forget the first day in the scripture class. The custom was to begin the class with prayer. The instructor, not knowing any of the students, looked at his roll and arbitrarily called upon Doug Snarr to give the prayer.

As usual, I was in the far corner of the back row, hoping I would not be seen. When I heard my name called, I reluctantly walked to the front of the class, folded my arms, bowed my head, and once again fought the battle. Nothing came out—just a sweat-drenched silence.

The teacher, perceiving my plight, came over, put his arm around me, bowed his head, and said the prayer for me. On walking back to my seat at the far end of the room, I felt the furtive glances, the stares. Again, I knew how a freak must feel.

As we left the classroom, the instructor pulled me over to the side saying,

"Please continue to come to my class. I will never call on you to speak again. I promise you that. Please come."

I was grateful for his concern, but his solution to my problem was not the answer for me, and I knew it. Somehow, if ever I was to compete in this world, the gift and privilege and blessing of speaking had to be realized, I had to learn how to talk.

I went into the special speech therapy class with high hopes. I was given a battery of tests. Following the tests, I was interviewed by the head of the department. He was kind and gracious as he told me that science does not know why people stutter. He explained that stuttering is not a disgrace and that everyone has a problem. Some problems are more obvious than others. The apostle Paul had a thorn in the side. Some people have a finger missing, a wart on the end of their nose, a blind eye; and generally the solution to the problem is to learn to develop the proper attitude so that the problem doesn't destroy you—learn to live with the problem.

He told me many stories about success and how people made the best of their predicaments. He concluded by saying,

"Here at B.Y.U. we cannot cure you of your stuttering, but we can teach you how to live with the impediment and can help to integrate you into society where you will succeed and be a socially secure and sound person."

It sounded good. It sounded logical; but it was wrong, and I knew it was wrong. He was asking me to quit, give up, surrender to stuttering and all of the limitations stuttering would impose upon me in life before I even started to fight. I was told that my impediment was extremely severe and that I would always be a stutterer.

I asked him if he had ever stuttered in his life. He said no, and I then somehow told him,

"You don't know how I feel, or how anyone else feels who suffers from stuttering; and if it's the last thing I do, I will learn to speak."

I knew I was talking to the wrong man, and as I got up and walked away, I felt so low!

The dream of an easy classroom solution had come to naught. The hope that somewhere within the framework of an esteemed university, filled with distinguished professors with endless credentials, I would find the secret to my success, evaporated before my eyes. I was alone on the street facing the hard reality.

My stuttering worsened, and I was reduced to writing on a pad when I wanted to communicate. I would even go out of my way to avoid someone I knew. I just crossed the street or turned my back so that I would not be recognized nor feel compelled to talk.

At the end of the school year, I found myself in a barber shop. While waiting my turn, I was browsing through the dog-eared magazines. In one magazine I noticed a small ad. Two words caught my eye, *"stuttering"* and *"free."* An address was listed where one could write for information on how to be cured of stuttering. I immediately dashed off a letter to the Benjamin N. Bogue Institute for Speech Correction, Indianapolis, Indiana.

In two weeks I received a package filled with testimonials from all kinds of people who had learned to stop stuttering. I devoured the letters of success and exploded with enthusiasm to take the course. I hitchhiked from Provo to Idaho Falls, about 300 miles, and told my parents I was going to go and get cured.

Being responsible and concerned, they checked out the Bogue Institute by calling Ricks College at Rexburg, the University of Idaho at Moscow, and Idaho State University at Pocatello. They were told that the Bogue Institute was a school of quackery and that Bogue had no credentials. He was neither recognized nor did he have a degree from a suitable university in speech correction. He was a loner who had stuttered as a child and who claimed to have developed a method by which he was able to cure himself. That method became the basis for his course. My parents were told that the course was a gimmick, that it would not work.

The tuition was $1,000, and I was informed that if I wanted to go I would have to pay my own way. I told my parents I was going even if I had to crawl!

It was May, and I wrote to Mr. Bogue that I would be there the first part of September. I got together with Don Bybee, my mouthpiece, and we clearly defined the objective.

"Come hell or high water, at the end of August we will have enough money to pay for that tuition!"

We agreed that there could be no dates, no movies—just work.

The words of my grandfather Snarr kept coming back to me.

"Man at work and money at work."

I decided that, in addition to painting wall signs, window banners, signs on the sides of trucks, store fronts, etc., I would go out on the highways, rent locations, build billboards, and sell advertising space. From the billboards I would collect rental income over a three- or four-year period. That way I could have money making money for me while I was back at the school for stutterers.

By September we had cleared enough money so that I had that $1,000. In addition to that, we had built five billboards which would earn monthly rental income for three years. Money at work!

My father knew I did not have enough money to pay the train fare, so he gave me a round-trip ticket, for which I was very grateful. As I stepped aboard the old steam train at Pocatello, he said,

"Doug, you had better come back talking a lot better than you're going!"

Upon my arrival in Indianapolis, I was greeted at the train depot by Mr. Bogue's secretary, who arranged an interview.

Mr. Bogue's office was simple. He stood about five feet ten inches tall and was crowned with a full head of white hair. He was in his early seventies and was exceedingly affable. He took me in and said,

"Welcome to the Bogue Institute, Doug Snarr. I know
you have worked hard and have sacrificed in order to come
here. Someday you will look back and realize that the
decision to come here was the most important decision of
your life."

His words were strong, reassuring, positive, and sensi-
ble. He continued,

"When we are through with you, you will be able to talk,
and I assure you that you will be a success in life."

He conditioned me; he prepared me; he gave me hope—
and I believed. I was unable to restrain myself, and I wept
openly.

Next, I met my teacher, Mrs. Meyers, who was in her late
seventies and was blind. The classroom was located in a
poor section of town, up about three flights of rickety,
wooden stairs lighted by incandescent light bulbs. A
microphone stood at the far end, and folding chairs rimmed
the three walls. Of the six students, I was the youngest.

Mr. Bogue's theory regarding stuttering was very simple. Since the problem is not a physical disability, it must be
a mental problem. Being a mental problem, stuttering can
be corrected. The question was not one of overcoming the
impediment, but rather to forget the past—to take a fresh,
clean slate and start over again as if you had never spoken
at all.

Our first assignment was to be completely silent for ten
days—not to utter a sound, under any condition, at any
time, for ten days. If one needed to communicate, the
instruction was to write on a pad like a deaf mute and to
communicate only through the written word.

The results were interesting. The terrible pressures
incidental to speaking were immediately lifted, and a
marvelous sense of relief set in. To a minor degree, it was
even a forgetting, a dimming, a partial loss of memory of all
those countless and painful failures. The escape was
exhilarating.

At the end of ten days I was told I would learn how to
speak as a little child learns. I was to be "re-programmed!"

The first thing we learned was how to breathe properly.
We learned to take a big breath of air at the beginning of
every single syllable—not every word, but every syllable.
Inhale only through the nose—nose for breathing and

mouth for speaking.

Ironically, stutterers can sing. They can't talk, but they can sing. The reason they can sing without stuttering is because of melody, the process of rhythm, the flowing from one word to another.

Bogue was shrewd enough to understand this and introduced the rhythm process to speaking. As a choir director swings his arms in tempo, I was asked to swing my arm in a half circle in tempo with each spoken syllable. At the commencement of each syllable, and prior to the arm swinging in the half circle, I would press together my thumb and index finger while the remaining three fingers were gripped firmly in the palm of my hand.

The slower, the better; the flatter the monotone, the better; the longer the pauses in between the syllables, the better.

I discovered on the first day after the silence that I could stand before a microphone and enunciate words without stuttering or stammering. I talked so slowly and in such a boring fashioin that no one would listen. But I could talk.

The first few days following the silence were spent mastering difficult sounds. Stutterers always have an especially hard time with consonants such as B, D, K, P, M, and R. And W is murder. We practiced "B©-Ka, B©-Ke, B©-Ki, B©-Ko, B©-Ku," etc.

And Mrs. Meyers, that marvelous, dedicated, altruistic instructor, unable to see a thing, but hearing every sound, inspired all of us.

I can hear her now, imploring,

"Speak slower, Doug, speak slower,"

"Aim for the stars, even if you only hit the treetops."

"Hitch your wagon to a star."

"What I shall be, I am now becoming."

She was a walking encyclopedia of inspirational quotations.

I often think of that little old lady in that rickety, hot room without air conditioning or carpeting. I see her standing with that big smile, all those beautiful wrinkles on her face, bursting with enthusiasm. She lived a full life. Every day she was the first one in the classroom and was always the last to leave.

I was prepared to go through life swinging my arm,

talking slowly, and I would have considered myself the luckiest man in the world.

The cardinal principle was to never speak a syllable without the use of the swinging arm.

I remember going into a "Ma and Pa" greasy-spoon cafe located off the main beat, bent on ordering a hamburger. I walked to the counter and, following the question of the waitress asking for my order, I took a deep breath, swung my arm into position and started to order,

"May I have a ham-bur-ger with ev-er-y-thing ex-cept the on-ions?" My arm was swinging with every syllable.

The waitress was startled. All of the greasy-spooners sitting on the stools along the curved counter stared at me. Moments later when she delivered the hamburger, I couldn't resist the chance to crank up my arm and reply,

"Don't laugh, sis-ter. Some peo-ple talk with their mouths, oth-ers with their arms. Me, I talk with my arm."

Then I placed my arm behind my back and moved my lips as if I were trying to talk. The waitress was bewildered, as were the others who were looking on. I repositioned my arm, and said in that long, drawn-out monotone while swinging my arm,

"See, with-out my arm I can't say a word."

I took the hamburger and left.

My enthusiasm for speaking was untrammeled, and I found myself experimenting in many ways. My favorite place was a little park near the school where I would sit on the bench with a newspaper, over my lap. Under the newspaper my arm would swing back and forth during an exchange with some illustrious "wino." He would usually lie prostrate on a bench, his cap strategically perched to provide shade for his eyes, recalling his war stories with imagination and mountains of exaggeration. I would respond, using every chance to practice hard sounds and difficult words—big, long words like "everywhere", and "somewhere."

After about two months, I began to doubt the magic of the swinging right arm when I experienced moments of relapse. Occasionally, when I would swing my arm, I would again stutter. Fortunately, these moments were infrequent. However, the fact of the relapse disturbed me to such an extent that I dug deep into my own soul. I knew I was struggling for more than speech. I was battling, fighting, warring for survival. I had put everything on the line. I had risked all, and I had to win. I would have rather died than to go home a stutterer.

The moments of failure were so damaging, and my morale so negatively affected that I quickly reached a crisis and wondered if even the Bogue Institute with its re-programming, the arm swinging, and all the hours of practice would free me from the chains of stuttering.

I felt myself sinking deeper and deeper each day as if caught in some undefinable quagmire with no support, grasping frantically for anything, even a straw, but feeling only the suction that pulled me down, down, down to the very depths of hell.

I started to read, study, search, and literally devour everything I could get my hands on. I searched the words of the great minds, searching for that missing link—that ingredient that would make the solution whole, complete, and successful.

Henry David Thoreau talked about people leading lives of "quiet desperation." He also said, "Desperate men do desperate things." I was ready to do something desperate.

Of the many things I had read, the words of Plato drove home the hardest.

"The first and best victory is to conquer self. To be conquered by self is of all things most shameful and vile."

How do you conquer self? I had already done everything in my power. I had followed the rules, adhered to the program, paid the price, and still success was beyond my reach.

I had nightmares of returning home and of having my father sitting me down and saying,

"O.K., Doug, talk!" and having nothing come out.

I needed a miracle. I needed a home run with all the bases loaded.

All my life I had heard about prayer and of the vital role it can play in a person's life. I had listened to many prayers. I had heard stories about how prayers were answered. I had even prayed myself, but it was always the routine kind of prayers made up of phrases others had taught me to say.

I had been taught that there is a God, but I was not convinced that God even knew I existed. I was at the end of

my rope with nowhere to go. I had relied upon man's ways—
the best available—but I knew they were not enough. I
realized that if I were ever going to speak, I needed to use
my knees as well as my arm.

For the first time in my life I really prayed. I pleaded
with God to show me the way. I talked, I pleaded, I begged! I
lost track of time. Finally, when I was completely ex-
hausted, I felt a warm, peaceful reassurance. My spirit had
touched a power. I rose with something extra.

It was Sunday and I felt impressed to go to my church;
so I called a taxi and gave him the address. Unfortunately,
it was late in the afternoon, and when we arrived, the
services were over. The building was empty and the doors
were locked. A small plaque with the name and address of
the elder in charge gave me direction.

The sky was dark, and it was raining fiercely when I
arrived at the elder's home. I asked the taxi driver to wait. A
large man in his thirties greeted me at the door and asked,
"What can I do for you, young man?"

Still standing in the rain, I took a deep breath, lifted my
right arm to its proper position and introduced myself,
speaking one syllable at a time. I told him why I had come
to Indiana and that I wanted to attend church.

After talking with him, I waved the cab on and spent the
rest of my stay in Indianapolis at the home of Wilbur and
Hope Lawrence. They became my parents away from home,
giving me a bed, and, most of all, their hearts.

Two weeks later, the Lawrences decided to travel to
southern Indiana, where both of their parents lived, to
spend the weekend. They invited me to accompany them.

The fall beauty of southern Indiana was in vivid
contrast to eastern Idaho where one's gaze is somewhat
restricted to blue sagebrush, potato vines, and boundless
space.

I spent Saturday night at the home of Mrs. Lawrence's
mother. She immediately became fascinated by my "arm
swinging" business. She wanted to know how the "swinging arm" could produce words out of the mouth. It was the
greasy-spoon restaurant all over again.

She became so excited by the magic of my "talking arm"
that she ran to the phone and called the elder in charge of
the local branch. She asked him if I could give a short talk

the following morning in Sunday School to demonstrate my technique.

My immediate response was, "No, never. I can't do it; I have never done it before." But she, along with the elder in charge of the church, prevailed; and I was scheduled to give my first major talk before the congregation the following morning.

I spent a sleepless night. At times, when I pictured myself facing the congregation, perspiration literally jumped out on my forehead and my back. It would get so bad I would have to get out of bed and take a towel to wipe the sweat from my body. The problem was compounded by the fact that I couldn't think of anything to say.

At the appointed hour the following morning my father-away-from-home, Wilbur Lawrence, introduced me to the congregation and explained that two weeks earlier I had stood at his doorstep in a rainstorm, had introduced myself, and had asked to come in. He told them that I was now their guest and that I had never before spoken before a group and that this was my first talk. He told them that I had always been a stutterer and was going to a special school to learn how to speak all over again. He wisely prepared them with a brief demonstration, then he turned the time over to me.

I reached the podium, stood firmly, took a deep breath, raised my right arm and began to speak.

In that moment I felt a warm, powerful influence attend my presence—a feeling of light and substance. I knew that I could drop my arm, forget the past, and speak out— normally, forcefully, as any other man speaks, just as I had always dreamed of doing. Without question, that moment was the most sublime and joyous in my life. The sweetness and ecstacy transcended all that I had ever known before or since, because I could talk.

I then dropped my arm and told the congregation of my deepest and most secret wish.

I told them that throughout my youth I had wanted to go on a mission for the Church, but I knew that that was impossible. I couldn't go on a mission because I couldn't talk. How could one teach and not talk? How could one convert and not talk? And so the desire remained a hopeless wish.

Whenever the subject of a mission was discussed, I

would communicate, one way or another, "That's not for me; that's for the 'do-gooders.' I've got bigger and better things to do such as to paint signs." But deep inside I dreamed, almost incessantly, of going, of talking, of teaching, and even of converting.

Now, in an instant, cowardice became courage. I knew I could go, and I knew I would be able to talk and to convert.

I testified that God had loosened my tongue. I told the congregation that I was going to go on a mission to let the world know that there is a God who performs miracles. I would tell the world that everyone's wish, if it were righteous, could become a reality if one paid the price and made God his partner.

I choked, I cried, I wept.

When I returned to my seat, I knew that I was just like I had been before. I had to go back and continue to rely upon the arm. But I knew for a surety the greatest reality of all— that God does exist and that I would win my battle against stuttering.

I had experienced a miracle. The simple prayer of a 19-year-old who wanted to speak was heard and was answered.

I reasoned that if God would answer one prayer, He would answer others. Armed with that hope, my entire life was changed. Anxiety, apprehension and doubt vanished, and I knew I was going to make it because God was going to help me. I was no longer alone.

Eventually, I advanced from swinging my arm in a half-circle to putting my hand in my pocket and swinging my index finger. The tempo of my speech had tripled.

I graduated from the "winos" on the park benches to the main street where I would stop and ask all kinds of people many different questions, such as,

"Sir, where is Penn-syl-van-ia Av-en-ue?" while swinging my index finger in perfect time with my faster speech.

I left Indiana enthusiastic and anxious to face the world. I was a lucky man to have come in contact with Mr. Bogue, Mrs. Meyers, the Lawrences, and my God.

Part II
I returned to the sagebrush and to the unrelenting,

blowing winds of eastern Idaho.

I made four decisions: "I am going on a mission!" "I am going to be a millionaire by age 30!" "I am going back to my girlfriend's house and say to her father, 'I'm Doug Snarr!'" "I am going to marry Carol Stanger!!!"

Upon my return, I went directly to Carol's house. I rang the doorbell and once again her father answered.

"Doug, can you talk?" he asked.

I couldn't wait to answer. But to make sure of myself, I decided against the index finger and raised my right arm to the heavens.

"Good-eve-ning-Sir-my-name-is-Doug-Snarr!"

I met with my business partner and told him I no longer needed him to do the talking but that I wanted to stay together, sell together, paint together, work together, and build a great big company. He agreed to remain partners with me.

I visualized hundreds, even thousands of billboards from Canada to Mexico, San Francisco to Kansas City—all property of Snarr Sign Company—each billboard bringing in a monthly income. This was money at work!

Along with going into business in a big way, I decided to get engaged. I went to the biggest jewelry store in Idaho Falls and asked to look at the best diamond ring for sale. The price then, in 1954, was $750. I was shown a beautiful blue diamond. It was flawless. The jeweler sold me on the setting and the stone. I had to have it. I asked him if he would hold it for me for two weeks, and I would be back with a proposition he couldn't resist. He agreed, even though he looked at me rather strangely.

I created a design for a billboard. The main rectangular part of the sign was ten feet high and thirty feet wide. Then I designed a huge diamond ring—a cutout, circling the sign in the most dramatic and eye-catching manner—which extended above and below the rectangle. I made sure the jeweler's name was extra large. He had named the store after himself. I painted the model in vivid colors, an inch-to-a-foot scale.

I figured that by digging the holes and building the sign, myself, I could do it for $250. I put a price of $1030 on the rental space for a three-year period. This would give me, in addition to the diamond ring, enough money to buy the materials.

I warmed up my right index finger. I was vibrating with so much enthusiasm that my mouth literally watered. I arranged an appointment with the jeweler and with my sketch under my arm ran to the store.

Luck was on my side. There wasn't a soul in the store except the owner. Two- and one-half hours later I signed a hand-written agreement promising that I would build the sign for him during the month of June. In April, I walked out of the store with the $750 diamond ring. And Carol Stanger became my fiancee.

I had passed my first real talking test. The index finger worked; I could sell a sign all by myself. I figured that if I could sell one sign, I could sell hundreds.

At age 19 I had finally learned to talk. I spoke slowly, swung the index finger, but I talked.

I built 36 billboards throughout eastern Idaho, bringing in enough rental income to service the debt and to provide enough cash flow to get married. I had purchased a Studebaker pickup, hired three additional men, and had all the business I could handle. The prospects for the future were exceedingly bright.

I visited Carol every day. We were fast making plans for the future. My life was beginning to find order and balance.

Then, during the month I turned 20, I received the most important letter of my life. It was from the Church, asking me to devote two years of my time as a full-time missionary at my own expense, starting in 60 days.

I said goodbye to Carol and my business partner, closed down Snarr Sign Company, and asked my grandfather Snarr to collect the rents. I wished my parents and family well and left for London, England. My first area of assignment was Belfast, Northern Ireland.

I discovered what it was like to shave and bathe in cold water, to get up every morning at 6 a.m. and to have the room so cold and damp that you could take your finger and write your name on the wall in a thin sheet of moisture. I learned to eat smoked herring for breakfast and potatoes prepared five different ways for supper. I learned to drink room-temperature milk, and like it, because refrigerators were unheard of. After a while I could see only the good— the green, the beauty, the charm, the quaintness, the cobblestones, and the earthy warmth of the people.

Although I went to Ireland with the assumption that I was going to teach, I left fourteen months later with the realization that I was the one who had been taught. With tears streaming down my cheeks because I had learned to love and respect those good people so deeply, I boarded the ship at Belfast Harbour to sail to Liverpool, England, and to my next field of labor in Stockport.

While in England, I learned much from many people, but mostly from a newly converted member, William "Bill" Bates.

Bill was a young industrialist who owned a large metal fabricating business. He gave me the one thing I needed— perhaps the most important thing next to being able to talk. He gave me acceptance. He told me, "Elder Snarr, you're all right. You're my favorite missionary and I love you as a brother."

With that statement, something wonderful happened in my life. Because of his accepting me, I was now able to accept myself. Until Bill Bates came along, I was always the boy from the farm who could not talk, the sign painter who had a partner talk for him, Carol Stanger's boyfriend who was learning how to talk. But because of Bill Bates, I was Elder Douglas T. Snarr who could talk with the best of them.

Bill told me that when I talked, he listened, because I usually had more to say than others. He further stated, "You're going to be as successful as, and I believe even more successful, than most of the other missionaries."

Previously, I had considered myself inferior to the other missionaries. But when I received Bill's expression of confidence in me, an expression from a successful businessman who employed over 300 people, who was a considerate father and a loving husband, who was a *somebody*, I was able to make the transition from boy to man.

I now believed I *was* as good as anybody else. I was able to put the past behind me—the image of failure, the memory of bitter speaking disappointments, and all of the other failures incidental to those tragic moments.

Bill saw me as I really was—a child of God—hoping, aspiring, working, teaching, sharing, and giving everything I had.

The mission itself provided the perfect context for positive change. I now carried a dignified title—that of Elder Snarr. I held the Melchizedek Priesthood—the authority to act in the name of Jesus Christ—and was now a missionary for Christ's Church. I was a new person, and now even people of Bill's stature looked up to me.

Ten months later I returned to Idaho. I left behind a great deal of my heart and my "swinging index finger."

My business partner, who was working on his MBA at New York University, felt the call of the big corporation more promising than painting signs in Idaho Falls. We agreed on a price, and I bought him out.

Carol had waited for me, and 40 days after my return, we were married.

My immediate objective was to earn enough money to go to school to learn advertising art. I chose the Art Center School in Los Angeles.

I also concluded that I could not realize my financial dreams without an understanding of accounting and bookkeeping. I hired an accountant to tutor me once a week at 5 a.m. for three hours. Art had always come easy, but figures came hard and slow. But I stuck with it.

I have made it a habit to keep track of all financial transactions, both personal and business. Every check is entered into a journal and a ledger. Because of this I have always known where I stood. Many times I didn't like where I stood, but at least I knew the truth. Record keeping forced me to deal with facts and realities rather than dreams, hopes, and "pie in the sky."

Next, I set out to prepare myself to deal on a meaningful and intelligent basis with the banking community. I needed the banks because I had to pay for the signs as I built them. Yet, the income from the signs came after they were built, when they were rented. I needed immediate capital. I had 36 signs, a pickup truck, experience, but no money. I needed collateral to obtain financing. I figured that the best collateral I could give a bank would be signed contracts from substantial companies for the advertising space on the yet-to-be-built billboards.

I drove around Idaho Falls and nearby towns and made a list of owners of major motels, restaurants, clothing stores, sporting goods stores, photographers, automobile dealers, farm machinery companies, furniture stores, service stations, etc., making sure to pick the ones that looked prosperous and had been in business for many years.

In order to screen the prospects, I chose a few "old-timers" in the area in a determined effort to pick their brains. I talked to the old fellows who sit on their porches in overalls and straw hats, playing checkers and chatting about "times past." I had already become an expert at listening while occupying the park benches in Indiana.

The "old-timers" told me what I needed to know. I learned about the various family ownerships, the intrigue, who had the say and who didn't, of the potential prospects. I found out who had money, who pretended to have money, who paid their bills, and who didn't pay their bills. With this information, I narrowed my prospect list to a chosen few.

Next, on the agenda was the drawing board, the creating of an outdoor advertising campaign for each business on my list. I had enough "horse sense" to see what each was doing in the newspapers and the yellow pages. I made sure each billboard advertisement was a marked improvement over what the prospect already had.

Next I went out and took pictures of existing billboards—the backs, the sides, and the fronts. I prepared a booklet of leaning, tipping, bending, falling-down, and fading signs to show the prospective customer how it shouldn't be done.

Then I built some sample models out of balsa wood in fresh, bright colors, three-dimensional, showing how a Snarr sign would actually be.

I decided on some basic policies. The backs of the signs would be painted as well as the front, and the backs would be maintained, too. Another policy was to depart from the conventional horizontal format used by all my competitors. Snarr signs had to be different, vertical rather than horizontal, free-form rather than rectangular. I designed a unique shape for each customer. Snarr designs reeked with personality.

It was obvious to me that, when driving down the road, the monotony of the horizontal, rectangular, look-alike signs lulled the motorist into a state of non-recognition—a state of unawareness. I was convinced that motorists would be jolted by my "personality spectaculars" scattered among the ordinary, typical road signs.

The entire process had taken all my cash and four months of my time. But I had conducted a sophisticated market research program, had carefully selected my potential clients, and had designed a series of different outdoor advertising campaigns for each of them.

Now I mustered the raw courage to go out and sell the billboards. I left the sanctuary of the drawing board and stepped onto the cold, brutal pavement of the street. I methodically visited each prospect "cold turkey" and introduced myself. I showed them the designs I had created for them. I talked, talked, talked, begged, pleaded and called back over and over again. I discovered that I could obtain a contract on 75 percent of my presentations.

Within 90 days I had over $50,000 worth of leased billboard space on contract. I worked out a pro forma cash flow statement, along with cost data, showing I could build the signs for $20,000. To be safe, I decided to ask for a bank loan of $25,000 to be repaid in monthly increments as the lease rental flowed in.

I called on three banks in Idaho Falls. All three turned me down. They told me, among other things, that I was too young. I learned for the first time, a number of big words like "performance contracts," "bankable collateral," "track record," "reserves," "compensating bank balance." I was told, in short, to find a "sugar daddy."

In my search for someone to back me, I met one of Idaho's wealthiest men, Mr. Howard Dougherty, an old Irishman. His office was in the top of a two-story building. He had six desks and 20 file cabinets, but no secretary. When I met him, he was alone in the building. He sat smoking a cigar and had his feet propped up on his desk. Once in a while he would interrupt the routine by going to the window to pour bird seed on the sill. He talked to the birds as they carried off his seeds. He was in his 70's. He wore suspenders and a belt and was worth many millions of dollars.

I introduced myself and explained my program. Then he gave me some of the best advice I have ever received. He said,

"You know, Snarr, you are not going to sell just $50,000 worth of billboards. Before you are through, you will be selling millions of dollars worth. You are not after a loan, you are really after loans."

"Let's assume I loan you the $25,000 you are asking for, and you pay me back as agreed right on time. Now, after you have paid me back, what do you have? Absolutely nothing. All you have is the satisfaction of knowing that I won't take your company away from you because of default and that you have paid me $25,000 plus interest."

"Now, let's assume you borrow that $25,000 from a bank and you pay them back. What do you have?"

He then pointed his round, stubby finger at me, and with a twinkle in his eye and firmness in his jaw, said,

"Credit! And once you have credit with a bank, you can borrow again. Bank credit is the most important thing in business. Remember, individuals come and go, but a good bank is always there. Go find a bank."

I told him I had gone to three banks and they had turned me down.

"So what?" he said. "You mean to tell me there are only three banks in all the United States of America? This great big country of ours is full of banks."

"I'll tell you what to do," he continued, "Find a young, brilliant loan officer, establish a relationship, and ride him all the way to the top. All the presidents of banks started off first as bright young loan officers."

"Go to all the banks in Idaho Falls. Go to all the banks in the nearby towns. Then go to Boise, and if they all turn you down, start working the banks in Montana."

"But I will bet you will get a bank to say yes before your 25th presentation. In fact, I'll bet you $1,000 right here and now you will get the job done before the 25th presentation."

As I left the second floor and started down the stairs, I could hear that marvelous old Irishman talking to the birds. I was surely glad he had talked to me. I knew he was right—dead right.

All the banks in Idaho Falls said no. But in nearby Rexburg, I found my young, bright loan officer. He was the son of the president of the major bank there, a country bank with money and heart. After hearing my presentation, he asked me to come back in one week. I felt hope. I went back, and he said,

"We are not only going to give you the $25,000, but we are going to finance all the signs you can sell."

He further said, "In determining credit, many factors, of course, come into play, the major ones being the three C's, collateral, capital and character. We have made this loan entirely upon your character."

When I left the bank that day, I had a loan for $33,000 and a friend in Steve Meikle, Jr.—my banker, by advisor, and next to my wife, at that time, the most important person in my life.

I was 22 years old and on my way.

I built signs during the late spring, summer, and early fall. Then, when the snows came, I packed up my little family and headed for Los Angeles to study advertising art at the Art Center School. This pattern continued for three years.

The average age of the students studying art at the Art Center was 27. I started at age 22. When I looked around the school, I saw a sea of unshined shoes, faded blue denims, unpressed shirts open at the neck. The students respectfully called the teachers by their surnames—Mr. Harris, Mrs. Brown, etc., and the teachers called the students by their first names—Jim, Bob, Barbara, etc.

I was different. I wore Florsheim wing-tip shoes which were shined every day, a suit, a starched dress shirt, and a tie. I was a young businessman in a hurry. And the teachers addressed me as *Mr. Snarr."*

By the time I returned from my third trip to California, I had several hundred signs sprinkled all over southern Idaho and northern Utah, and my line of credit at the bank was $200,000.

It was then that William Harrah of Harrah's Club at Reno and Lake Tahoe was driving through Idaho in his white Ferrari. There he experienced the jolting effect of the vertical, free-form "Snarr spectaculars" that reached out and grabbed his attention.

Mr. Harrah phoned his advertising agency and instructed them to visit Idaho Falls to see for themselves the Snarr billboards and to find out about Snarr. I received a call telling me they were on their way. I borrowed my grandfather's big, red Buick, deciding against using my

Studebaker pickup, and met them at the appointed hour at the airport. The first thing they asked me was if they could meet my father. I told them I would be happy to drive out to the potato farm but that he was on the tractor cultivating potatoes and the dust might be too much for their alligator shoes. When they learned that I was the Snarr they had come to see, their hearts sank, and their enthusiasm vanished.

As I drove them up and down the Idaho Falls highways, showing them the "Snarr spectaculars," they started warming up. But then, when we went to lunch at LeBarons, the biggest thing in Idaho Falls, famous for broasted chicken, they all but ignored me.

When they boarded their private twin-engine Cessna to fly back, I was unable to contain myself any longer and I exploded.

"Gentlemen, you have flown all this way from Reno to see my signs. Where do I stand?"

The account executive, figuring he would never see me again, said,

"Ah, shoot us a deal," and then flew away.

I was only 24 years old. I had a Studebaker pickup truck but no office, no desk, nor even an adding machine. But I knew I could design and build better signs than anyone else around. And I was determined to show Harrah's that I was better than even the "big boys."

The following day I shifted into high gear. I barreled my Studebaker down to Reno and launched another little market research program. Among other things, I photographed Harrah's existing outdoor advertising billboards. I moved around town looking, talking, and listening. I introduced myself to a number of "old-timers," service station people, and motel owners. I asked how Harrah's was doing, and about Harold's Club. I asked which was best, who goes to each one, and why.

I then raced back to Idaho Falls, knowing that I could beat the "big boys." I spent about a month preparing my billboard campaign, including seven different designs. I built models an inch-to-a-foot, out of balsa wood, showing the back braces, the gussets—all the parts incidental to a billboard. The backs were painted green, and the fronts were colorful, exciting free-form shapes standing vertically.

When built, the signs would stand about three stories high.

My mother chipped in and sewed together special capes to cover each model.

The most exciting part of all was the buying of a huge map of Western America. I literally blanketed the map with colorful dots, each color representing a specific design, on all the roads leading to Reno and Tahoe. When I finished, the colorful dots covered a nine-state area. It was beautiful. I felt terrific standing back looking at that map as I imagined "Snarr spectaculars" all over the West.

I phoned Harrah's Club and informed the account executive that I had a deal all prepared for him. The meeting was arranged, rather strangely, for 8 p.m. The following Monday evening, I borrowed my grandfather's red Buick, loaded the models, and headed for Reno.

We met in an impressive board room. The head of the advertising agency was at the end of the table, and beside him was his account executive and artist. Mr. Harrah was unassumingly seated at the side with various executives and advisors filling the rest of the table.

I was so excited I could hear my heart beat. I started my presentation by showing them photographs of their existing signs, pointing out that they were just about the same as those of everyone else. Their signs were common, ordinary, regular, horizontal—fitting nicely into the standard sizes and formats arbitrarily imposed by the outdoor advertising industry.

I prepared Harrah by saying, "We have no limitations in size, color and shape. Our only objective is to create signs that motorists always see and never forget."

I then laid out the seven models in a row, covered with the capes. I could tell they were anxiously waiting for me to remove the capes, but I continued to talk. They kept looking at the capes while I discussed all the major roads leading to Reno and Tahoe, and how the signs would be strategically located on those roads, funneling people into Harrah's casinos. Everyone still stared at the capes. I talked; they looked.

After about an hour, I stopped talking and stepped toward the capes. Everyone in the room leaned forward. Then, with a grand gesture, *I removed each cape.* They were startled when they saw those vertical "Snarr spectaculars."

The slogan on each sign was,
"I hit the jackpot!"
One of the vice-presidents asked me if I would step out
and wait in the adjacent room. I was called back very
shortly and asked to give them a price on 150 signs. I
stepped back into the room, dazzled by the reality of what
was happening.

To date, the biggest contract I had entered into was for
$7,200 with Farr Ice Cream in eastern Idaho—seven signs
in three counties. We were now talking about 150 signs in
nine states. And Harrah wanted them up in six months.

Using my modern accounting system—a pencil and my
fingers—and a lot of guess work, I arrived at a price in
about 15 minutes. As I was about to leave the room, I was
struck with the thought that I might be a little too low. To
make sure I was safe, I doubled the price. I went into the
board room and told them I would do the job for $400,000
rental fee over a 48-month period.

What was interesting about the meeting was that Mr.
Harrah never asked one question—never said one word.
After I quoted the price, he merely smiled, got up and left
the room. All the others stayed behind, threw their arms
around me, shook my hand, and said I had a deal.

To celebrate the victory, I went out and ordered my first
New York cut steak—rare.

The first problem facing me was to borrow the $200,000
needed for the materials to build and erect the signs and for
two trucks, two trailers, additional equipment, and a fancy
desk with a lamp. My banker said I had already borrowed
close to their legal loan limit and that another $200,000 was
out of the question. I had grown a lot faster than they had
ever dreamed. They told me to find an additional bank.

I went to Boise and introduced myself to the president of
the Bank of Idaho, Mr. James Byers. I pitched hard until he
arranged a second meeting in Idaho Falls where he could
see our operation first-hand. The day following that second
meeting, he said he would give me the money if I could get
Harrah to personally guarantee the contract in the unlikely
event Harrah's Club were to default. I asked him if he would
instruct his attorney to write the guarantee. Upon receipt of
the guarantee, I went to Reno and a day later brought back
Mr. Harrah's signature personally guaranteeing payment

of the sign contract.

I had a strong feeling that the bank did not think I could get that personal guarantee. Maybe they were hoping I couldn't.

After I laid the personal guarantee on his desk, Mr. Byers, a man in his 50's, articulate and opinionated, gave me a piece of his philosophy:

"You know, young Snarr, I sit here behind this desk day after day—smiling, having to put my best foot forward—listening to people like you who come in here for a loan. Each person has a great idea and is convinced it will work and that the bank must put up the money."

"Do you know what I look for?" he continued, "I look for enthusiasm, the most important ingredient in a businessman's makeup. Of course, the collateral has to be there. But many bank loans that have good collateral are turned down because the individual involved lacks enthusiasm, the stuff that sees a project through to the finish."

"My problem is how to tell the difference between enthusiasm and baloney! The difference always reveals itself later on after the loan is made when the project runs into difficulty and the best laid-out plans fail and the outcome hangs in the balance. At that point the man with baloney fades away. The man with baloney has starting power but does not have the staying power. On the other hand, the man with true enthusiasm seems to get better when things get tough."

"By hell, young Snarr," and he looked me straight in the eye with a piercing gaze that I could feel clear down to my toes, "What I am seeing and feeling had better be enthusiasm and not baloney!"

For a 24-year-old, I was in business in a big way. The signs were built on schedule, and the $200,000 loan paid for all the trucks and trailers and the signs, plus the additional equipment needed to build them. Bill Harrah taught me that the "big boys" are no harder to sell than the "little boys." They just take a little more time and a great deal more homework.

Part III

After Harrah's signs were erected and while the salesmen were bringing in the bread and butter sales to keep the
company going, I decided to go after a company far bigger
than Harrah's. I arbitrarily chose Phillips Petroleum of
Bartlesville, Oklahoma. I liked the Phillips logo. It lent
itself to a "Snarr spectacular."

I first visited the district headquarters of Phillips in Salt
Lake City and asked to see the advertising manager. His
name was Dick Taylor, a 40-year-old extrovert who knew
and understood the ways of the big corporation.

I informed him I was going to design a regional outdoor
advertising campaign for Phillips covering five to fifteen
states and asked if he would show me some samples of their
current advertising. He looked at me as though he thought
me to be insane. He said that all of their advertising was
handled by J. Walter Thompson of New York City, the
biggest and best advertising agency in the world. He told
me that the advertising was programmed two and three
years in advance, that the media selections were scientif-
ically mixed, each supporting the other, exactly in the right
proportion.

He further stated that he did not want to hurt my
feelings, but there was absolutely no way I would ever sell
an outdoor advertising program to Phillips.

I replied that I appreciated his advice, but I would still
like to see some samples of what they were doing—point of
sale, newspaper, magazine, television, etc. I walked out
with an armload.

A month later, I had created and built five balsa models.
I took Dick out to lunch, my objective being to find out who I
needed to see in Bartlesville, and also to get Dick's reaction
to my models.

He gave me the name of Ollie Bettis, a 64-year-old
bachelor in charge of outdoor advertising. I showed Dick
the signs, and he came "unglued." "By gosh, Snarr, this is
the best I have ever seen in my life. We need them, but you
will never sell them.

"Those guys further up the corporate ladder," he contin-

ued, "are so afraid to do anything different or make any
waves. You know how it is. They don't want to lose their
rung on the ladder. I just don't see any way you could sell
those signs to Phillips."   I began to think that maybe he
knew something I didn't. One thing that occurred to me was
that at Phillips I would have to sell a number of people, not
just one, as was the case at Harrah's. Also, Harrah's had
come to me first, but at Phillips, I was taking the initiative.
It was a completely different set of circumstances.

I figured I would have to show my signs to the right
people. If I went in as a complete stranger and showed my
signs to this fellow, Ollie Bettis, who probably didn't have
much to say in the final outcome, anyway, I would probably
be wasting my time. I needed a go-between, someone who
could help me get the attention of some key people.

Then I found that one of the biggest stockholders in the
church's lived in Salt Lake City. He happened to be a
general authority in the Church of Jesus Christ of Latter-
day Saints and was absolutely inaccessible. His name was
Henry D. Moyle, and he was the second counselor in the
Church First Presidency.

I went to Salt Lake City and met his son. I was honest
with him and told him my problem. I told him how
determined I was, that I was going to sell Phillips, but that
they didn't know it yet. I told him I needed the help of his
father.

I then showed him the model signs and introduced him
to Dick Taylor. Taylor agreed with me that my signs would
be a great thing for the company.

It never occurred to me that I might be taking advantage
of the generosity of young Moyle or his father. I knew my
signs would help the company sell more of its product,
resulting in a material gain for stockholders. It was a clean,
honest business arrangement all the way.

The son went to his father and told him the problem. The
father respected the son and agreed to help, but only after I
had arranged an appointment with the advertising people
in Bartlesville, Oklahoma.

I called Ollie Bettis, introduced myself, and told him I
had the most fabulous outdoor advertising campaign he
had ever seen. I asked if I could come to Bartlesville and
show it to him. He answered in a slow, southern drawl that

there was no need for me to come, that it would be a waste of time for me and for him. He said the company was satisfied with J. Walter Thompson and that their outdoor advertising was buttoned up for the next three or four years.

I told him I knew all that, but that what I had was so much better, there was no comparison. I asked for 15 minutes to show it to him. After all, I told him, I was paying my own way and he had nothing to lose. If he didn't like my work, he could throw me out of his office.

He finally agreed to let me come, but reminded me that the interview was for 15 minutes only. The appointment was set.

I contacted young Moyle who then contacted his father. The father phoned Bartlesville and talked with the executive vice-president in charge of advertising, Mr. Kenneth Rugh. Mr. Moyle informed him as to when I would be meeting with Mr. Bettis and asked to receive a written report of the meeting. He also asked Mr. Rugh to give him his personal opinion of the Snarr signs. A letter was written as a follow-up to the telephone conversation.

I flew to Bartlesville with the models and went to Ollie Bettis' office. After the perfunctory introductions, in walked Mr. Rugh, wearing a Brooks Brothers suit. It was "Ivy League," natty, neat, crisp, and to the point. He introduced himself, looked at his watch, and said,

"You have 15 minutes, Mr. Snarr. Please proceed."

Three- and one-half hours later, they took me to lunch. Mr. Rugh kept saying,

"Ollie, we've got to look into this. These signs are a lot better than anything we have, and better than anything anybody else has. Ollie, we have got to look into this."

They asked for bank references, credit references, and insisted I send a written resume. A follow-up meeting was scheduled in my Salt Lake City office in one month. They also wanted feedback from the boys in the field, people like Dick Taylor in Salt Lake City. I knew I had a chance, and I wasn't going to let it slip through my fingers. Mr. Rugh wrote a positive letter to Mr. Moyle who sent me a copy. Everything looked good.

I was worried about the people from Phillips coming to my Salt Lake office. All I had was a big, empty room with one desk and two drawing boards, one for another artist

and one for me. We looked like a two-bit outfit. My assets
were not in the office, but out on the highways generating
income and in my manufacturing plant where the signs
were built. If they judged me by my office, I was doomed.

So, the day before the meeting, I rented six desks from
Salt Lake Desk Company, hired a battery of secretaries
from Kelly Company, and organized makeshift work.
Towards the end of the day, I told my artist that I thought
we needed one more design—something new to show the
Phillips people. He objected, saying that their coming was
based on what they had already seen, and a new product
might confuse them, muddy the water. He thought I should
stop while I was ahead.

I felt, however, that I could do something better. The
stomach signal was there, telling me I was right. We worked
together all night and finished the new sign at 4 a.m.

The Phillips people walked in at 9 a.m., and 2H hours
later they bought a half-million dollars worth of billboards,
covering a ten-state area. Each billboard was the same
design, the one we had created during the night.

Phillips Petroleum gave me legitimacy. I was for real,
and with the Phillips account, Idaho's biggest bank, the
Idaho First National, extended my line of credit to
$1,000,000. I was 27 years old and my signs covered states. I
was starting to think I had a few answers, but little did I
know what lurked ahead.

Part IV

In June of 1965, I decided to take my wife on a full two-
week vacation, our first extended vacation together since
we had been married. I was 29 years old and thought I had
the world by the tail.

Just after breakfast on the second day, as we were
walking through the lobby of the Sahara Hotel in Las
Vegas, I noticed the headline on a Las Vegas newspaper,
"LBJ Decides Billboards to Come Down."

My heart sank, and the vacation was cut short. Later on,
my worst fears were confirmed. On October 22, 1965, the
Highway Beautification Act was signed into law by President Johnson, given as a gift to his wife "Lady Bird" for her

birthday.

The law required that all billboards along federal roads in areas not zoned commercial or industrial be taken down by July 2, 1970. It said the government would pay for any sign it removed, providing they were not erected after October, 1965. It called for hearings to be set up in each state to determine how much it would cost to take down the signs and how it would be done.

Seventy percent of my signs were on rural highways and would have to come down. When I arrived home, the employees had a thousand questions about our future. I told them that all I knew for sure was that the signs were out on the highways making money and that nobody was sawing them down, not yet anyway.

But shortly thereafter, I received a letter from my bank that sent a cold chill through me. I opened the letter to read that my loan of nearly $800,000 was called due and payable in 30 days. The shock of the letter made me literally sick. I was unable to sleep for the next few nights. Big chunks of hair started falling from my head.

There was no way I could repay that loan. The lease money on the signs was coming in monthly installments and there was no way I could raise that kind of money immediately.

I flew to Boise. The banker now in charge of my loan said that even though I had over a million-dollar backlog of signs waiting to be built, he would not finance any new sign construction because the new law stated that there would be no compensation for new signs built after the passage of the law. He said his bank would not finance illegal assets.

He then said that because of the uncertainty of the law, my existing assets were jeopardized. He said the bank had more secure places to put its money and that, therefore, our line of credit was being withdrawn. The full payment of the loan was due immediately.

I tried to explain that nothing had really changed, that the existing signs were still on the highways generating rent and income, that I was making my payments on schedule as agreed and that the note would be paid in the time specified. I added that if the government did start chopping down signs, I would be justly compensated as outlined in the new law. So either way, the bank would get its money.

The banker didn't see it that way. He said he believed that when the bureaucrats sat down with me to figure the cost of my signs they would take me through the meat grinder and not pay me anything. He then told me many stories of people entering government contracts and being ruined. He got specific and asked me how much the government would pay me for my "State Street Motel" sign located between Boise and Caldwell, Idaho. He said that if I couldn't prove how much the government would pay for that sign, that I couldn't prove that the government *would* pay for it. And if I couldn't prove that, then as far as the bank was concerned, that multi-million dollar figure on the asset side of my balance sheet—capitalized costs—would have to be changed to zero. He said that in that case, I was unbankable. He gave me two weeks to find that information; otherwise, the loan was due immediately. He added that the bank was ready to take over and run my company if I failed to perform. I realized that the bank's fear was that I would get involved in a lengthy and costly legal struggle that would drain cash from the company. They could see complex litigation with various government agencies.

I went directly to the Idaho Department of Highways to see the chief engineer. I told him of my conversation with the banker and asked him what the state of Idaho would pay for the State Street Motel sign between Boise and Caldwell.

He said the state could not pay anything for the sign because there was no money and no allocation program. He said that before an allocation could be made to the state, there first had to be an appropriation made by Congress— that the Highway Beautification Act was merely an authorization, not an allocation or appropriation. I then asked him how much he would pay for the sign if he had the money in hand.

He said that before he could make an appraisal, federal guidelines determining the appraisal method would have to be written and published in the Federal Register. Then state guidelines would have to be written and approved by the Highway Board. He said he couldn't give me an estimate until these guidelines were finished.

I asked how long he thought it would take to complete

the guidelines. He guessed at about five years.

I asked him if he thought I would eventually be compensated for my signs. He said the act specified "just compensation." I asked what "just compensation" meant in terms of the State Street Motel sign. He said he had no idea.

I then asked him what he would do if he were me. He said he would sell the signs to somebody else and get into another business.

Upon leaving his office, I decided to get a second opinion and compare his words with those of his counterpart in Utah. The following day I was introduced to Henry C. Helland. He was different in that he seemed concerned. He confirmed everything the Idaho chief engineer had said, but added, "Mr. Snarr, I can see that the Highway Beautification Act, if not properly administered, could bring great hardship upon many people. I would like to assist if possible. My door is open to you at any time. Please feel free to keep me informed."

I asked him what he would do if he were me. He advised me to keep fighting—not to give up.

I went back to the bank and told them that my findings had confirmed their assumption, that the government couldn't tell me the value of the State Street sign. I begged the bank to be reasonable because it would take a great deal of time before any signs would come down. The banker partly consented by agreeing to renew my note every 30 days, provided I made a personal visit to the bank every 30 days to report on the status of the Highway Beautification Act. They reserved the right to insist on full payment if the situation deteriorated. They also insisted on acceleration of the payment schedule and on no new sign construction. Snarr Advertising had 80 employees and was supporting, counting wives and children, nearly 500 people. The employees were my friends. I had personally hired nearly everyone.

I walked away from over a million dollars worth of business when I asked the salesmen to contact the clients who were waiting for new signs and tell them that we couldn't deliver. Because of the uncertainty of the law, we could no longer guarantee existing contracts, and some had to be cancelled. At the end of 30 days, I was down to 12 employees.

At my lowest point, I received a letter from the Utah Highway Department ordering me to move seven signs located 10 miles east of Salt Lake City. The state was widening the freeway. If I didn't move the signs in one week, a bulldozer would do it for me, and I would have to pay the cost of removal. This kind of thing is common in the sign business. After grumbling about it, you send out a crew to move the signs out of the state's newly purchased right-of-way and put them up over the state fence onto private land.

This time, however, I took a different approach. I first visited the contractor who was building the road and he agreed to work around my signs for two weeks. Then I went to the Highway Department and told Mr. Helland that his department was breaking the law by ordering me to build seven new signs in areas prohibited by the new Beautification Act. Then I laid copies of my seven leases on his desk and explained that the roadway was not free of encumbrances, as his department had certified to the contractor, because my claims had not been satisfied. The landowners had entered into a legal lease agreement with me which was not terminated with the sale of the land to the government. I informed him further that his department had allowed and encouraged the construction of 60 illegal signs from other sign companies along the same right-of-way in direct violation of federal law. I asked him what he thought would happen if this information were leaked to the major newspapers, radio and television stations.

Mr. Helland immediately phoned the attorney general who agreed with every one of my conclusions. They asked me if I had any suggestions. I told them to hire the smartest appraiser they could find, determine the value of the signs, and pay me a fair value for them—and pay for the other sign companies' signs, too.

Two weeks later I had an offer for the seven signs. It was fair, and I accepted. The state of Utah had appraised and paid for a sign.

I now had evidence to show the banker that the government would pay for a sign. Signs are real property, deserving compensation under the law. I had a check to prove it. Signs could be converted to money.

The bank was pleased but stubbornly insisted that I would never be paid for a sign taken down to beautify a highway. I had been paid because of road construction; that was different. I decided to find another bank.

I began to wrestle with the basic idea of highway beautification. Every sign company, without exception, had taken the side against the beautification program. As I wrestled with the problem, I came up with a different conclusion and decided to support the beautification program. It seemed that the regulation of outdoor advertising was an integral part of the fundamental question of controlling our environment. I considered myself an artist with an appreciation for beautiful things. I loved the countryside of Ireland and England where signs are restricted to commercial areas only. These countries are magnificently unspoiled, even after centuries of civilization. Maybe we Americans could take a lesson from our mother countries.

But I also understood the terrible financial realities facing the sign companies, particularly the small and medium-sized companies. Their crisis was my crisis.

At first, I was labeled a traitor and stood alone, but I went ahead anyway. I figured that if the State of Utah could appraise seven of my signs, it could appraise all of my signs and enter into a contract with me, agreeing to pay me a fixed sum for each sign at the time the sign is removed. That contract became my single most important objective. Appraisal determines value, and value is collateral. With collateral, the asset side of my balance sheet would be restored, and I could find a new bank.

I started by visiting each small and medium-sized sign company that had signs in Utah—27 in all. I presented my solution, which I believed was also their solution. They all agreed to go along and sent letters to that effect to the state.

The Beautification Program called for independent appraisal and removal of each sign. In Utah that meant 7,000 individual negotiations. My plan called for 27 negotiations with the 27 companies. The Beautification Program specified that the government take down the signs. Under my plan, the owner companies would take down the signs. After receipt of the letters, backed up with plenty of publicity in the local media, the Department of Highways conducted a study comparing the two methods of sign removal and concluded that administration costs would be cut to less than half with my plan. The 27 companies selected me to be their spokesman with the government in obtaining the contracts.

Part V

In April of 1967, I flew to Washington, D.C., to attend a hearing on highway beautification. Two sides had polarized stiffly against each other. The ecologists were saying the signs must come down. The big sign companies were on record as agreeing with the concept of beautification, but discouraging funding and implementation at this time.

I was introduced by Utah Senator Frank Moss as the spokesman for the Utah sign industry. My suggestions surprised everyone. I outlined what became known as the "Snarr Plan for Billboard Blight." I explained that Utah's 27 sign companies were all for it, and that the state had studied the plan and concluded it to be right. I exhorted the Congress to follow through, fund beautification, and get on with the show.

Newspapers and magazines began to write about the "Snarr Plan." Problems become public issues when they become possible to solve.

Finally, in Utah the State agreed to appraise my signs and enter into a contract with Snarr Advertising. It took two years, and I spent at least six hours every working day in pushing, nudging, and helping them get the job done. In the end, it was worth it. I had a contract.

I found a new bank, Walker Bank of Salt Lake City, and I figured I was on my way from third base to home plate. But the contract had one hitch. The state wouldn't pay a penny until the federal government authorized funding, appropriated funds, allocated money to Utah, approved Utah's contract with Snarr Advertising, and paid their share of matching funds.

My contract with Utah was for a little over a million dollars. I decided to take it to Washington, D.C., and get the money. I delegated the management of my signs and chopped off all extra activity in order to become a one-man lobbyist. I figured the government would do nothing unless someone moved them to action.

I decided to become the most influential and powerful figure in the country in regards to highway beautification. I figured no one would bestow the power upon me, so I would have to assume it on my own.

I met with the president of Walker Bank and told him what I was going to do. He didn't think I could do it, but he agreed to spread out my loan payoff schedule so I would have sufficient cash flow to mount a one-man lobbying effort in Washington.

I had one more financial need, but I didn't have the nerve to ask the president of Walker Bank. I went to another Salt Lake City bank and asked for $12,000 with which I intended to buy a new wardrobe—a series of beautiful, tailored wool western suits, all with vests; a collection of handmade cowboy boots; and the brightest and finest silk ties available. I told them I needed the $12,000 wardrobe so I could go to Washington to get Congress to pay me for my signs. At first they thought I was joking, then they said it would be the most ridiculous loan in the history of the bank, but they gave me the money.

When I first went to Washington, D.C., I observed that it was a city of gray men in gray suits, men with gray faces and personalities. Gray is an in-between color; it says nothing. It lacks life. "Old Glory" is bright red, bright blue, and a clean, honest white.

I figured the "gray men of Washington" might not remember what I said, but I wanted them to remember me. So I decided that I would smile, whistle, radiate enthusiasm, be bright and joyful and sunny, and provide color and resilience.

That $12,000 wardrobe turned out to be the best $12,000 investment of my life. The press wrote about my clothes. Congressmen and senators wanted to know where I bought my ties. Some called me "Tex." It worked—they were talking.

I packed the wardrobe and flew to Washington where I found a one-room apartment five blocks from the White House. I rented it for 90 days. I was there for five years.

Senator Moss arranged an appointment for me with Mr. Frank Turner, director of the Federal Highway Administration. There, Senator Moss explained that Utah had acted, and that I had a contract. He asked that action be taken to have the signs paid for and taken down. Mr. Turner told me that everything stood at a big question mark. Things were at a standstill. There was no funding, and nothing could be done.

He did say that it was too bad the government couldn't experiment with the Snarr Plan on a trial basis. It could then be determined if signs could economically be removed on a company-by-company basis. He added, however, that that couldn't be done because there was no enabling legislation.

Senator Moss said he would immediately get a bill ready to get the enabling legislation. From that meeting, Senate Bill 1442 came into existence. It authorized five million dollars for pilot projects in two or three states for removal of billboards on a company-by-company approach.

I decided I needed exposure. I had to mobilize the national press to get public pressure on my side.

In the meantime, the big sign companies were spreading the word that my bill was private legislation to help Doug Snarr out of financial difficulty. They were men with lots of money, expensive luncheons, lavish dinners, and unlimited expense accounts. I was one man without an expense account. I needed help.

One day I noticed a lead article in *Fortune* magazine which advocated the take-down of signs on a per company approach. Here were conclusions that coincided with mine and yet were independent of me, proving that I was on the right track.

I flew to New York City. At Kennedy Airport, I called *Fortune* magazine from a phone booth and asked for Edmund K. Faltermayer, author of the article. As he was on vacation, at home in Brooklyn painting his house, I took a cab and headed toward the famed Brooklyn Bridge. When I got to his home, I told him the whole story; and the first thing he asked me was what motivated me to try to lobby a bill through Congress. I told him the truth. First, money. Second, preservation of my property rights. Third, beautification, because it was right. I asked for his help.

Soon thereafter, *Fortune* magazine did an article on me. It opened doors and paved the way to many other articles.

The Snarr Plan was becoming a national public issue, although a small one.

But the big sign companies successfully stalled the legislation in committee, and I reached a time when nothing was happening.

I needed help, but didn't know where to get it. I needed knowledge and experience but couldn't afford a Washington legal firm. One night I prayed earnestly for an answer.

The next day I ran into a young lobbyist, J.C. Penney's man in Washington. I had known him years ago as a fellow missionary in Great Britain. He was from Utah. I told him my problem. He listened, he cared.

William K. Daines became my teacher and the most important person in my life during those Washington years. He had forgotten more about government than I would ever know. He taught me, and I soaked up his knowledge like a sponge.

With a new understanding of how laws become reality, I leaned hard on Senator Moss, asking him to arrange an appointment with the chairman of the Senate Public Works Committee, Jennings Randolph of West Virginia.

The three of us met in a little private room in the capitol. There, I asked Senator Randolph if his committee would hold hearings on Senate Bill 1442 and discuss the plight of the small and medium-sized sign companies. I stressed the fact that the Utah sign companies were willing to cooperate and that the state of Utah was ready to start taking down signs.

He agreed to conduct the hearings on one condition, that I persuade sign companies from West Virginia to support S.B. 1442. He instructed me to see his Chief of Staff who would give me the names and addresses of the sign companies I should contact.

I headed for West Virginia and met with the sign owners. They agreed with me, and I had them send telegrams to Senator Randolph, stating so. Upon receipt of the telegrams, Mr. Randolph lived up to his word, and hearings were scheduled.

Next, I asked Utah Congressman Laurence Burton to enter the same bill into the House of Representatives. He did.

Next, the sub-committee on roads of the House Public

Works Committee, under the direction of John C. Kluczynski from Illinois, was persuaded to hold hearings. That resulted in more news, more articles, more pressure.

Even though the Senate Public Works Committee was sympathetic to highway beautification, the House Public Works Committee was not. The big sign companies had done their homework, and they immediately lined up a brilliant attorney to speak for them in the hearings.

I asked Mr. Henry Helland, director of the Utah Department of Highways if he would testify. He agreed and arranged for Utah's chief appraiser to explain the sign appraisal techniques that Utah had developed. The appraiser would discuss the findings of the internal study and show the savings Utah would make through the adoption of the Snarr Plan.

I then found five small sign comapnies from several states who had been irreparably damaged and who would also testify. Brigham Young University did an independent study on the feasibility of the Snarr Plan, and agreed to testify as to how the Act was causing a growing monopoly in the advertising industry.

First, a two-hour hearing was scheduled in the House of Representatives. The lawyer for the big sign companies spoke first. It was understood and agreed that each witness had only 15 minutes to speak. The Congressmen sat smiling while the lawyer took one hour and forty minutes.

We were left with only 20 minutes for the eight witnesses. Mr. Helland took the balance of the time. Brigham Young University, the appraiser, and the five sign owners were asked to submit testimony for the record, and we all knew it would be buried deep and never looked at.

I had been outstructured and outsmarted by the big boys with the big expense accounts. They had beaten me, and I realized it was my own fault. I vowed never to be made a fool of in Congress again. From this humiliating defeat, I realized for the first time that I had a good chance of winning. If I didn't, why would they try so hard to keep the truth from being heard?

I informed Senator Randolph that I didn't want the same farce to occur in the Senate hearings. I didn't want my witnesses to waste their money coming to Washington if they were not to be heard. I told him the national press would be at the hearing and that I would brief them about what had happened in the House hearings. The Senator assured me we would get equal billing.

A month later, when the Senate hearings were held, the smooth attorney again tried to take up all the time. Senator John Sherman Cooper of Kentucky cut him short, and Chairman Randolph dismissed him. We all testified, and Senator Cooper invited us back the following day.

The Senate Public Works Committee acted, and the bill was amended from five to fifteen million dollars and passed the Senate unanimously. From there it went to the House.

I went back to Congressman Burton who arranged a luncheon with Chairman John Kluczynski. My objective was to get the House Public Works Committee to send the bill to the floor for a vote.

Chairman Kluczynski was a man in his 70's, his width nearly matching his height. He had beautiful white hair combed straight back. He was jolly with a natural smile. I had heard it whispered around from many sources that behind that smiling face was an empty head. He was the formal leader of the subcommittee on roads, but he took his marching orders from others.

During the luncheon, his Chief of Staff, Richard Sullivan and Sullivan's attractive assistant, Audrey Warren, did all the talking. They told me all the reasons the Snarr Plan would never get through the House.

Finally, Mr. Sullivan gave me some sagely advice. He said that a lot of people are devoured by the processes of government, and that I ought to go home before I got hurt. Something inside told me he was not counseling, but threatening.

I clenched my fist and hit the table, looked Sullivan in the eye and raised my voice sufficiently to command respect. I asked him if he thought I should lie down and die, give up, quit, when he and I both knew I was right. I had listened for 45 minutes to a thousand flimsy excuses but not one substantive reason. I told him I was not going back to Salt Lake City but was staying in Washington until the bill left the committee and the Congress had a chance to vote on it. I told him I was sick and tired of words, words, words. All I wanted to know was what I had to do to get the bill out of committee and onto the floor.

Kluczynski looked up and finally spoke. He said he was a machine politician from Chicago and that his leader was Mayor Daley.

"The first thing you do is get Mayor Daley to approve Moss's bill. The second thing you do is to get Secretary of Transportation, John Volpe, to write me a letter saying he approves the bill. And the third thing you do is to get the Bureau of Budget to budget the funds for Moss's bill. Then I will get it out of committee so the full House can vote on it."

They all sat back because they knew they had me. I was possessed to say that I would do exactly that. I would see Mayor Daley, John Volpe, and handle the budgeting.

Chairman Kluczynski looked at me and said, "Young man, I like you. I like your spirit. You know, I believe you will do it. I'll tell you what I will do. I will phone John for you and arrange an appointment."

He turned to Audrey and said, "Audrey, call John and make arrangements for this young man to meet him."

He then added, "I want you to go with Mr. Snarr and tell me what Volpe has to say."

I gulped. Having Audrey Warren along would be like going into a boxing match with my hands tied behind my back. The appointment was arranged for Friday at 5 p.m., the end of that week.

Part VI

I was determined not to be outstructured in the meeting with Secretary Volpe. I decided to present my case to one of Volpe's trusted aides before the meeting so the Secretary could be properly briefed.

Friday morning, I had breakfast with Secretary Volpe's most trusted aide. I didn't know him, and he didn't know me; but we were talking.

After hearing me, the aide offered hope. He said I was morally, legally, and politically right and that he would recommend the Secretary to hear me out.

Following the breakfast, I returned to my apartment. As I mulled over the conversation and contemplated the seriousness and the magnitude of the upcoming meeting with Secretary Volpe, I became ill—so terribly ill that I was forced to bed. I was sweating all over. I guess it was the pressure, knowing that if I failed, my dreams and aspirations would go up in smoke, and I would be left in the ashes of eventual ruin.

At 4 p.m. I pulled myself together, took a quick bath, then stood at the door of my closet looking at that $12,000 wardrobe. I thought that if ever there was a time for color, texture, style, and cut, it was now. I chose a bright royal blue suit accentuated with fine, white pinstripes, a vest, suspenders (never a belt), a white shirt with French cuffs, a white handkerchief puffed in the coat pocket, and a scarlet red tie. I slipped into my black alligator cowboy boots, spit-shined, which lifted me an inch-and-a-half higher into the air. I said a little prayer and headed for the Department of Transportation where Audrey Warren met me.

At 5:15 we were ushered into Secretary Volpe's office. Secretary John Volpe, Frank Turner from Highways, James Washington, Jr., General Counsel, and the Secretary's aide were there.

The Secretary energetically embraced Audrey, saying how wonderful it was to have her in his office, and would she please sit right by him.

Then, he introduced himself to me and introduced me to the others in the room. He asked me to sit across the desk off to the side so at a glance I could establish eye contact with the Secretary, General Counsel, and the Chief of the Bureau of Roads. I liked the seating arrangement, except for Audrey who was too close to the Secretary. They chatted as old friends, and the more they talked, the more apprehensive I became.

A voice from the phone box sliced through the conversation. "Mr. Secretary, the House has just voted on the authorization bill for the SST, and the victory was substantial. It has passed."

Secretary Volpe sprang from his seat, hit both hands on the desk, and shouted into the phone box, "Get President Nixon on the phone."

The box responded, "I am sorry, Mr. Secretary, the President is not at the White House."

"Get Halderman on the phone," demanded the Secretary.

"Mr. Secretary, Mr. Halderman is out of his office."

"Get Ehrlichman on the phone!"

"Mr. Secretary, Mr. Ehrlichman is also out of his office. Is there anyone else you want to speak to?"

"I don't talk to second-stringers," responded the Secretary in a more subdued voice.

He turned and lectured us with power and conviction, "Do you know what's wrong with the Congress of the United States? They are a bunch of damn lawyers. We need more businessmen. It is impossible on a project as immense and costly as the SST for a company like Boeing to finance it. Boeing can't walk into a bank and ask for money to build a prototype when they can't prove it will fly. It's the public's responsibility in this case to provide the money to build one or two working models, to prove it will fly, that it's safe, and that it will not be detrimental to the environment as its opponents claim. I am happy the House sees it my way."

He looked right at me and said, "Mr. Snarr, the time is yours."

I knew one thing for sure. I had to present my case in such a way that Audrey Warren wouldn't be allowed to speak. If she did, I would lose control of the meeting.

I stood on my feet, took two steps forward, clenched my fist, raised my arm, and hit the Secretary's desk. Looking him straight in the eye, I said, "Mr. Secretary, do you know what's wrong with the Congress of the United States? They are all a bunch of damn lawyers. Do you know what Congress needs? More businessmen."

"Now take the highway beautification problem," I continued. "Do you know what the highway beautification program needs? A prototype, a working model, a pilot project in one or more states to prove that signs can be taken down with the cooperation of the sign industry, without law suits, in harmony with state governments."

I then talked as hard, fast, furious, and enthusiastically as I had ever done in my life for approximately one hour as I outlined the Snarr Plan. When I was through, the Secretary asked me to come back Monday morning at 9 a.m. and meet with his top aide. I was dismissed.

The aide stepped out into the hall with me, saying, "You have just sold Secretary Volpe. See you Monday."

I felt great all over as I walked to my apartment. A few tears of supreme delight rolled down my cheek. Monday came off as expected. The Secretary would fight for the program all the way, but he needed help. He asked me to stick around. He had problems in his own department. Frank Turner of Highways placed his loyalty with his friends on the House Public Works Committee. Turner was part of the clique and Volpe was a mere cabinet officer, an upstart, a newcomer telling the old guard what to do. The bureaucrats in the agencies see cabinet officers come and go. They build lasting bonds with the staff officers of congressional committees—bureaucrats clinging to bureaucrats.

Next, I went back to Senator Moss and asked him to help me get a hearing with Mayor Daley of Chicago. He agreed, and the following day I was on a jet to O'Hara Field.

Mayor Daley said, "I see nothing in Senator Moss's bill that would have a negative effect on Chicago. We will pass the word to Chairman Kluczynski."

Getting what we wanted from the Bureau of the Budget was far more difficult. President Nixon had centralized all policy-making decisions in the White House. All congressional action by Nixon's cabinet had to receive White House approval, and that normally takes a long, long time.

Secretary Volpe decided that before he exposed himself to the White House, he had to double-check everything I had said. He sent two aides to Salt Lake City to talk with the governor, the department of highways, small sign companies, large sign companies, banks. They drove the highways and found all the facts they could. Their findings proved that I had said it as it was. In every instance I had told the truth.

Secretary Volpe and his staff launched a White House attack. They hammered away. Days, weeks, and then months went by, but the White House would not move.

I was worried. I knew that beautification was dead without the support of the Nixon administration. The thought occurred to me that if the pilot program were expanded to include all states willing to remove signs, the administration could win a lot more friends by supporting the project.

Finally, I discovered one man in the White House who had clout, who could get the job done. His name was Charles Colson. He had the ear of the President; he knew how to deliver.

It took some doing, but a meeting was arranged with Colson, my teacher Kay Daines, and me. Daines and I spent the week prior to the meeting writing a five-page single-spaced brief explaining the company-by-company approach to sign removal and how it could be done on a national basis, thus allowing the Nixon administration to take the credit in an area where the Democrats had failed.

I visited Senator Moss, the Democrat who had helped me get the bill together, and explained to him how the bill had to be broadened in order to win White House support. I was afraid he might withdraw his support, but he assured me it was the right thing to do and that he would continue his support because he cared about good government. With that assurance, I was ready to tackle Mr. Colson.

We met him in his office in the Executive Office Building and handed him the five-page brief. I had handed out many pieces of paper in my lobbying efforts, and the typical response of the recipient was to put the paper aside and ask me to explain the contents. Colson was different.

"May I read this?" he asked.

He read it very slowly, very thoroughly, page by page. When he finished, he looked at me as if he were staring through me. He then read the five pages a second time, page by page, very slowly.

After 20 minutes, he raised his head and said, "This is so simple and so logical. Why didn't we think of this?"

"Mr. Snarr," he continued, "we will take action. I cannot assure you what the final form will be, but I can say that we will move quickly to resolve the problem."

And so highway beautification became part of the administration's 1970 Federal Aid Highway Act.

It was April, 1970, and three years had gone by since I first rented my apartment. About every three weeks I would catch a Friday afternoon flight home to Salt Lake City, collapse for the weekend, see my banker Monday morning, borrow more money, make all the business decisions that had to be made, and fly out again Monday afternoon—week after week, month after month, year after year, this hectic schedule continued.

I had four children, three boys and a girl. The older boys would ask, "Dad, when will it end? When are you going to come home and live with us again?" My wife Carol never complained, knowing I had to do it.

In May, 1970, we decided we'd rather live together like sardines in my little one-room apartment than be apart. We packed the four kids and the dog in our Chevrolet Suburban and drove across America to our new home in Washington, D.C. We spread sleeping bags on the floor. Carol bought a little sign, "God Bless This House," and nailed it to the door.

Carol often accompanied me to interviews with the press. She added a feminine touch that humanized me. With her at my side, a highway sign became more than lumber, steel and paint. Behind the signs were human beings, families, children, tears, laughter, hopes, and dreams.

Even though our apartment was wall-to-wall people, we grew closer. Always the children would pray, "Please help Daddy win so we can go back home." When school started, the children attended the Washington, D.C. city schools.

The hardest time of my life became the happiest time of my life. I was striving for that which extended me, demanded the utmost effort and the help of God. It involved the full support of my family.

In the summer evenings, we often went to the Capitol steps and listened to the Marine Band, the Army Band, the Air Force Band. We visited the National Art Gallery, Williamsburg, Gettysburg, Bull Run, and Fredricksburg. I introduced my children to congressmen and senators. They were in the galleries when the key votes were cast.

During the month of June, the battle lines were drawn. The Snarr Plan was incorporated into the Senate version of the 1970 Federal Aid Highway Act where it sailed through the subcommittee on Roads, the Committee on Public Works, and with a big majority, the full Senate.

On the other hand, the House omitted the Snarr Plan from its version of the 1970 Federal Aid Highway Act. Instead, it added a scheme set up by the big boys for a two-year study commission. Now it was up to the House and Senate conferees to work out the differences.

Early in the fall, the conferees started to meet, beginning the process of reconciling, line upon line, the many differences that plagued the huge highway act. Highway beautification was one small part, sandwiched deep inside the hundreds and thousands of words that comprised the major legislation.

Days and weeks passed. October came and Congress recessed. All the representatives and a third of the senators went home to fight for re-election.

In the middle of November, the conferees were meeting again.

By the first of December, they were still arguing. Issue after issue was discussed—some were readily agreed upon, others only with great difficulty.

Then came highway beautification. Hour after hour it was discussed.

The Senate conferees argued that the government had been studying the beautification program for five years and that a lot of small sign companies had been hurt because of the dillydallying around. They insisted that the best way to study and learn about a program was to implement it, then refine it later, if needs be.

But the House conferees wouldn't budge. They argued that perhaps the Snarr Plan was right, but perhaps it was wrong. The government could not act prematurely on such a matter. Sure, some people would be hurt, but it was still better to study the matter for an additional two years, to make sure the government was right before it acted.

Hours went by—a day, two days, a week—the pressure was constantly mounting, becoming unbearable.

For me, everything hung in the balance. I had invested half a million dollars and five years of my life. For those five years, I had lived and breathed highway beautification. I, my wife, my children, my business, all those small sign companies in Utah, and all the small and large sign companies throughout the nation waited on the verdict of that committee.

For the larger sign companies, this decision meant millions of dollars—for the smaller sign companies, this meant life or death. We worried. We waited.

Finally, when the conferees were weary and a solution was desperately needed, the Republican conferees of the Senate conference committee proposed a compromise. They agreed to the House's insistence that there be a study commission, but they also insisted that the government recognize the plight of the small sign companies. They suggested that, until a decision was reached by the study commission that money for beautification should not come from the Highway Trust Fund, as had been proposed by the Senate, but that money be immediately authorized from the general fund for the singular purpose of billboard removal. They suggested that it be given to states in chronological order, according to when they achieved complying legislation, and then to be given first to the smaller sign companies that were irreparably damaged because of the original highway beautification legislation. This way, the smaller companies would be able to take down their signs and receive just compensation, while the big companies could bide their time for at least a couple of years until the study commission reported back to Congress. The House conferees agreed, and the stalemate was over.

In mid-December, the 1970 Federal Aid Highway Act came out of conference and back to the floor of both the House and Senate for final vote, then to President Nixon for signature.

I was elated, for $100 million had now been authorized for highway beautification to be spent specifically for billboard removal over the next three years. I knew my signs would be removed, paid for, and the principle of "just compensation" for property rights, pursuant to highway signs, preserved.

On December 20th, we loaded up the Suburban and headed back to Utah, arriving the day before Christmas Eve, just in time to enjoy the best Christmas of my life.

The hard part was over, but there was still a lot of work to do. It took four more years to get all the states where I had signs, to comply with legislation and to get funds appropriated, the federal guidelines written, the signs appraised, approved, and removed. I had to secure contracts, similar to the contracts I had with Utah, with the 12 other states where I had signs in order to take the signs down and collect the monies.

In Idaho, for example, I rented a motel room for six weeks and personally lobbied the state law through the legislature. I testified before the committees, worked with the press, and met with the governor over and over again until finally the act was in compliance with federal law.

In all, it took nine years and $550,000 to finish the job. In the end, I paid off the bank and made good my signature on every single loan. Financially, I would have been miles ahead if there had never been the Highway Beautification Act. My banker knows that, and so does my accountant.

Finally, my battle was over.

The three reasons I gave Edmund Fatlermayer of *Fortune* Magazine at the beginning of my fight in Washington had been accomplished. I had fought for the money I felt the country owed me in order to have my signs taken down, and I had won. I had fought for my property rights and those of other sign owners and had won—my property could not be confiscated without my being paid for it. I had fought for the beautification of America's highways, and signs were being taken down across the nation. I had won.

I had fought for the contract to produce billboards for Phillips Petroleum and Harrah's Club, and numerous other companies, and had won in my efforts.

I had fought for the blessed and sacred ability to talk and for a personal relationship with God, and had won.

And, most important to me, I had fought for the hand of the most beautiful girl I have ever known or shall ever know, and had won.

I won these many battles and many more because I knew I was a child of God and had within me a spark of divinity—that as God was a winner, so could I, one of his children, win.

And I won these battles because of the help and encouragement of many people. I especially remember one man, my boxing coach, who, when I was a freshman in high school, believed in me and gave me encouragement.

Coach McHargue (W.H. "Walt" McHargue) my high school boxing coach, gave me confidence. He taught me how to win. Because he taught me how to win with my fists, I later became convinced I could win with my tongue.

The words he spoke, to this very day, still ring in my ears, "Doug, it's in you! I can see it, I can hear it, I can feel it. When the day comes that you see it, that you hear it, that you feel it, *nothing will stop you.*"

Part VII

Doug Snarr periodically descends upon Washington like

a whirlwind out of the West, takes up temporary headquarters in the Senate Office Building, and prowls congressional corridors to push his program.
                          —*Deseret News*, April 9, 1969
    His is currently the loudest voice pleading for imple-
mentation of the dormant anti-billboard provisions of the
Highway Beautification Act of 1965. (*Fortune*, September,
1969)
    Douglas T. Snarr has a plan to make sure that three-
quarters of the billboards in rural America are torn down.
That may seem an unlikely goal for a man who owns 1,300
roadside signs in 13 western states, but he is serious....
(*The National Observer*, Aug. 24, 1970)
    ...is currently a one-man lobby to get the government to
obey its own law. (*The Washington Post*, Aug. 29, 1970)
    Douglas Snarr, 35-year-old self-proclaimed "billboard
king of Utah," came to Washington, complete with suits of
green, purple, and orange, and ties, iguana cowboy boots
and personality to match. (*The Minneapolis Tribune*, Oct. 4,
1970.)
    Mr. Snarr is the unlikely catalyst in the anti-billboard
operation. (*The Christian Science Monitor* Dec. 5, 1970)
    ...two years ago there was little hope of halting, much
less reducing, the onrushing billboard buildup. But the tide
has turned. And beyond doubt, this dramatic shift is
attributable to the efforts of a single citizen. His name:
Douglas T. Snarr. (*Readers Digest*, December, 1971)
    "Believe in yourself," Snarr cried toward the close of his
50-minute bit that brought the crowd leaping to its feet in an
ovation. (*San Francisco Chronicle*, March 11, 1978)
    ...is currently the fast-rising star of positive-thinking
rallies being held in major cities across the United States....
He has been involved with political debate and successfully
lobbied two bills through the U.S. Congress, testified at
Congressional meetings and with the national press.
(*Church News* [The Church of Jesus Christ of Latter-day
Saints], March 25, 1978)
    What Snarr brings to rally audiences is hope—hope that
ordinary folks can dream big dreams and achieve big goals.
(*Parade* Magazine, May 21, 1978)
    Everybody seeks some form of it; not everybody agrees
what it means. Some see success in terms of wealth,

position, honor—and some, in peace of mind. However you describe it, if success is getting what you want, Douglas T. Snarr has it." (*The Anchorage Times*, March 11, 1979)

Douglas T. Snarr is a genuine success story, a story so downright American that no decent Republican could hear it without having to blink back the tears. (*We Alaskans* [feature magazine of *The Anchorage Daily News*], March 14, 1981)

Editor's note: The preceding chapter is an abridgement of part of a forthcoming book by Douglas T. Snarr which will cover his life and also his philosophy of success in greater detail. The book will further present his life following his Washington, D.C., battle, which is not discussed here. The book will relate how he became one of America's foremost public speakers, speaking on the same platform as Paul Harvey, Art Linkletter, Zig Ziglar, Ira Hayes, Earl Nightingale, Cavett Robert, Dr. Robert Schuller, and Dr. Norman Vincent Peale. This soon-to-be published book will also discuss his term as mission president of the Alaska Anchorage Mission and how he became the chief executive officer and majority stockholder of Positive Thinking Rallies, Inc.

Robert Allen—author of *Nothing Down*, the best-selling book on how to buy real estate with little or no money down (44 weeks on the New York Times best seller list). Approximately 12,000 people signed up for Bob's Nothing Down seminars in 1981. He personally buys about $1,000,000 worth of real estate each year using the methods featured in his book and seminars.

Robert Allen

I can think of many examples to support the idea that my mother has been watching out for me, her little Bobby, even though she died the day I was born. My uncle always accused me of being born under a lucky star. I will mention some of those incidents in this story.

As I said, my mother died the day I was born. They couldn't stop the bleeding, so they moved her from the Raymond, Alberta, hospital to Lethbridge, about 20 miles away, but she never made it.

My father didn't remarry. He just never wanted anyone else. From the things my father and friends said about my mother, I concluded at an early age that she must have been a terrific person. I believe that because she was taken early, she made some kind of a deal with God wherein she had special privileges as my guardian angel.

I had a brother and a sister, both much older than I. They both left home by the time I was ten years old. Most of the time it was just me and Dad.

Raymond had a population of about 2,000 people, mostly Mormons. My grandfather was sent to southern Alberta by Brigham Young. He started a store in Cardston, but later moved to Raymond. When my grandfather died, my uncle took over the store and my father became an accountant for the Raymond Sugar Company. He worked his way up to be head accountant and eventually was in charge of the accounting departments of a number of Alberta sugar factories.

One day as my father and I were driving to Lethbridge, he looked over at me and said, "Son, don't ever work for anybody else." He didn't go into any detail as to why he felt that way. I imagine the statement was the result of frustrations in his work at the sugar factories. Nevertheless, those words had a tremendous impact on my young mind, and I have never forgotten them.

In an effort to head me down the road to independence, Dad started buying penny stocks for me. The stock prices were always listed opposite the funnies in the local paper, and every day after I read my favorite comics, I would look over across the page and see how my penny stocks were doing. I would watch the values go up and down, mostly down. Sometimes I would own several hundred shares in a single company, but the total dollar value would only be about $150.

Dad was always dabbling in the stock market, himself. He read every book ever written on the Dow Theory. It was exciting when one of our stocks would suddenly go up, but there were plenty of downs to offset the ups, so it seemed we never made any substantial gains, but it was fun watching things happen.

Whereas my older brother was an outstanding student in the local school, I was rather mediocre, especially in math and math-related subjects like chemistry and physics. I flunked my 10th grade algebra class and had to take a make-up course during the summer in Calgary, about 160 miles away.

I think Canadian schools are more difficult than those in the United States. In order to graduate from high school, a student must pass a government exam covering in great detail the subjects taught in high school. If you don't pass the exam, you don't graduate. Students are forced to study very hard if they want to graduate.

Even though I was not a good student, and I didn't excell in athletics, either. I was very sociable, and as a result, was elected student body president during my senior year. We raised money selling magazine subscriptions and candy. We bought a new time clock for the basketball gymnasium and left about $1,000 in the bank for our successors. I wasn't one of the best salesmen, but when the magazine company, for which we sold subscriptions, held a drawing among all the salespeople for a motorbike, I was the lucky winner. The lucky star was beginning to shine.

After graduation I rode my new motorscooter to Banff, Alberta, and got a job driving a taxi and limousine for a tour guide company. It was a great experience driving people around, telling them about Canada.

At the end of the summer I enrolled at Ricks College in Rexburg, Idaho. The first exam I took was in zoology. I had already learned the material in my high school zoology class, so after a brief review I was able to earn an A on the first exam. I remember how good it felt, for the first time in my life, to be at the top of the class. I began studying in all my classes in an effort to get more A's. Suddenly, I became a good student, earning five or six A's in the second semester.

After school was out, I submitted my application to become a missionary for the L.D.S. Church, then returned to Banff to guide tours. This summer I wanted to drive buses instead of the taxis and limousines, because bus guides made more money. The company didn't have any formal training program for bus drivers, it was just a matter of getting other drivers to take you out after hours and teach you what you needed to know.

By the first of July, they assigned me to an old 30-seat bus, and I began driving groups of tourists through the Canadian Rockies.

In August, I was assigned to a group from the Philippines. None of the other drivers wanted the Philippine group because they would be on the bus for two weeks, which would probably mean a single tip for the assigned driver. The drivers preferred new groups every day so they could get tipped every day. I ended up with the Philippine group because no one else wanted them.

I picked them up at Lake Louise, and I'm sure they thought I was a little young to be driving their bus over those narrow mountain roads. I went out of my way to give them excellent service, even to the point of having half of the sky windows covered over with paper so they could enjoy more shelter from the sun. They had been on a

worldwide tour for some time and were more interested in
being comfortable than in looking at mountains all the
time. I left the windows at the back uncovered so they could
go back there whenever they felt like looking up at the
scenery.

The head of the group was "Mr. Lopez", the brother of
the vice-president of the Philippines. He owned many
companies including the main newspaper, a television
station, the electric company and other concerns. He was a
multi-millionaire. The group consisted of his friends and
relatives.

They appreciated my helpfulness and soon were inviting
me to eat with them and stay with them in the fancy hotels.
We had a great time. I felt like one of the group.

At the end of the tour, Mr. Lopez asked if I wanted to quit
my job and continue on with them to the Philippines and
Japan. I called Dad from Jasper to see what he thought of
the idea. He, in turn, checked out the group with the Royal
Canadian Mounted Police to make sure they were legitimate. It was decided that I would go with them.

My father agreed to drive up to Banff to get my
belongings and bring them home. I really didn't have
anything with me other than a spare uniform and a
shaving kit. Mr. Lopez took me down to a clothing store in
Jasper and outfitted me with new clothes—suit, shoes,
shirts, socks, everything I needed. He rolled off three extra
$100 bills which he gave to me in case I needed any pocket
money.

We flew to San Francisco where Mr. Lopez owned a
mansion. He bought me three more suits at Roos Atkins. A
few days later we flew to the Philippines. From the airport,
we went straight to the Marcos mansion where Mr. Lopez's
son presented some new dresses to the first lady. A picture
of Mrs. Marcos and me appeared in the family-owned
newspaper. They assigned one of the company executives to
show me around the Philippines. We had a limousine and
an airplane at our disposal and spent the next 14 days
visiting many of the thousands of islands. Then we went on
to Japan.

After about a week in Japan, the group decided to go to
Europe, and invited me to come along, but I figured I had
been gone long enough, and was expecting my missionary

assignment any day. I thanked Mr. Lopez for his kindness, and flew back to Alberta, remembering, once again, that lucky star. I still had the three $100 bills given me at the beginning of the trip.

A few weeks later I received a mission call to go to French Polynesia. After spending two months at the language training mission at Brigham Young University, I went to Tahiti to be a missionary. During the next two years I became very proficient at speaking French and Tahitian.

At the conclusion of the mission I enrolled in Brigham Young University's semester abroad program at Grenoble, France. My older brother, Richard, was director of the German study-abroad program for B.Y.U. and was living in Salzburg, Austria, at the time.

They made me tour director for the Grenoble students. I would go down to the local bus company and charter a bus and design a tour to ski in Switzerland, or visit the bull fights in Spain, or perhaps sightsee in Marseilles. If I couldn't sign up a large number of kids to go, I would get a smaller bus. The vast majority of the students in the program were female, so it was usually me, the driver and 40 or 50 girls who would go on my tours. I made sure the accommodations were suitable, that the girls were fed on time and didn't get lost or kidnapped. We had a ball.

I returned to B.Y.U. and began working towards a degree in French. Financially, I didn't have any problems, thanks to another stroke of good luck which my uncle would have credited to my lucky star.

My sister's brother-in-law, who was a successful stock broker, put together a shell corporation, which he intended to sell to a large private company that wanted to go public. Apparently it was more convenient and less expensive for a private company to buy a shell corporation, assimilate the stock, then resell it under their own name, than to go directly public themselves. I was hired to be the puppet president of this shell corporation at a salary of $500 a month while they were setting it up. The job lasted about a year, and my only responsibility was the occasional signing of papers. I never met a college student with a better part-time job than that.

I went on to graduate with a degree in French. At first my intention was to become a French tutor or teacher, but

as graduation neared, and I was faced wtih the realization
that I could never earn a comfortable living as a french
teacher, I looked to other things and enrolled in BYU's
MBA (Master of Business Administration) program for the
following fall.

During that summer I ran into a fellow named David
Filmore, an entrepreneur's entrepreneur. He worked out of
his basement. He had been on a mission to Japan, and
when he came home he started importing a product that can
best be described as a permanent match. It was a little
plastic box containing a metal match with a wick in it. The
match would light whenever it was struck against the flint
on the side of the box. You could blow it out and light it
again as often as you wished, occasionally refueling the box
with lighter fluid.

David talked me into helping him sell the matches. I had
never liked selling, and my sales experience was limited to
the magazine and candy projects in high school, but David
convinced me it would be a great thing. Our first sales trip
was to the Portland-Seattle area. At first I was reluctant to
approach store owners, cold turkey, without an introduc-
tion, in an effort to sell them the matches, but David quickly
helped me break down the barriers.

He kept saying the worst thing that could happen would
be someone saying "no," and that couldn't hurt anybody.
Besides, I would never see the people again, anyway. I had
nothing to lose, but everything to gain.

Whenever we'd see a store, we'd decide whose turn it was
to make the sale, then go inside to make the presentation. It
was a very visual presentation, striking and blowing out
the matches. It was funny, too, and it usually didn't take
very many minutes until the store owner was laughing so
hard he had to buy the matches. If one of us ran into a hard
objection, the other would step in and help. We had a ball,
and after all the expenses were paid, we each made about
$1,000 on that first trip.

David and I got along so well, that we started talking
about putting together a company to import other products
from overseas. I still had two years of school ahead of me, so
we didn't get much going.

David taught me that it was possible to start something
from nothing. All one needed to get into business was a

dream and a plan.

The next winter, while I was hitting the books, David went to Italy and found a line of glass bottles which he began importing. He shipped them to an old warehouse in Salt Lake City where he made them into terrariums by adding dirt and plants. He began putting the terrariums on consignment in stores around the Salt Lake area, then he talked me into trying to introduce them to stores outside the area.

I'll never forget my first trip. I rented a U-Haul trailer, filled it with terrariums and permanent matches and headed for the Denver area. Once I sold the first Albertson store, it was easy. I'd go into the next Albertson store and say "Fred, at the other store, just bought one," and they would buy, too. Within four days I had sold the entire load and returned home, about $500 richer.

My next sales trip was to the Phoenix area, where again I was able to sell out in just a few days. I continued to sell the matches and terrariums while working towards my MBA degree.

While David Filmore was teaching me how to make money, the MBA school was teaching me how to fit into a large corporation as an employee. The classes were tough, and the competition fierce. There were 60 or 70 students in the class, divided into small groups, working on seemingly meaningless projects. There was constant pressure, and the ranking of students by performance; number one, number two and so on. There was a lot of math and technical material, including computer science, sophisticated corporate financial analysis—everything except how to make money. I almost didn't make it through the first year.

One day, during that first year, I was visiting my sister and browsing through her library, when I discovered a little paperback book titled, *How I Turned $1,000 into a $1,000,000 in Real Estate in My Spare Time,* by William Nickerson. Hundreds of thousands of copies of this book have been sold since it was first published in 1959 or 1960. I think it is probably the best book ever written on real estate. I sat down and read the first three chapters, and became convinced that real estate was the best way to make money. The book showed how it was possible to turn a small nest egg into a fortune by investing in income properties. It was all so simple and reasonable. It was a revelation to me, a bright light on a dark night, a clear answer to that nagging question as to how I would achieve financial security.

As I thought about it, I realized that here was a way to make a living and become financially independent without working for someone else.

During the second year of the MBA program, we were allowed some elective courses and I signed up for every class having anything to do with real estate. One of my teachers, Glenn Nielson, who always taught by the book, made us go out and appraise a piece of property. On that assignment I felt like I was really learning something important, so when it came time to do the big senior project, I put my heart and soul into developing a sophisticated appraisal technique for commercial properties. It turned out to be a highly technical workbook, wherein one plugs in all the details about a particular property, then works them through a complex formula to eventually come up with the value of the property. It was over ten pages long and covered every detail that could effect the value of a property. As I look back, the elements in that report have helped me earn several million dollars.

The teacher, however, thought my project to be rather dull, and gave me a poor grade. I was very disappointed—in the teacher, not the project, which turned out to be the most significant learning experience of the entire MBA course of study.

During the last semester of the MBA program, I was involved in the usual interviewing with possible employers. My plan was to get a good job with a big company, continue living on a shoestring and invest every extra penny in real estate.

The national economy was struggling through the 1974 recession at the time, and the competition for the available jobs was fierce. In terms of grades and class ranking, I was near the bottom, and I didn't have a technical background. While my classmates were bragging about their all-expense-paid trips to visit this or that company, I was having a tough time getting ten-minute interviews in the placement office. I received nearly 50 reject letters from various companies around the country.

There was one bright spot, one moment of hope in what

otherwise was a very discouraging recruiting experience. Somehow, I had impressed the Proctor & Gamble representative who visited the campus, and was one of two students invited to visit their corporate headquarters in Cincinnati, Ohio. They are one of the most attractive companies to young MBA's because they have a brand manager program wherein it is possible for a new employee to quickly move into a position of nearly full responsibility for an assigned product—everything from production and packaging to promotion and advertising.

I went back to Cincinnati and interviewed with all the necessary people. There was a Mormon fellow who took me under his wing; and after all the interviewing was finished, he took me out to dinner. The interviews had gone so well, that at that point I assumed I had the job, and my escort seemed to have the same opinion. We talked about where I ought to live in Cincinnati, locations of the local Church wards, and things like that. I felt so good about the situation, and was so relaxed and at home with this fellow, that I began talking about things that probably should have been left unsaid. I told him about my intentions to invest every extra penny in income properties. I told him how excited I was about the investment possibilities in real estate and how I intended to make a fortune in part-time real estate investing while working for his company.

I returned to Provo and began making plans to move to Cincinnati. About a week later I received the much-anticipated letter from Proctor & Gamble. Instead of offering me the job, as I was sure they would, they turned me down. I was devastated. I had wanted that job so bad I could taste it. I had been so sure that it was in the bag.

Then I made one of the major decisions of my life. My entire MBA training had been preparing me to go to work for a big company. I had tried to follow the expected path, and thus far had met only with rejection, culminating in the big rejection by Proctor & Gamble. If the big companies didn't want me, then I would do my own thing in my own way. Instead of becoming a slave for somebody else, I would work for myself, looking to my own intelligence and resourcefulness for survival, rather than to some company for a regular paycheck.

I sold some Conoco stock my father had bought for me

as I was growing up, for about $4,300. Then I started
looking around for some kind of job to keep me alive while I
was beginning my investment program.

The second counselor in my local LDS branch at BYU
was named Paul Jewkes, an aggressive real estate developer with projects all over. He is a workaholic, a bundle of
nervous energy, one of those guys who is working all the
time. And very successful, too.

✗   At that time, Paul was just beginning a big recreational
development near Mt. Pleasant, Utah. When customers
bought the home sites, they received a share of the
clubhouse, riding stables, swimming pool and other common areas. The project was named Pine Creek Ranch.

I bought one of the building sites myself in an effort to
impress Paul that I was successful and had a little money to
invest. Then I asked him if I could go to work for him selling
home sites. I didn't really care how much money he paid me.
I was mainly interested in learning all I could by working
closely with him. I wanted to find out exactly how he had
become so successful. The project was over 60 miles from
Provo and I conveniently arranged to commute with Paul.
He didn't seem to tire of my endless questions, and he
shared freely his real estate experience with me. He told me
about the first apartments he built in southern California,
how he slept in them as they neared completion to prevent
theft and vandalism, how his wife did the decorating. He
told me about his many battles with city administrators
and city councils in his efforts to get the proper permits and
zoning approvals. These kinds of things were all new to me
and I eagerly tried to digest everything he said.

Occasionally Paul would surprise me, like the morning
we arrived at the project just as they were beginning to pour
cement for the swimming pool. Paul could see that the
concrete was not being handled properly, so he grabbed a
pair of dirty boots out of the trunk of his green Riviera and
jumped right in the middle of all the wet cement, grabbed a
long board and started shimming it across the surface. I
was impressed to see this multi-millionaire wading around
in cement, working side by side with guys earning three or
four dollars an hour. I don't know how many of my MBA
classmates would have been willing to do that.

In finishing up school and beginning to work for Paul I

had somehow let about half of my nest egg slip through my fingers. Of the initial $4,300, I had only $2,000 remaining when I finally got serious about going out and finding a property to buy. I had been studying Nickerson's book, and finally realized it was time to go out and do it.

I began reading the real estate classified advertisements in the local newspaper, and responded to an ad describing a duplex that could be purchased with a low down payment. It was located at 700 North and about 400 East in Provo. It was owned by a student working on his master's degree, and his mother. The student didn't want to manage it, and neither did the mother, so they wanted to sell. They had had it listed with a realtor for $26,000 for more than a year with no success. Now they were trying to sell it themselves at a reduced price of $25,500. They were making monthly payments on a $19,000 contract.

I met with them, inspected the property, and they explained all the details. I felt lost, like I really didn't know what I was doing. I didn't know if it was a good buy, or if I was getting stung.

Partly as a stall tactic, and also in a sincere effort to get a better idea of what the building was really worth, I told them I would have to get an appraisal. I located a realtor named Paul Brown who did the cheapest appraisals in town, at $40 each. The appraisal came in at $22,500, three thousand below the asking price. It appeared that they were asking too much, but I still liked the property because it was close to BYU and was producing rents totaling $300 a month. It didn't appear to be a bad investment.

I sat down with the student and negotiated the price down to $25,000. I told him I had only $1,500 for the down payment, so he agreed to take another $1,000 two months after we closed, and another $1,000 two months after that. I would assume the $19,999 mortgage, and pay off the remainder of the student's equity at a rate of $75 a month at nine percent interest.

Once we had all the details worked out, I sat there at his kitchen table for a full fifteen minutes without saying a word. I was scared to death, not knowing whether to do it or not. I had no idea how I would come up with the additional $2,000 for the rest of the down payment. Finally, I said, "Let's do it," and signed my name on the earnest money agreement. We closed the deal at Paul Brown's (the appraiser) office and set up the escrow there, too.

I immediately went over to my new property, made friends with the tenants, and started cleaning up. I rented a truck and hauled three loads of junk to the dump. I mowed and watered the lawns which were really a mess, cleaned out the flower beds and fixed all the leaky faucets.

Four days after I bought the duplex, a realtor came to see me. He said he had a buyer willing to pay $28,000 for my property. I asked how much his commission would be. He said $1,500. Very quickly I figured that that would leave me a $1,500 return on my $1,500 investment, not bad considering the money had been tied up for only four days. I told the salesman I would accept the offer. A few days later, on the way to Mt. Pleasant, I bragged to Paul about the terrific investment I had made. It probably seemed like a tiny deal to him, but to me it was the greatest thing in the world because it was my first successful real estate investment.

I sold cabin sites for Paul during the summer, and made what I thought was pretty good money. I was also in a play that summer, the BYU production of *South Pacific*.

In my continuing search for another piece of real estate, I ran into a salesman who talked me into becoming his partner in purchasing a seven-plex. I put up the money, he put up his commission, and we were partners. It didn't work out very well so I started thinking about getting my own real estate license so I wouldn't have to work through realtors all the time. I figured it would be a valuable learning experience, plus a chance to keep at least part of the commissions on the properties I purchased.

In October, when things began slowing down for the winter at Pine Creek Ranch, I passed the test for my real estate license and went to work for Paul Brown, the old fellow who had appraised the first duplex for me. We had become good friends. He could see that I was a go-getter, and he welcomed me into his office. Paul Brown Realty was one of the small, old-time offices, specializing in house sales. They didn't have any computers for fast appraisals, or any fancy advertising—just a quiet small-town real estate office, everyone in shirt sleeves.

I felt very uncomfortable in Paul's office. I had been trained as an MBA, a business professional. Now I was nothing more than a house salesman in Provo, Utah. I hoped none of my classmates would find out what I was doing. That would embarrass me.

I didn't like selling houses. I was more interested in investments, and wanted to put together investment packages. That's the direction I wanted to go. I took every real estate investment course that was offered in my efforts to learn all I could.

That Christmas the BYU football team was in the Fiesta Bowl in Arizona, so my roommates and I decided to hit the bowl game and go down to Acapulco, too. It was a fast trip, almost all driving, covering about 2,500 miles, and we did the whole thing in 52 hours. It was tiring, but I had a lot of time to think, and decided that if I was going to be a big-time investment counselor, rather than a small-time house peddler, I had to start acting the part. First I would look the part, no more short-sleeve sport shirts. From now on, I would wear a coat and tie every day. I would have my own private office, with a good desk. I was going to be a professional businessman.

As soon as I arrived home, I set up my own private office in the back of Paul Brown Realty. My office looked sharp, and so did I. But most important of all, I began to feel like a young professional who was going places.

Not long after I had put on my new, successful look, an employee from the LDS Church real estate department came into the office to have Paul Brown do a quick appraisal on a four-acre field owned by the Church and located in an apartment area near BYU. He asked if anyone in the office was interested in taking an option on the parcel.

I didn't know anything about options, but asked him to explain how it worked. He said that if I would give him $5,000 I would receive a 12-month option to buy the property for $280,000. If I could find a buyer during the 12 months who would pay more than $280,000, I could keep the difference. If I was unable to sell it during the 12 months I would forfeit the $5,000. I told him I didn't have $5,000. He said that maybe he could get it through the committee for $2,500. I didn't tell him that I didn't have that much, either. I had put all my money into that seven-plex and was suffering from a negative cash flow. I also had to pay $100

every month on the recreation lot I had purchased from
Paul Jewkes. I didn't have any money, but I told him I
would think about it.

Paul Brown did the appraisal and advised me not to take
the option at $280,000. He said it was too much, but if I
could get them to go $200,000 on the option, it might turn
into a pretty good thing for me, a way to get my feet on the
ground, and get off to a good start in the real estate
business. I drove to Church headquarters in Salt Lake City,
went to the real estate department to gather more information on the property.

This was the kind of deal I wanted to be involved in,
rather than selling houses. As I became more wrapped up in
the option on the four acres I realized that Paul Brown and
the rest of his salesmen were more interested in residential
selling than investment projects. I started looking around
for another place to work.

I ran into Lowell and Paul Christensen, Patrick Wyman
and some of the other people at Lincoln Realty in Provo.
They wore suits and ties to work as I did. In addition to the
normal residential selling, they had investments and
developments all over the world. They knew how to work
the numbers and were into real estate investing in a big
way. They offered me a job and a nice office. I moved to
Lincoln Realty.

After some negotiating I was able to get the option on
the four-acre parcel at $200,000 by putting up $2,500. I
obtained the $2,500 by getting a local dentist to co-sign with
me on a bank loan. It was April of 1976.

Now that I was getting into what I felt to be big time real
estate, I wanted more education. I talked my roommates
into going to Miami, Florida with me and sharing the gas
expenses, so I could attend a convention of the National
Association of Home Builders. I wanted to rub shoulders
with the big hitters, to expand my thinking and broaden my
horizons. I was not disappointed.

One of the first things I noticed at the convention was a
fellow riding up in a Rolls Royce. He was in the back seat
talking on a telephone. There were a lot of guys like this
attending the convention, heavy hitters, people who had
succeeded in real estate. For three days I attended dozens of
mini-sessions with these fellows, hearing them discuss their

real estate transactions. My horizons were indeed expanded, and I became more convinced than ever that there were a lot bigger things to do than sell houses in Provo, Utah.

As we drove back from the convention, I re-read *Think and Grow Rich*, by Napoleon Hill. I decided it was time to get serious about setting goals. One of the first goals I wrote down was to build $100,000 in personal net worth by the time I was 30 years old. That amount seemed like a fortune to me.

After arriving home and settling into the routine of things at Lincoln Realty, I began to understand one of the big differences between the poor and the rich. Whereas most people are living from one paycheck to the next, using credit to spend more than they are earning, the more successful and more wealthy people are planning ahead—two, five or even ten years down the road.

The people at Lincoln taught me how to make financial plans. They were numbers people, with their H.P. calculators, always working out projections, year by year, as far as five or ten years down the road, taking into consideration appreciation, inflation, income, tax benefits and all the other financial considerations concerning real estate investments. They showed me how an income property that might appreciate only ten percent a year could give the owner a 50, 100 or even 200 percent return on his investment, if leveraged properly. Gradually, I began to realize that my goal to have a $100,000 net worth was peanuts. I began to understand that with a handful of good investments, I could have $1,000,000 net worth by the time I was 30 years old.

I began putting together projections on the four-acre option parcel. I made sketches, showing how many apartments could be built on the property. I gathered all the legal information, what could and could not be done, and I did a lot of dreaming. I read everything I could get my hands on that had anything to do with developing rental income properties.

I attended a seminar in Salt Lake City taught by Charles Considine, one of the foremost real estate tax accountants and attorneys in the United States. I think it cost me $250 to attend the seminar, and it was worth every penny as I learned about corporations and real estate investment organizations. They plugged me into a network of people out of California who teach creative real estate seminars, and soon I was off to California to attend those seminars.

Of course, I wasn't making any money traveling around the country attending seminars. Most of them cost $250 or $300 to register, plus I had to pay for gas, food and lodging. Some people thought I was crazy spending so much money on these expensive seminars. Some months I hardly had enough money to pay the rent, but somehow I would manage to scrape together enough money for another seminar. When friends would criticize me for spending so much time and money on seminars, I would answer with a quote from the president of Harvard University, "If you think education is expensive, try ignorance." At the seminars, I was discussing real estate investments with some of the most successful real estate people in the country. As far as I was concerned, the price of the seminars was dirt cheap, considering what I was learning.

Between seminars, the guys at Lincoln began indoctrinating me in big-time real estate, getting me involved in listing and selling apartments, the big ones. I put together several deals on major apartment complexes in the Provo area and earned some pretty good commissions. Every time I received a commission check I thought, "Wow, I'm getting paid to go to school."

There were some hard knocks, too, as I became the victim of several "commission-dectomies." That's where the seller tells himself that he has sold too cheaply and cannot afford to pay a sales commission as he agreed to do before the sale was made. I still have scars from one or two of those, but I learned some lessons which I doubt could have been learned any other way.

I had no ambitions of becoming a real estate broker. My goal was to learn all I could while building up my own holdings to the point where I could become a full-time investor, buying and selling my own properties.

I believe that one of the keys to success is becoming an expert at something other people need. It doesn't matter much what the chosen profession is, as long as it is something people need, and you become an expert at it. Once I chose real estate as my profession, I did everything possible to become an expert, a true real estate professional. When money was scarce, I didn't jump back and forth from one thing to another, but continued to concentrate on real estate.

There was one time, however, when financial pressures almost got me headed in another direction. It was in the winter of 1975. There were only three months left on the option, and no buyers were in sight. One or two commission-dectomies had put me in a serious financial bind. I didn't have enough to pay my rent, which was only $55 a month. Out of desperation I went up to BYU and applied for an opening in their program bureau, falling back on my experience in heading up excursions for their semester abroad program in Europe. The job offered a salary of $10,500 a year. I was so low that I figured I just had to go to work for someone as a salaried employee. As with the Proctor and Gamble job, I was again fortunate enough to be turned down. If I had been offered the job, I'd probably now be earning $1,000 a month lining up hotel reservations for groups of dancers and singers. As it was, the rejection forced me back into real estate where I belonged.

A few days later I received a call from a company in Salt Lake City offering me $280,000 for the four acres. I told them to put it in writing, fast, and I might take it. They did, and I did. After paying the sales commission, a return to the dentist who had co-signed the note, various costs, and a portion to Lincoln Realty for helping me put the thing together, I ended up with $30,000 cash—not bad for a single guy just out of school, paying $55 a month rent.

I was back in business. I formed a corporation for tax reasons, bought an airplane so I could attend more seminars and set ten personal goals for 1976, including finding a wife, earning $100,000 in commissions, taking a major trip out of the country.

About that time I took a listing on a 12-unit apartment on Center Street in Provo. It had a terrific price, and the attorney who owned it was willing to sell for only $5,000 down. I presented it to a friend who owned one of the exclusive clothing stores in town, thinking I would make a nice commission on the sale. It was perfect for my friend. Because of the location it was appreciating better than 15 percent a year, and the depreciation write-off alone would

save him more on his taxes in the first year than what he
would spend to make the down payment.It was a steal, one
of those once-in-a-lifetime opportunities.

When an opportunity like this one presents itself, you
have to act fast. If you don't, someone else will. My friend
talked and talked, and haggled, and consulted, and finally
sent his mother and brother over to check it out. The mother
didn't like the pink carpets, and the brother, who was a
builder, could see that it needed repairs. They told my friend
it was a dump, and that he shouldn't buy it no matter how
low the down payment. My friend just couldn't see past the
pink carpets and leaky faucets. He couldn't grasp the
numbers.

Finally, in exasperation I asked myself, "Why am I
doing this? Why am I beating my head against the wall to
get someone else to make an investment that will earn a
better than 200 percent return the first year?" I bought it
myself, and still own it today. In fact my corporate offices
are to be located there, shortly. I began to change my
thinking about what I wanted to be doing in real estate. In
the future, instead of spinning my wheels trying to get other
people to snap up good investments, I would spend more
time and energy trying to buy those investments myself.

About that time I obtained another listing on a 12-plex,
this one priced a little over $300,000. I couldn't buy it myself
because the owner needed more cash than I could raise. I
was planning a trip to Europe that summer and wanted to
get it sold before leaving. I tried very hard, but was
unsuccessful.

That summer I bought a Volkswagon bus in Germany,
and together with two friends from BYU, spent two months
traveling through 17 countries. I brought the bus back to
Provo, and moved into a duplex which I had purchased.

At the end of the summer, our student LDS ward
sponsored a Hawaiian luau. Up until this point in time I
had been too busy to make any progress towards my goal to
find a wife, but I hadn't been at the luau very long when I
began to notice Daryl Lieurance. I had known her for a year
or so, but she was a little too flashy for me, and we were just
casual friends. She had been working in Salt Lake City
during the summer and drove down to the luau. She was on
a physical fitness kick, had lost some weight, and looked

just fantastic in the new white outfit she was wearing. We began dating, and one month later I proposed to her in my airplane at 10,000 feet above the Provo temple. The wedding date was set for the following February. As far as I was concerned we could have been married that week, but she wanted time to get ready, send out invitations and those kinds of things.

In the meantime I attended a seminar, in Las Vegas, another in San Diego, and another in Hawaii. I was really learning the ins and outs of apartment investing. I loved it, every detail. Of course there were sometimes problems in the application. I remember unloading a 7-plex at a loss because the resident manager was selling heroin, holding wild parties, and I was getting calls in the middle of the night.

Not long after I started courting Daryl, I flew to Los Angeles to attend a seminar in creative financing by a fellow named Bob Steele. He said that the conventional way of buying real estate with a down payment followed by monthly payments is just one of many ways to make a purchase, and he proceeded to blow my mind away with countless creative ways to finance transactions, using paper instead of money.

While I was at the seminar I received a long distance call from the owner of the 12-plex I had been unable to sell the past summer. He said he had an offer for $295,000 and my listing had expired, but he wanted to give me one last chance to buy it because I had worked so hard at trying to sell it. He would let me have it for $300,000. I didn't have nearly enough for the big down payment he wanted, but I told him I would get together with him in the next few days to work something out. I returned to the seminar, more alert than I had ever been in my life, looking for some creative angle that would enable me to buy the 12-plex.

The following weekend I sat down with the owner and worked out a nothing-down deal. He agreed to let me take out a new first mortgage on the property for $225,000 which paid off the $80,000 old mortgage, leaving $145,000 cash for the down payment. I agreed to come up with an additional $15,000, making a total down payment to the seller of $160,000. He agreed to take a $60,000 second mortgage at 12 percent interest.

When I told him I needed six months to put the deal together, he was concerned that I would tie up his property for the six months and not be able to put the deal together. His worries were probably well-founded. I was young and single, a basically inexperienced real estate agent. He asked for $5,000 earnest money.

I didn't have it, but finally convinced him to go ahead with the transaction by offering him my duplex—and its $8,000 equity—no strings attached if I defaulted at the end of the six months.

It was necessary to take in a partner with a strong financial statement in order to get the new first mortgage. Of the $15,000 cash that I had to come up with, $10,000 was obtained from the first month's rent receipts, and my partner and I borrowed the other $5,000 on a signature loan.

Not long after the transaction was closed, my partner offered to sell me his interest for $5,000. I didn't have the money, but I did have a $5,000 equity in the recreational lot I had purchased from Paul Jewkes. I talked him into taking that. I became the sole owner of a $300,000 apartment building with nothing down.

I realized that if I could buy one property with little or nothing down, I could buy more. It occurred to me that if I could get my name on $1,000,000 worth of income property without creating a negative cash flow, assuming an annual appreciation of 10 percent, all I would have to do is wait seven years and the appreciation alone would earn me $1,000,000! In the next 18 months I purchased $2,800,000 worth of real estate, some with partners, most on my own. Several of the purchases were bad decisions, but most were sound investments.

At the end of 1976, after completing the deal on the 12-plex, I felt I had graduated from the amateur status and was a legitimate big time investor. One of the first things I did in 1977 was move out of Lincoln Realty and open my own office. I didn't have a broker's license, so I maintained my affiliation with Lincoln as a branch office.

I wanted to be the classiest investment broker in Provo. I leased a brand new office near the University Mall for $300 a month, and filled it with $4,000 worth of beautiful furniture which cost me $141 a month on a lease agreement.

Just before Daryl and I were married in February of

1977, I traded my duplex for a nice home on Chokecherry Lane in Orem, another nothing down deal. We were married on Valentine's Day and went on our honeymoon to Hawaii.

We were there for fourteen days, and again the hand of luck fell upon me. One day I was out swimming in the ocean when by pure chance I came upon an older couple who were drowning. While they were swimming in the surf, the riptide had carried them out. They were out of shape and didn't have the strength to swim back to shore. They had just said their final goodbyes to each other and were going down for the third time when I came splashing along. I towed them to shore, and they couldn't do enough to express their gratitude. Of course, I wouldn't take any money for what I had done. They owned a plush condominium on Molokai and said I could use it, free of charge, whenever I came to Hawaii in the future. In fact, much of my book, *Nothing Down*, was written while staying at that condominium.

Daryl and I returned to our new home and my new office to begin our life together. Business was good to me as I was able to attract some excellent clients and put together some good transactions. I was subscribing to and reading the *Creative Real Estate Magazine* and was beginning to get involved in exchanging problem properties for people whom I referred to as "don't wanters." A typical example is the owner of a 12-plex who wants to trade for bare ground because he is tired of management problems. The fellow with the bare ground wants to trade for apartments because he needs a bigger tax write-off. My job was to get the two together. I began attending exchange meetings and seminars, around the country.

While traveling to and from the various seminars I did a lot of thinking as to which direction my career should take. I wanted to be my own man, not under someone else's umbrella, as I presently was with Lincoln Realty. I didn't want to be an agent, anymore, showing people property, trying to get them to buy something. I didn't like being a real estate salesman.

I wanted desperately to be on my own, but the income properties I was buying were, in most cases, not providing any cash flow. Without sales commissions I had no money to live on. I needed to find a supplementary source of income if I wanted to give up selling.

One day Jack Ayre, a fellow I'd met at a seminar in San Diego, called from his Salt Lake City office and invited me to drive to California with him to attend a seminar. Like me, he was also a seminar nut. He is a big thinker, and I welcomed the chance to travel with him and pick his brain. At that time he was just getting into a big mining deal in Nevada. I don't remember all the details, except that it was some kind of tax shelter angle wherein people would buy undeveloped silver claims for around $12,000 each, conduct some core sampling to establish the value of the ore, then reappraise the claims at about $200,000 each before donating them to Brigham Young University. The buyer would receive a $200,000 tax write-off for only $12,000. I don't know how the deal finally turned out for Jack, but I don't think the IRS liked it.

As we were driving along that day, we got to adding up all the money we had spent on seminars, and how much money was being spent on the present seminar we were going to attend. We concluded that seminars could be very profitable, and that we ought to conduct one ourselves. I realized that I was probably one of the foremost seminar attenders in the entire country, having spent more than $5,000 on seminar registration fees in less than three years.

Back home again after the seminar, Jack and I put our heads together and organized our little seminar. We called it "Pyramiding Your Buried Assets into Millions." Jack arranged for us to use the conference room at Western Savings in Salt Lake City where he had some money. We placed a $25 ad in the classified section of the newspaper offering a free lecture, call for details. The phone nearly rang off the hook. At the free lecture we gave them a taste of what we intended to teach in the seminar which was held one night each week for four consecutive weeks. The cost of the seminar was $75 per person. We also arranged to use the Commercial Security board room in Provo for the same program.

Our free lectures usually drew 30 to 40 people, and 10 or 15 normally signed up for the seminar. We took turns teaching the evening seminars in Provo and Salt Lake City. Except for advertising, our expenses were practically non-existent, so we were able to take home nearly all of the registration money. Each of us was making about $1,000 a month for teaching one evening each week.

I thought we had a good thing going, and I was finally able to pay my bills without having to be a real estate salesman. On the other hand, this seminar thing was just peanuts to Jack, when compared to his big mining deal in Nevada. After several months he backed out of the arrangement, giving his share of the business to me.

Now that the seminar business was mine, I decided to make some changes. It was the end of the year (1977), the time of year when I seem to make the most changes in my life. I decided to change the name to "Nothing Down." By this time I had purchased quite a few properties with nothing down, and as I taught the seminars I noticed people never seem to tire of hearing ways to buy real estate without using their own money.

The new name drew more people, and I began to make pretty good money on the seminars. My wife didn't like me running off in the evenings to teach classes, but I loved it. It was a real ego trip for me, showing people all the ways I had discovered to buy real estate without a down payment. It was very satisfying knowing I was helping other people be successful in real estate.

I didn't hold the seminars all the time. Whenever I needed cash, I'd just put the little ad in the paper announcing the free seminar where I would collect several thousand dollars in registration fees. It was a very simple, profitable business, allowing me to have my days free to manage the increasing number of acquisitions in my portfolio. I was like the guy in the circus trying to keep a number of plates twirling on sticks, all at the same time.

I remembered a statement I had read by Herb True saying, "What people don't realize is that successful people often have more failures than unsuccessful people, the difference is that the successful people keep trying." Thomas Edison invented concrete furniture, a new idea where furniture was produced very inexpensively by pouring concrete into molds. The concept was a big flop, but we don't remember him for that.

During 1977 and 1978 I was involved in two very bad investments. One was a 40-unit condominium conversion in Salt Lake City, the other a 41-lot subdivision in Pleasant

Grove. I got into both of them with nothing down, taking in partners by promising them double their money back in one year. I was thinking big instead of smart. In the subdivision I started 15 single family spec houses at once, right at the beginning of the big housing slump. I lost about $200,000 on both deals, and it has been just recently that I have been able to pay off what I owed the partners. I promised them going in that if things didn't work out, I would refund all their money plus interest, and I have done that even though I personally lost a lot of money.

Some nights, I had nightmares of Dan Rather and the cameraman from *60 Minutes* showing up at my doorstep, asking if I was the so-called millionaire investor who had sucked these unsuspecting partners into these shaky real estate transactions.

There always seems to be some good along with the bad. About the same time as the two projects above were going sour, Jack Ayre and I converted a 10-unit Provo apartment into condominiums. Again, it was a nothing down deal for me. I received a $50,000 mortgage the first year as the condominiums were sold, upon which I get $444 a month for the next 25 years.

While the bottom was falling out of the two bad investments, I was in a terrific cash bind. My biggest single source of cash income at the time was my seminars, so I decided to beef them up as much as possible. Instead of putting a little $25 ad in the classified section of the paper, I developed a display ad with my picture which cost $212 to run in the paper. Instead of using the Commercial Security conference room for free, I rented a larger conference room at the Royal Inn for $16. The free lecture was packed, and I signed up 40 lecture was packed, and I signed up 40 people at $125 each for the seminar. After all expenses were paid, I made over $4,000.

I began to realize that the seminars could be a big thing for me if I handled them right. First, I changed the format from one free lecture followed by weekly seminars, to a series of three, free lectures followed by a Friday night and Saturday seminar, getting the whole thing finished in one week. That's the way Albert Lowry, Nickerson and the other big seminar people around the country did it.

I decided to try the new format in Salt Lake City by

placing $2,600 worth of display advertising in the local papers and reserving space at the TraveLodge and Hilton. The free lectures were on Monday, Tuesday, and Wednesday nights with the seminar the following Friday night and Saturday. The free seminars were packed and we signed up 180 people at $195 each to take the seminar. I guaranteed the results of the seminar, offering people their money back if they weren't fully satisfied with what they learned. I had to give up only one refund, to an old fellow who complained the room was too crowded, too hot and that he couldn't hear what was going on. After all the expenses were paid, I made over $20,000 on that one seminar! Now I knew I was on to something big.

I decided to take the show on the road. We went to Seattle, Portland, San Francisco. We had a flop in Fresno, California, where only seven people signed up. We had another disaster in Denver, where, after spending a bundle in the local papers, only 20 people signed up for the course. I learned the hard way that in Denver you never schedule anything on a Saturday when the Denver Broncos are playing. My wife and brother-in-law helped me do the seminars.

The success of the seminars convinced me that there was a need for a book explaining my nothing down philosophy. On February 14, 1978, our anniversary, Daryl and I flew to Hawaii for a one-month stay. We had scheduled the condominium on Molokai for one week, the one belonging to the couple I had saved from drowning. The other week was scheduled at the large home on the beach near the Hawaii Temple.

Before leaving on the trip, I had roughed out a general outline of what I thought the book should contain. All that information was festering up inside me, wanting to burst right out. I could hardly wait to start writing.

While Daryl sunned herself on the beach, I pounded away, day after day on the typewriter. When it was time to come home, I had finished seven or eight chapters and had a detailed outline for the rest of the book.

I hadn't been home long when I ran into Dian Thomas, author of *Roughing it Easy* and other outdoor books. She wanted to take my course, hoping it might help her better invest her royalty money. In the course of our conversation

I mentioned my book. She told me I ought to go to the American Book Association (ABA) convention in Atlanta. She said every major book publisher in the country had a booth there. She told me to take my manuscript and show it to them.

That sounded like a good idea so I told her I would give it a try. I arranged to have a cover designed, and for a professional editor to edit some of the chapters. I did some research to determine which publishers I ought to go after. Nickerson's and Lowry's books were both published by Simon & Schuster. Sam Myerson, the fellow who had edited these books was still there. I decided that Simon and Schuster was the one I wanted.

When I arrived at the convention center, I found out that writers with manuscripts were not welcome. It was a convention for book business people—publishers, distributors, retailers. I told the people at the registration table that I was considering going into the book business, and wanted to learn more about it. I wasn't really lying. I have always wanted to own a bookstore.

I went up to the Simon and Schuster booth and asked one of the salesmen to show me the president. He told me to come back later and he would point him out to me, which he did. At first, I was too scared to go up and speak with Mr. Schneider. For two days I just observed him, while learning all I could from other publishers. As far as I could tell, I was the only author in the place. The fellow representing BYU Press said, "You sure got guts coming here."

Most of the publishers I showed my book to, loved it. Three or four wanted to sign me on the spot—Grossett & Dunlap, Dow Jones, Irwin and one or two more. I asked every question I could think of, learning as much as possible about the book business.

During the second day I approached Mr. Schneider, introduced myself and told him I had a manuscript I thought he would like. After briefly looking over the cover and sample chapters, he said he loved it and suggested that I show it to his associate publisher, Joni Evans, who also was his wife. I met her a little later and gave her the manuscript and art which she promised to take back to the editor.

As soon as I returned home, I began receiving calls and

letters from the other publishers who had expressed interest in the book. After several weeks, there was still no word from Simon and Schuster.

I called an editor from HP Books, a fellow I had become acquainted with at the convention. I explained that a number of publishers were after the book, but that I still hadn't heard anything from Simon & Schuster, my first choice. What should I do? He told me to call Simon & Schuster and tell them to "put up or shut up."

I called Joni and explained to her in detail the offers I was receiving, and from whom. She responded by offering me a $6,000 advance, $3,000 on signing a contract and $3,000 upon completion of the manuscript. I would receive a 15 percent royalty on each book sold. I accepted the offer, not sure how good of a deal it was for me. I later found out that it was an excellent offer. The best authors in the world usually receive no more than a 15 percent royalty, and first-book writers usually receive less than 15 percent. What I didn't realize going into the agreement, was that there would be another 18 months of writing, re-writing, editing, checking galley proofs, etc., before the book would finally appear on bookstore shelves.

Soon after Simon & Schuster agreed to publish my book, I received a call from a Roger Larson in Reno, Nevada. He explained that he had been in the real estate seminar business with Albert Lowry, one of the biggest real estate seminar people in the United States. While working for Lowry, one of Roger's assignments had been to check me out to make sure I was not copying them. He said that a Burns detective had taken my course and recorded every single word. He said Lowry was planning to sue me if the tapes proved that I was using his material, but instead, the tapes had confirmed my legitimacy, that I was indeed doing my own thing.

Roger explained that he had left Lowry to start his own marketing company, specializing in real estate seminars. He wanted to know if I was interested in letting his company take over the marketing of my courses. I agreed to get together with him to talk about it.

I was in the mood to listen to him, because a short time earlier we had had another seminar fall flat on us. Up until that spring we had never taught any courses further east

than Texas, but thinking we could succeed anywhere, we
scheduled one in Baltimore, on the east coast. It was
scheduled in the Jewish section of town. ✐

We arrived in a snow storm, but it was colder in our
lecture room than outside. The eastern Jews didn't appreciate my upbeat, western style, and the effectiveness of the
free lectures was ruined with heckling. Few signed up for
the seminars. It was a wasted trip.

We had planned to take the proceeds from the Baltimore
seminar and go on a brief vacation to the Caribbean. There
were no proceeds, but we went to the Caribbean anyway,
using my American Express card. My brother Richard and
his wife who lived in Baltimore talked with us about his
coming to work full time with me. He had an excellent job as
assistant dean of the evening school at Johns Hopkins
University, and was in line to become the next dean, but his
kids were entering the teenage years and Richard and his
wife were beginning to think it would be better to raise their
children in Utah. Shortly after the trip, the decision was
made for him to join me in Utah.

In July, Richard and I met with Roger Larson and his
people at the Rodeway Inn in Salt Lake City. They
convinced me that they would be able to sign up a lot more
people for my courses than I had ever been able to do. In
August, they took over the marketing of the seminars. I
received a handsome royalty on everyone who signed up for
the course. All I had to do was train the instructors.

With Roger handling the seminars, Richard and I began
setting up monthly RAND (Robert Allen Nothing Down)
groups to service graduates of the seminars with advanced
courses and newsletters. We now have over 50 functioning
groups in the top 50 cities in the U.S. We worked closely
with Roger and his marketing people.

During the last part of 1979, about 2,000 people took the
basic seminar. In 1980, when 7,000 people signed up for my
seminars I knew I had done the right thing in letting Roger
Larson take over the marketing. In 1981 we taught over
12,000.

The book was finally introduced at the end of January,
1980. Two months later it hit the New York Times best-
seller list and remained there for 50 weeks.

Simon and Schuster's best method of promoting the

book had been a display advertisement showing a picture of me with the accompanying headline, "Send me to any city in the United States. Take away my wallet. Give me $100.00 for living expenses. And in 72 hours I'll buy an excellent piece of real estate using none of my own money."

Advertisements with this headline sold a lot of books, but of course there were those who were skeptical of my claim. In November of 1980 I received a letter from the *Los Angeles Times* challenging me to go to a city of their choice (unknown to me) with one of their reporters at my side and buy a piece of real estate as I claimed I could in the advertisement. I wrote back formally accepting the challenge. They assured me that if I succeeded, they would give me some very favorable publicity, but if I failed, they would crucify me.

I flew to Los Angeles on the evening of Sunday, January 19, 1981. The next morning at 6 a.m., I met *Times* staff writer Martin Baron in the lobby of the Marriott Hotel near the airport. As we drove to the terminal, he asked if I knew where we were going. I told him I had no idea. He handed me the Sunday edition of the *San Francisco Chronicle*, indicating that was our destination. I opened to the real estate section where the lead story had the headline, "Median Home is $106,662 in the City."

I told him he couldn't have picked a harder city, except perhaps Washington, D.C., or New York City. He seemed delighted. He was in a no-lose situation. It didn't matter to him if I succeeded or failed. Either way, he had a good story.

While on the airplane, I explained to Baron that the key to making a nothing-down purchase is finding a "don't-wanter," someone who really wants to get rid of a piece of real estate. Maybe there are tenant problems, or an oppressive mortgage payment. Maybe he's been transferred and sky-high mortgage rates are killing plans to sell his home. Or maybe he's just read one of those best-selling books about the coming real estate crash.

I devoured the classified ads, marking the ones where the seller showed signs of being flexible. Some of the key words I was looking for were: rent with option to buy, vacant, only five or eight percent down, etc.

A lady on the plane overheard some of our conversation and recommended TRI Realty on Van Ness Boulevard because they were reported to be very good at putting together creative deals.

When the plane landed, Baron gave me the $100 expense money, and I gave him my wallet. He was insistent that the claims in my advertisement be met in every detail.

We took the airport shuttle bus to the central bus station where we checked our luggage into a locker, then headed for TRI Realty. We were introduced to salesperson Trish Bentzen. I told her I was interested in buying some properties where the seller would be flexible on the terms. She began showing me properties described in her listing book requiring down payments of about 10 percent. I wrote a no-down offer on one of the properties in her multiple listing book wherein I would assume the first mortgage, and the seller would take a second and third mortgage for the balance. There would be no down payment, and I would make the payments on all three mortgages.

She took the offer to show it to her boss, and returned a few minutes later saying there were too many loose ends, not enough security for the seller. She would not want her seller to accept such an offer. I realized I was in the wrong office.

I borrowed the phone and called a realtor across the bay in Alamo. His name was Richard Holzhauer. Even though I had never met him, I knew he had taken my course and was using my techniques. He agreed to present some offers for me, and to come to San Francisco early in the afternoon.

After a quick lunch at the Burger King, we went to the plush St. Francis Hotel where I used their lobby telephone to call the numbers listed in the ads I had marked in the paper. I was able to get an appointment to see a condominium priced at $158,000 in San Francisco's Diamond Heights district. The seller was asking only eight percent down.

Holzhauer was a little late picking us up, and had to make a stop on the way to Diamond Heights. We were 45 minutes late for the appointment and missed meeting the owner. Things weren't going well at all, so much wasted time and wheel spinning.

After visiting several more properties during the late afternoon, we checked into a TraveLodge motel in the seedy Tenderloin district. We ate dinner at a Jack-in-the-Box restaurant. I had only $100 for expenses and didn't want to end up spending a night on a park bench before it was absolutely necessary.

I spent the evening calling on more leads and making more appointments. At 10:12 p.m. I received a call from Rocky Lane, owner of the Diamond Heights condo. I told him I had seen the condo, and explained the kind of deal I would like to put together. He said he would be willing to look at a nothing-down offer. We arranged to get together the next morning. I told Baron to write down "10:12 pm." in his notebook. I was reasonably certain I would be able to buy the condo. After what had been a frustrating day, I went to sleep feeling pretty good about how things were developing.

The next morning, we met Rocky Lane at his office in Menlo Park. He was big, 28 years old, wearing an open collar and cowboy boots. His office was a plush, restored mansion with $60-hinges on the doors and 14-foot ceilings.

Baron seemed startled when, after only a few minutes, we signed an agreement. I assumed the $125,000 first mortgage. Lane took back a second mortgage for $21,000 and a third mortgage for $12,000, both at 10 percent interest. I was to pay interest only on the second and third mortgages for three years, at which time they were to be paid off in full.

The reason Lane was so willing to make a nothing-down transaction is as follows: He purchased the condo three months earlier for $122,500. Based on an appraisal from a savings and loan company of $165,000, he was able to get a first mortgage of $125,000, pocketing $2,500 for his trouble. Based on the $165,000 appraisal, he anticipated selling the $21,000 second mortgage from me to an investor at a discounted amount of about $16,000, all of which he could pocket as profit on the deal, in addition to the $2,500 he had already taken. Not a bad return after holding the property for only three months.

Baron asked me how I intended to handle the $1,800 a month payments on the three mortgages. I told him I would immediately place a classified ad offering half ownership in the condo to anyone who would move in and take over the payments. The party would have an option to buy out my half for $6,000 any time within two years. The purchase price including my $6,000 profit would be $164,000, one thousand below the appraised value.

We completed the condo deal 30 hours after arriving in San Francisco. By the time we had reached the 58th hour, I had purchased seven properties valued at $722,000. I must admit that some of them were not the kinds of investments I would make under normal circumstances, but I wanted to make sure Baron became absolutely convinced that I could buy real estate with nothing down as my advertisement claimed, that I was for real, that I was legitimate.

The publicity from the article was priceless. On Sunday, February 1, 1980, the story appeared in the *L.A. Times*, beginning on the front page of the business section and continuing through five consecutive pages. There were pictures of me, my advertisement and the properties I had purchased. Within days, the story was picked up by other newspapers in California, Hawaii, New Jersey and other states.

I have no idea how much that story will benefit book sales and seminar attendance, but I am sure a million dollars in advertising couldn't produce an equal benefit. Simon and Schuster has prepared a new book campaign based on the *L.A. Times* story, and Roger Larson is well on the way to signing up 10,000 seminar students in 1981.

Sometimes people ask me why, if I am so successful in real estate, do I bother with seminars and books. First, I tell them that I love to teach, both through the written and spoken word. Second, the book and seminars are very profitable undertakings and my entrepreneuring spirit will not let me turn my back on such golden opportunities. Third, I receive a trememdous amount of satisfaction knowing I am helping other people realize success and financial independence. A number of my seminar graduates have purchased in the neighborhood of $10 million worth of real estate. Many have become millionaires using the things taught in my book and seminars. I have achieved financial independence, and I enjoy helping other people do the same.

At present, I am writing a new book, planning for a nationwide real estate newsletter and buying about $200,000 worth of real estate phenomenon (all nothing down, of course). The opportunities are endless.

Occasionally, I think back on that day as a boy when Dad and I were driving to Lethbridge, when he told me never to work for anybody but myself. I wonder where I would be today if I had landed that job with Proctor & Gamble or some other company. It is difficult to say what would have happened, but I am sure I would not have achieved the freedom and independence that I now enjoy. Thanks, Dad.

Amy LaRae Grant—mother of four and major Amway Double Diamond distributor. She is co-founder of UHI Corporation, an international research and national marketing organization which distributes additives for fuel conservation. She works out of her home.

Amy LaRae Grant

As a small child, my bedroom was just off the living room of our Orem, Utah home. Many nights, I remember listening to my parents' earnest and sometimes heated discussions about money—after they thought I was asleep. They never raised their voices, but their differences were often intense as they tried to work out how to get by on too little money.

Often, I would lay there, tears streaming down my cheeks, trying to decide which parent I would go with if they split up over their money problems. As I grew up, I resented the fact that the lack of money caused unhappiness in our home. My father was a real estate broker, and some months he didn't have any income. I remember my great uncle coming to live with us. He gave Mother $50 a month to cover his room and board, and many months, that was the family's only income.

In his business, my father always insisted on telling potential buyers everything about the homes they were looking at—the bad points, as well as the good ones.

Sometimes well-meaning friends would tell him that he should be more careful about what he told potential buyers, but to Father, there were a lot of things more important than making a sale.

We thought times were hard, but when Father became bishop of our local Mormon ward, our financial troubles only worsened. Dad was totally dedicated to his calling as a bishop. It seemed he was continually taking time from work to visit the sick, cheer up the sad, conduct funerals, help people move, or see that something at the church was fixed in time for Sunday meetings.

Dad was always trying to teach his children that people were more important than things, and his actions spoke even stronger than his words. It was during this bleak period that one evening in late October, father arrived home without his hat and coat. When Mother asked where they were, he said he had given them to a man who needed them more than he did. He explained that in going to and from work the past several days, he'd seen an old tramp sitting on a park bench. It was getting colder every day, so he'd stopped the car and given his hat and coat to the tramp. Dad went that entire winter without a hat and coat.

As I lay awake at night listening to my parents' anxious discussions about money, month after month, year after year, I resolved that my life would be different, that money would not be a source of contention between me and my future husband, or cause my children to feel insecure.

I landed my first job when I was only six. Our neighbor, Roy Humphries, was a dentist and his wife, Betty, agreed to let me help her with the house work and children for 10 cents a day. I don't know how much help I really was, but I will never forget how important they made me feel.

When I was eight I tried to land my first real job. I went to see the owner of a local fruit orchard who was hiring cherry pickers. When he saw how little I was, he just laughed at me. I begged for a chance to show him that I was a good worker. He wouldn't do it. He told me to come back when I grew up. As I left the orchard, I vowed that someday I would be the best cherry picker he ever had.

The next summer I got a job at the Gappmeyer farm picking strawberries and raspberries. I worked there for three years before going back to the cherry orchard to prove to the owner that he had made a mistake in not hiring me earlier. By this time I was in the fourth grade and old enough to start babysitting too, two or three nights a week. I took every job I could get.

The summer I was 12 years old, I gave up the cherry and berry picking and started babysitting full time. I worked for the Murphy family, arriving at their home at 7:30 every morning, just in time to say goodby as they went to work. The four children were usually still asleep when I arrived. I would fix breakfast, then lunch, and clean the house. Many times I fixed dinner for the entire family which was ready when the parents arrived home at 5:30 p.m. I received 35 cents an hour, 10 cents above the going rate! At $3.50 a day, I was making more than the cherry pickers. I continued babysitting through the summers of the sixth, seventh and eighth grades.

Then in the meantime, my father's business began to pick up and we moved into a nicer home. Just before that my older brother, Charles, was called to serve a mission for the Church in Germany. My mother went to work in order to help support Charles for the two and a half years he would be away. She became a school secretary—so she worked when we were in school, and was home when we were home.

When my brother returned home at the completion of his mission, Mom continued working. What started as a job to get extra money, became a job to help with the necessities.

I was one of those girls who grew and matured quickly. I had reached my full height by the fourth grade, and by the time I was 13, I looked 17 or 18.

When I was 13, while my father was still bishop, I went with my parents to pay a social visit to an older couple in the ward, the Andreasens. To make conversation, I commented on a cute picture of a little cub scout hanging on the wall. I asked if the little boy was one of their grandchildren.

Mrs. Andreasen's face lit up. She said he was her grandson alright, but that he was now grown up. She said he was a senior in high school, and asked if I would like to meet him. She had no idea I was only 13 and still in the eighth grade, and I didn't volunteer to tell her. To my mother's chagrin, I told Mrs. Andreasen I would like very much to meet her grandson. We lived just a few blocks away and I told her to call me next time he came to visit and I would drop in to borrow a cup of sugar.

About two weeks later, Mrs. Andreasen called and said she was sending her grandson, Leo, over to see me. We began to go to church together in American Fork where his father was bishop.

We hadn't been acquainted very long when Leo began telling me that he loved me. I would laugh at him and tell him he didn't know what love was. I was too young and wasn't ready to settle down with one boy. We still continued to see a lot of each other and became great friends. Whenever someone criticized me for dating so early, and with an older boy, I'd tell them that he was just like a big brother, not realizing that such friendships lead to true love.

When I was in the tenth grade, Leo was called on a mission to Oklahoma and Kansas. Before leaving, he made me promise that I would be available when he returned. Actually, it was an easy promise to make since I was only a sophomore in high school.

Leo's plan was to go to dental school after his mission. The financial security associated with being married to a dentist appealed to me very much. If I married Leo, I would have the financial security I had been craving since early childhood.

At home, the financial worries were shadowed by a more serious challenge. My older sister was having serious emotional problems. She'd had a sad and traumatic childhood. She was the little redhead who was continually teased and picked on by the other children. For example, when she would call on the neighbor girls to walk with them to school, sometimes they would sneak out the backdoor leaving her sitting on the couch in the living room. This kind of treatment continued through high school and she unleashed her frustrations on the family with increasingly violent temper tantrums. My parents tried everything to help her develop a sense of self-worth, but nothing seemed to work. She didn't believe she could do anything.

I would leave for school with her yelling, screaming, crying—and return home expecting more of the same. I saw her knock my mother to the floor in her outbursts of anger and frustration.

Even though my mother's heart ached with anguish over her unsettled child, she would often tell me and my younger sister, Jan,

"Girls, every cloud has a silver lining. You have to look for the silver lining."

I tried to see the silver lining, but with my limited vision, could see nothing but the heavy black cloud hanging over our home. My father often reminded me, "Amy, we must all love her and make the best of this."

I began to appreciate my parents' emotional strength and never-ending optimism, and their ability to put the needs of others before their own.

Every morning as I shut the front door and headed off to school or work, I consciously turned a key in my mind, leaving the sadness behind and putting a smile on my face. I was determined to smile and be happy, in spite of the heartache at home. That smile made me popular at school, and all the kids thought I was happy all the time.

Sometimes friends would tell me that they could be happy too, if they were like me and didn't have any problems. I would think to myself, "If they only knew what real problems were." I avoided taking friends to my home, except for Venice Whitwood, my best friend and trusted counselor during those teenage years.

I learned that real happiness does not come from external circumstances or happenings, but from within, based on a personal relationship with God, and always looking ahead to a brighter tomorrow, not getting caught up with the disappointments of today. I was determined not to let my sister's unhappiness, or my parents' financial difficulties, make me unhappy, too. It wasn't easy.

Upon returning home from dates, I would hurry into the house, fearing that if I lingered to talk, my older sister would come out and embarrass me by pulling on the door handle and ordering me into the house. She did this on various occasions.

At times like that, I would go to my room and play Nat King Cole's popular record, "Smile." It had become my theme song. The following words comforted me and became part of me while I continued to look for Mother's silver lining:

"Smile though your heart is aching,
Smile even though it's breaking,
Although a tear may be ever so near,

That's the time you must keep on trying.
Smile, what's the use of crying?
You'll find that life is still worthwhile
If you'll just smile."

With tears streaming down my face, I would play that song again and again, saying to myself, "I must keep trying, I must smile. Life is still worthwhile. Be happy!"

In time I developed that power to be happy, regardless of what was going on about me. I discovered, too, that my happiness was contagious, that I had the power to help other people be happy.

The silver lining began to surface, and as the years went by, I realized that the problems with my sister had helped me develop an inner strength or toughness which would be instrumental in later successes.

At Christmas, my senior year, Leo's father came to see me, an engagement ring in his pocket. Leo was going into the Navy two months after the completion of his mission. He had asked his father to give me the ring now, so I would have plenty of time to prepare for the wedding in June.

All my life I had had dreams of receiving a romantic marriage proposal—moonlight, words of affection, gentle kisses. It had never even occurred to me that in the United States in the twentieth century, a girl could receive a marriage proposal from the groom's father!

As soon as I realized why Leo's father had come to see me, I told him if he hoped for any chance of success he would have to get on his knees. If I couldn't have a romantic proposal, at least I could have the appearance of one.

It wasn't easy for me to accept the ring. While Leo was gone I had dated other fellows whom I liked very much, who also had promising futures. Several had already talked of marriage. Choosing someone to marry for time and eternity in a Mormon temple is probably the most important decision of a lifetime, and I spent many worrisome hours trying to decide if Leo was the one for me.

There was another concern. Everyone in my family had gone to college, and I had always planned to go, too. If I married Leo and went with him to live at a Naval base, I would have to give up my chance for a college scholarship.

Pushing my doubts aside, I began making preparations for the wedding, sending out over a thousand invitations to relatives and friends.

Leo arrived home from his mission and surprised me by announcing that he loved teaching and helping people. He had decided to become a schoolteacher instead of a dentist. I was very disappointed because I didn't want to spend the rest of my life pinching pennies. On the other hand, I knew that if Leo really wanted to be a teacher, it would be wrong for me to steal his dream.

On June 5, 1961, two days before the wedding, I began to panic. After two years of separation, we hadn't had time to really get to know each other again. I still had some special feelings for other fellows I had been dating. Even though all the invitations had been sent, I didn't know if I could go through with it. As I got off work that night, one of the fellows I had been dating was waiting for me in the parking lot. He said he had to talk with me. He told me I was making a big mistake, that I was marrying too quickly without giving him a chance. We talked until 3 a.m., and I began to wonder if I was making a big mistake.

I asked him to take me to see my best friend, Venice, so I could discuss the situation with her. When we arrived she was still up, talking with another fellow I had dated who was on the track team at BYU. He was trying to get her to talk me into calling off my wedding. I stayed there and talked with him until 6 a.m.

By that time I decided that if I couldn't be sure about marrying Leo, I had better call it off. I had no idea how I would un-invite over a thousand families, many of whom had already purchased wedding gifts.

I drove over to Leo's home and knocked very quietly on his bedroom window so as not to wake his parents. He came quickly to the door and asked why in the world I was calling on him at 6 a.m.! I told him I had come over to call off the wedding.

Of course, Leo was upset. He had been in love with me for a number of years and knew that I was the one he wanted to marry. He hadn't been dating anyone else, as I had, and didn't have any of the doubts that were bothering me. He tried to persuade me otherwise, but there was no talking. I didn't want to get married for eternity unless I knew for sure I was doing the right thing.

After about an hour of unproductive discussion, we

knew the conversation would have to end soon because his parents would be getting up. Leo suggested that we pray, that perhaps a prayer would give me a better feeling about the direction we should go. He agreed to stand behind me, whatever my decision.

We knelt down by the side of the sofa. Leo poured out his heart to the Lord asking for me to be able to know what I should do—to let me know if it was right for us to share eternity together, as he loved me very much. I had never before heard a more sincere prayer. When I stood up, I knew that Leo was to be my eternal companion. Something deep inside said I should marry him, even though I believed I would be giving up the prosperity I had always wanted.

Five weeks after our marriage, Leo entered the Navy. I stayed home while he was in basic training, then joined him in California. I went to work as a secretary for the California Farm Bureau in their legal and natural resources departments. Several months later Leo was transferred overseas. We were expecting our first child, and since I couldn't go with him, I returned to Utah to live with my parents and have our first baby. Terry Leo was almost a year old when Leo returned home.

The first year after Leo's return, we managed the Hillcrest Motel in Orem while Leo attended Brigham Young University. The plan was for me to work while he went to school. As soon as he received his degree and was teaching, I would give up my job and stay home with the children.

In 1964 I became a dental assistant for Dr. John R. Bench where I learned a great deal about people—but soon it became apparent that I wasn't earning enough to support the three of us and keep Leo in school, too. If Leo took a part-time job in addition to his studies it would take him longer to get through school, and I didn't want that, so I took a second job as a fashion consultant selling women's clothing at evening fashion shows.

I would leave for work at the dentist's office at 7:45 a.m., and usually arrive home about 6 p.m. Sometimes there were dental emergencies that kept me longer. After a brief dinner with Leo and Terry, I would run off to do a fashion show, returning home about midnight. Every Thursday night I stayed up all night cleaning house, doing my paperwork and ordering merchandise.

My goal was to help Leo get through college as soon as possible, and I was willing to do whatever was necessary to reach that goal. All my life I have been willing to do what other people would not do, if I felt it was necessary in order to reach my goal.

There were times, however, when I didn't know if I were going to make it. I remember one day coming home on my lunch hour to do a little catching up on my housework. First I checked out the kitchen where every single dish was stacked in the sink, dirty. Next I looked into my little boy's room. The floor was covered with bedding, clothing and toys—a complete mess. I walked into the bathroom and saw how filthy it was. The dirt and mess really got to me. I had grown up in a clean, well-organized home and wanted my home to be that way, too.

I lay on the bed not knowing if I could continue living this way—the demanding schedule and the mess. My hands felt too heavy to move. I sensed that I was on the verge of having a nervous breakdown. It would have been so easy to give up—all I had to do was let go.

I was working hard at my two jobs to put Leo through school, but to come home and see that I was failing as a wife and mother by not taking proper care of my home was more than I could bear. With a nervous breakdown I wouldn't have to worry about or face reality anymore.

After struggling with my emotions for half an hour, I came to the conclusion that if I were going to make it through my present circumstances I would have to learn to live with some dirt and mess, and not be a perfectionist. I told myself the people who lived in the house were more important than dirty dishes and messy rooms. I decided I could continue, knowing the condition of our home was only temporary, and that I would keep a neat and spotless house as soon as circumstances permitted. Meanwhile, I would be content with doing my best.

This was a turning point in my life. I continued to work hard, but stopped worrying about things I couldn't change, and realized all negative circumstances were temporary if I continued to have faith in the future.

In January of 1967 I was suddenly confined to bed with a threatened miscarriage. Our second child was to be Leo's graduation present. It was hard for me to call Dr. Bench and tell him I could no longer assist him. In three years I had become very attached to the doctor and his patients. Also, I had become a district manager for the fashion company, and my district was leading the nation in sales. Our annual sales had grown from $10,000 to $300,000. From my bedside I ran the business, even conducting sales training meetings with chairs around my bed. I lived with the expectation that at any moment I could give premature birth to my unborn child, and each additional day was a blessing from the Lord.

In May, Leo graduated from BYU. For his graduation I gave him a new car and a healthy second son, Paul Raymond. I was so happy. My dreams were finally coming true. I would be able to stay home and take care of my two little boys while Leo supported us by teaching school. I quit my job as a fashion consultant, having saved enough money to get us through the summer until Leo received his first teaching check.

I'll never forget when Leo's first paycheck arrived the following October. We both ran into the bedroom to open it. When we saw the amount of the check, we both cried. We had worked so hard to get Leo through school, and the check was for less than I had been earning while putting him through school!

There wasn't enough in the check to support our family, and we would never be able to own our own home. I realized that in order for Leo to continue as a schoolteacher, I would have to go back to work. It was a great disappointment to me, but it never occurred to me that Leo should do anything but teach.

I returned to my job as a fashion consultant, and immediately began to sense disapproval from family and friends. It was alright for me to work while Leo was in school, but now that he was working full time, my place was in the home with the children.

Sometimes my mother would call and recite the familiar quotation that, "No success outside the home can compensate for failure in the home." She told me I was failing as a mother and should be home with my children. I tried to explain that I was working because I had to, not because I wanted to. I would have liked nothing more than to stay home with my children, but financial necessities dictated otherwise. I felt so torn.

At times like this I would get on my knees and pour out my heart to my Father in Heaven. I didn't think it was his will that we spend the rest of our lives in poverty, unable to progress, or lighten the load of others, and I felt the only way for us to get above the poverty level was for me to work. I often remembered one of Brigham Young's favorite sayings that, "It's no sin to be poor, the only sin is to remain poor." I believed that then, and I believe it now. To me the message in the scriptures, especially the Book of Mormon, is clear that God gives prosperity to those who keep his commandments. Nevertheless, even though God will give a bird its food, he doesn't drop it in the nest. You have to go after it, and that's what I was doing.

I wanted to do what was right. The more I prayed, the more I felt that I could be a good mother, a good wife, and still be successful in business, as long as I kept my priorities in order, and always tried to stay close to the Lord for guidance.

With Dad's help and the extra income from my clothing business, we were soon able to make a down payment on our first home. It was small, and needed a lot of fixing up, but the price was right, only $10,000. Not long after moving in, I gave birth to our third son, James Melvin, May 19, 1969.

In the spring of 1972, Leo's uncle, Juel Andreason sold us a beautiful view lot on the Orem bench, overlooking the Provo River and the Wasatch Mountains. Immediately we started planning our dream home, the place where we would live the rest of our lives.

In May of that year Leo brought home a little booklet with horoscopes in it. Neither one of us really believed in the predictions, but it was fun reading them. The one for me said that by the end of the month I would embark on a totally new career. That was ridiculous. We had even planned our new house around my clothing business so I would be able to handle everything from home, allowing me to be close to the children.

A few days later Leo was reading the business page of the newspaper when I leaned over his shoulder and noticed the picture of the appointed manager for the new ZCMI store at the University Mall opening soon in Orem. I pointed at the picture and told Leo that that man was going to be very successful. I could see it in his eyes, having always had a special sixth sense when it came to judging people. Leo folded up the paper and neither one of us said or thought any more about the man.

Several days later I was picking up the newspaper from the living room floor to throw it away, and it just happened to be folded so I couldn't miss a ZCMI employment ad for a personnel manager. I threw the paper in the garbage.

The next day I noticed the same ad again as I was throwing the newspaper away. I remember thinking that it would be kind of nice to be the personnel manager at a big prestigious department store. Maybe I would have a chance for the job. After all, I had plenty of experience managing sales people in the fashion business. I had even written a sales training manual. I didn't have any other qualifications, however, so I didn't think any further of it. The third day the ad was ironically on top as I threw the paper away.

When Leo came home I asked him how he would feel if I called about the job. He said, "Go for it."

Keeping it a secret, I called regularly for two days before I finally got through to a Mr. Mitchell. He asked when I could come to Salt Lake City for an interview. I told him I had business in Salt Lake on Friday and I would be happy to meet with him then.

I remember walking into his office the next Friday and suddenly realizing that Mr. Keith Mitchell was the same man whose picture I had seen in the newspaper, the man I said would be very successful.

He walked around the desk to shake my hand. Then as he returned to his chair he asked if I had ever written a training manual. When I told him I had written a sales manual for clothing sales people, he stopped in his tracks, stared at me for a second or two, then returned to his seat. I knew I was off to a good start. As the interview progressed I began to realize that I lacked many of the desired qualifications. He told me about the MBA's and professional personnel people from all over the country who were applying for the job because they wanted to move to Utah. He had received hundreds of resumes for the personnel position. As I left his office I remember thinking that the interview, and meeting Mr. Mitchell, had been worthwhile experiences, but there was no way I would get the job.

A day or two later, Leo and I went out to our new building lot to clear off some of the brush. Leo cut and chopped while I piled the brush into neat little piles for burning. It was a pleasant change-of-pace activity, working in the spring sun and planning our new yard.

It wasn't until the next day that we discovered the lot had been overgrown with poison ivy. Both of my legs were soon covered with oozing sores. I was miserable.

When the sores were at their worst, Mr. Mitchell from ZCMI called and asked me to come up for another interview. He said he wanted me to meet the vice-president of ZCMI.

The doctor had ordered me not to put anything on my legs. The irritation had spread clear down to my toes and all I could wear on my feet was a pair of loose-fitting sandals. I was about to cancel the appointment but Leo made me promise to go through with it. He said the condition of my legs wouldn't influence their decision. That was easy for him to say, but I still didn't want those men to see my oozing legs.

Just before the interview, I had an ingenious idea. I wrapped my legs with gauze and then a brown elastic bandage from the knees to the ankles, then pulled on my nylons over that. I hoped that if I wore a big enough smile they wouldn't notice my legs.

The interview seemed to go well. On May 28, Mr. Mitchell called and offered me the job. I started May 30, as the personnel manager of the new ZCMI store which was still under construction.

I was third in the pecking order after the manager and assistant manager. My first assignment was to hire and train 350 employees, the entire staff for the grand opening.

I placed an employment ad in the local newspapers and the applicants started calling in faster than the secretary could handle them. I conducted thousands of interviews, all day every day for several weeks. After the manager and assistant manager went home between 5 and 6 p.m., I would stick around to process the applications and work on the training program. I didn't mind putting in the extra hours because I was told ZCMI gave bonuses to management personnel who helped in the opening of new stores. I figured my extra time and effort would be reflected in my bonus.

I set up the training program to handle 25 people at a time. The first group came in at 8 a.m., and finished at 3 p.m. The second training session went from 3:30 until 10 p.m. After the last session I would answer questions for a while then tackle the day's paper work. The training sessions continued day after day until all of the new people were trained.

I was very proud of our employees when the store opened. Our store immediately took the lead in sales among all the other ZCMI stores.

When the bonuses came, the manager and assistant manager received theirs, but there wasn't one for me. I couldn't believe it. I had put in countless hours, and everyone above me in the management heirarchy seemed so pleased wtih what I was doing. I told the vice-president that it had been my understanding that all managers would receive a bonus when the store opened. I asked him why I hadn't received one—possibly an oversight, I hoped.

He looked me right in the eye and said that ZCMI had never paid a bonus to a woman for helping to open a store. At first I thought he was kidding, but he wasn't. He said they would make it up to me in some other way. One year later, they gave me a $50 a month raise.

We had a high turnover rate at the store and occasionally I would come up with a new idea or program in an attempt to correct this problem. The typical response when I offered a suggestion was, "We have been doing it this way for over 100 years, Mrs. Grant. What makes you think you can do it any better?" I would return to my office thinking that because something was done one way for a hundred years was reason enough to look for a change, or a better way.

When I accepted the job at ZCMI, I was naturally concerned about being away from my children. Even though the normal quitting time was 6 p.m. I asked if I would be able to go home at 5 p.m. I was told that was fine, as long as my work was finished. I soon learned that a personnel manager's work is never finished. It was common for me to arrive home after 7 p.m. and once a week as late as 10 p.m. As an executive, I was expected to work overtime without extra pay. Terry and Paul were in school now, and no one was in the home to greet them when they arrived home each day. I dropped little James off at the babysitters on my way to work in the morning.

To make matters even worse, Leo and I found ourselves in the situation where we were unable to keep up with inflation. The price of our new home went up $13,000 while we were building it, and we had to take out a second mortgage. We moved into the home soon after going to work for ZCMI, and even though we pinched every penny, we were about $30 short each month. To make up the difference we began using the ZCMI charge card. Of course, I was unable to make regular payments on the charge card. When we reached our limit of $1,000, the credit manager called and firmly suggested that as a ZCMI executive I needed to take care of my credit problem right away.

I never cease to be amazed how resourceful people can become when enough pressure is applied. I borrowed from the credit union to pay off the charge account. Soon after that our refrigerator quit working. I applied to the credit union for the money to buy a new one, but I already owed them too much. They turned down the request. Luckily, we were able to borrow an old refrigerator that had been in the basement of Leo's parents' home.

About this time Leo decided to go back to school, part time evenings and summers, to earn his masters degree so he could earn a little more money as a teacher. The way inflation was going, we didn't kid ourselves into thinking that a masters degree could eliminate our financial bind— but every dollar would help, and the masters degree would mean about $50 more a month on Leo's paycheck.

Just before the Church's general conference in 1974, I received a long distance telephone call one evening from my lifelong friend, Venice. She was now living in South Carolina with her husband and family. She called to say that she was coming out to Utah to attend the Church's semi-annual general conference and that she would like to get together with me. She told me about her husband and children, and how well things were going. I told her how very busy we were at the store preparing for Christmas, and that Leo was going to full-time night school finishing up his masters degree. She replied that I needed a maid, and went on to explain how much she enjoyed having a maid to do the housework so she could spend more time with her children. I couldn't believe the differences in our lives.

Then she made a statement that struck me like a bolt of lightning. She said, "Amy, we are going to retire in five years, and spend the rest of our lives traveling with our family, and serving the Lord—and you can do it, too. I'll tell you all about it when I come." She didn't give me any more details over the phone.

One week later Venice came to conference, and after her Saturday leadership meetings she came to Orem to see us. She arrived just as Leo and our oldest son, Terry, were leaving to attend the priesthood session of conference. Terry had just turned twelve in July and this was his first general priesthood meeting, an important occasion for both father and son.

I had waited an entire week to hear what my friend had to say and I couldn't wait any longer. She said that Leo needed to hear it too, but I insisted that she tell me immediately how we could retire in five years. She opened her purse to get her notes, but they weren't there. Apparently she had left them in her hotel room in Salt Lake City, 40 miles away. Her husband had written everything down for her so she would be able to explain it correctly, and he had told her to carefully follow the notes so she wouldn't blow it. She was hesitant to tell me about it without the notes, but I insisted she proceed from memory.

She tried to draw out a business plan but couldn't get the figures to balance. She kept insisting that there was a lot of money to be made, and that she and her husband were going to retire in five years, but she couldn't remember exactly how it was going to happen.

She said the business was called Amway. I had heard of Amway, but I had never dreamed that it provided an opportunity to achieve total financial security to anyone willing to work, and that once the business was built up, it could be inherited from generation to generation.

At first I was disappointed. As personnel manager at ZCMI I held a highly respected position in the community. In fact, I was the only female executive at the store. There was no way I wanted to give up my title to sell soap!

By this time, all my enthusiasm was gone. I knew Leo wouldn't go for it either. He was so shy that he avoided answering the door bell if anyone else was around to do it.

When Leo came home, he listened politely to my friend as she tried to explain the program. When she finished, he told her we would think about it and let her know what we were going to do in the morning.

After she went to bed, Leo said there was no way he was going to do it, and that neither of us had the time to do it. During the night I kept thinking about what my friend had said, that we could achieve financial freedom in less than five years. We could be free to do, to go, to have—free to be more of what God intended us to be.

I realized that perhaps I wouldn't have to wait to the year 2002 (my scheduled retirement from ZCMI) to become a full-time mother again. Our children would never have to feel the financial insecurity that I had known as a child. I began to see a ray of hope for a bright financial future.

The next morning while we were in bed talking about Amway, and Leo had already decided that we weren't going to get ivolved, Terry walked into our bedroom, a bright smile on his face. He had overhead bits and pieces of our conversation and was excited about the new business.

He repeated what President Kimball had said at the priesthood meeting the night before, that every boy should save enough money to pay for his own two-year mission by the time he was 19, that boys shouldn't expect their parents to pay mission expenses. Terry said he hadn't slept most of the night worrying and praying about this great responsibility. He knew he could never save enough from mowing lawns and doing other odd jobs. Then this morning he heard us talking about this new business, and knew it was an answer to his prayers. He promised to do his part to help build the Amway business.

There was no way either one of us was going to tell our son that we wouldn't help answer his prayers. We called in Paul and James to get their votes of support. They promised to help, too. From that time on it was a family business.

We carefully checked out the Amway Corporation. It was founded in 1959, and appeared to be legitimate and forthright in every way, including a 100 percent money-back guarantee on all products purchased by distributors and customers. The company was growing at an annual rate of 40 to 60 percent, with new products being introduced almost monthly. The ultimate goal was to become a full-line department store, person to person, revolutionizing department store purchasing. By eliminating middle men, they were able to return a substantial percentage of each revenue dollar to the distributors through profit sharing and earned bonuses while giving the consumer the finest merchandise at competitive prices.

We caught the excitement of Amway and with less than $100 in investment capital, we became Amway distributors. We had nothing to lose and everything to gain.

Leo was finishing up his masters degree, evenings, while teaching days, so there was no way he could get actively involved in the new business, but he gladly offered his moral support even though he didn't feel comfortable in the business himself, as self-conscious as he was around people. It was totally up to me to make the business succeed. We were getting further and further behind financially, and I felt it was just a matter of time until we would lose our new home, unless we found a way to bring in additional income. I had worked two jobs before, and I could do it again. I had two immediate purposes, to help Terry save money for his mission, and to save our home—then on to my real dream of financial security.

As I became acquainted with Roland Hughes from South Carolina, who was helping us get started, I discovered that only men were active in building large distributorships. I had serious doubts about how I, as a woman, would be accepted. I wondered if I could be successful in sponsoring men into my organization.

As soon as the manual arrived, I brought Lee Pope home for lunch. Lee was one of our young, ambitious store executives with a degree in business management. He had come to work for ZCMI thinking it would be a good place to start his business career, but had become frustrated when he found himself in a dead-end situation, with little hope for meaningful advancement. Several times, he had come to my office to discuss career alternatives.

I showed him the manual and said, "Lee, our business is here. We can retire in five years!" I hadn't read the manual yet myself and didn't know how else to present the plan, so I opened it up and let Lee read about it himself, while I followed along. When he finished a page, I would say, "Isn't this exciting? See, it really works!"

My enthusiasm was contagious, and Lee decided to become an Amway distributor, too. Almost before I knew what the company was all about, I had succeeded in sponsoring a well-qualified individual into the organization.

One weekend, Leo's sister and brother-in-law came up from California and took us fishing. On the way I listened training tapes. They thought it ridiculous that Leo and I were going to be selling soap, and teased us, incessantly. When they could see that the Hee Haw approach wasn't changing our minds, they attempted to talk us out of it with serious conversation. But we were determined to stick it out, even when friends began to laugh at us.

The next week, I sponsored my secretary, still wondering if successful men would listen to me on how to build a million-dollar business. I worked out an arrangement with Lee Pope wherein he would give the formal business presentations while I did much of the support work like setting up the meetings at our home and inviting people to come.

I remember inviting an unemployed friend to one of our meetings, thinking that by helping him find work I was going to help him. He was enthused about the plan, but refused to sign up saying he didn't want to lose his welfare check. There were others like him, people I wanted to "save," but who didn't want to be bothered. After these experiences, I followed Roland's counsel more closely, to share the business with individuals who were already successful in whatever they were doing—doctors, lawyers, teachers, and housewives. I found that the more they were oriented towards success, the faster they caught the vision of Amway.

During my lunch breaks I was on the phone inviting people to our evening meetings, which usually consisted of five to ten couples. At home, the boys cleaned the house and tried to be quiet during the sessions. Leo attended night school, then studied at the library until he knew everyone would be gone.

One day Lee Pope informed me that he would have to miss our next meeting and I would have to present the plan myself. I was terrified, and didn't eat a single bite of food the day of the presentation. It seemed so presumptuous for

me, a woman, to be telling men how to become successful in
business.

That night when four or five couples were in our family
room waiting to find out about a new business opportunity,
I went into my room and prayed with all my heart that the
Lord would help me get through it successfully. To bolster
my confidence and help break the ice, I said to the couples
as I began: "Pretend I am over six feet tall, weigh over 200
pounds, and my name is Leo."

Once I got over the initial jitters I lost myself in the
excitement of what I was doing. I wasn't trying to sell the
people something to get their money—I was opening a door
for them to reach their dreams, to become more of what they
really were, deep inside.

My enthusiasm in Amway was contagious. I didn't ask
the people to work for me, but to become partners with me so
I could go to work for them. I showed them how the unique
Amway plan works, people helping people to be successful
by providing top quality products everyone wants and
needs.

After I had completed the presentation, someone came
up to me and said, "You know, you don't have to apologize
for being a woman trying to build a business. It doesn't
matter if you're a woman or a man. It matters that you care,
and that you are enthusiastic and really believe in what you
are doing."

Even though I was the one building the business, it was
a family project. The children understood that the success
of this undertaking was directly related to how much time
mother could devote to it, and that the business suffered
whenever I had to take time off for housework. Since we all
shared in the success of the business, the children took over
the basic household duties. The boys, ages 12, 8 and 6,
learned to cook meals, clean house and pick up after
themselves. It was their way to earn their share of the
income, and they knew someday they would inherit whatever we built. Late at night Leo handled the inventory and
shipping. Everyone did his part to help build the business,
and the boys really learned how to keep a clean house.

Teenagers are often very sensitive to teasing, and our
oldest son Terry was no exception. His teacher in our local
ward or church unit began to call him Soapy because of his

involvement with Amway. When the teacher would bring Terry home from an activity, with a carload of friends, Terry would get out of the car as the teacher teased loud and clear, "See ya later, Soapy." Terry would come in the house fuming.

I had my problems, too, at work. I was just getting the business off the ground, when the new store manager called me into his office and expressed concern that a ZCMI executive was moonlighting. "It doesn't look good for the company," he said.

Leaning over his big desk, he added, "Do you realize you're in direct competition with this store?" Amazed at this remark, I asked him how I could be in competition with an exclusive department store like ZCMI.

"Well, we sell soap in our cosmetic department," he replied.

He ended our conversation by saying, "Mrs. Grant, I'll give you one half hour to make up your mind, whether you will continue your promising career with us, or whether you will sell soap." He was aware of my financial difficulties, and knew he had me over a barrel. He knew I was working not because I wanted to, but because I had to. He figured I had no choice but to remain a slave of the store.

He sent me back to my office to decide my fate. I went in and shut the door. The minutes began to tick away.

I didn't know how big I could build the Amway business alone. There wasn't another woman in the Amway organization to whom I could relate. As yet, no one in Utah had built a Diamond organization—one that has helped six partners become Directs. At the Diamond level, one's income normally exceeds $60,000 per year. That was my goal.

The only successful people I knew in Amway were in the southern states, and I had never been east of Utah. Roland Hughes, our Direct, was a total stranger to me except for a few telephone conversations and the tapes I had listened to.

I stared at the walls of my office, wondering what I should do. We were already on the verge of losing our home. We simply didn't have enough money to pay all our bills. How could I give up my secure and steady income from ZCMI?

On the other hand, the Amway experience had made my

heart burn with a new excitement, a hope of a bright financial future where I would be able to stay home with my children.

As the minutes ticked away, I tried to look into the future. I could see the dark tunnel that Roland Hughes had told me about, with a tiny pinprick of light at the far end. He promised me that if I would exercise faith and build the business in the right way, that that light at the end of the tunnel would get bigger and bigger until we came out the other end into a beautiful new world of light and financial freedom.

I wondered if he was really telling me the truth. Did I dare choose a pinprick of light over an excellent position with a secure future?

When the 30 minutes were gone, I expected the phone to ring. I had decided that a pinprick of light, and a glimmer of hope were worth whatever price I had to pay, even the giving up of my security at ZCMI. I had made one of the major decisions of my life.

I waited another half an hour, and the manager still didn't call. I opened the office door and peeked outside. He was not in sight. As I hurried about my work, I expected him to confront me at any moment, but he didn't—not that day, nor any of the days that followed.

Every day, I worked under the dark cloud of wondering if it would be my last. I figured the manager had read my body language and would let me go as soon as he had found a replacement for me. As personnel manager I was all too familiar with the company's attitude that, "Anyone can be replaced, and probably at lower wages."

I received an unexpected answer to my prayers. A few weeks after the confrontation with my boss, I received a call from Mr. Charles Bates, president of Valtek, a large manufacturer of automatic control valves. His wife was a longtime friend of mine. He said he was looking for someone to set up his new personnel department and would like to talk with me. I tried not to seem too excited about the call, but quickly agreed to meet him on my lunch hour.

In the interview I told him about my commitment to Amway, and my intention to eventually retire from my personnel career. He asked if I would be willing to spend six months helping organize their personnel department. After discussing the situation with Leo and realizing that six months was probably not enough time to do what they wanted me to do at Valtek, I agreed to stay with them a minimum of one year.

The day before I left ZCMI, the manager told me that if I stayed he could see me progressing into higher executive positions within the company and possibly eventually even have a store of my own someday. As far as I knew, no woman had ever been manager of a ZCMI store, and that would have been a real honor for me, but I didn't want to be a ZCMI store manager. I wantd to be free to be a full-time mother, and Amway offered me a hope to achieve that freedom in just one or two years. As I mentioned earlier, my retirement from ZCMI was scheduled for the year 2002, long after my children would be grown and gone.

Little did I know how fast our business was going to grow. During my first month at Valtek, June, 1975, just seven months into Amway, we "broke Direct," by exceding 7500 points that month. Suddenly my income from Amway exceeded my executive salary as a personnel manager. The following month, our eighth in the business, our Amway income exceeded Leo's salary with nine years of experience.

In our tenth month, Roland and Molly Hughes flew out from South Carolina to be with us to celebrate the completion of our Direct qualification. Roland had visited us five times during that first year to make sure we were laying a proper foundation for our new business. Each time he came, he would gently encourage Leo to take a more active role in building our organization.

We were late to our Direct celebration party with Roland and Molly and the rest of our Amway family. The transmission in our old Pontiac stuck in reverse gear. We couldn't fix it and ended up having a service station attendant drive us to the party in his truck.

Roland suggested that since we were Directs, we should consider buying a new car. It was exciting going from an old, rusted-out Pontiac to a brand new, gold Lincoln Mark IV.

I'll never forget the first day I drove the new car to work at Valtek. I was in the middle of figuring employee pay raises, and hadn't been in my office long when Mr. Bates, the President, called me into his office.

"There are two things I would like to ask you, Mrs. Grant," he began. "First, how big of a raise do you expect? Second, did you know that you drove to work this morning in my dream car, the one I could never afford to buy?"

I stayed with Valtek a full year, just as I had promised, even though during the last few months I spent a lot of time in bed with the threatened miscarriage of our fourth son. Even though Valtek is a large, rapidly-growing, multi-national company, they still know how to treat their employees with integrity and respect. The spirit of Valtek has always stayed with me. If I ever were to work for someone, I would want to work for Valtek.

Today there are over 10,000 partners or distributors in our Amway family world-wide, including Wales, England, Germany, Australia and Japan. Some great leaders have emerged. Bob Cook, a postal executive, and his wife Ardis, were one of the first successful teams to join us. They sponsored Curtis Ledbeter, a professor of ancient scripture at Brigham Young University and his wife Virginia, who became Diamonds in only a few months.

Harold Thompson, an electrician, and his wife Marva shared the business with Bob Moss, a professor at the College of Southern Utah, and his wife Roberta. They had just lost their dream home to a dishonest partner in a business deal gone sour. They quickly became Diamonds, and purchased another dream home. Together with Bob and others we have purchased a dude ranch in Colorado which fulfills Bob's lifelong dream of teaching youth positive self-image and success principles in a natural environment.

Becoming financially independent has taken a back seat to the thrill of watching people progress. I have seen thousands of people benefit, financially and otherwise, from our involvement with Amway. I have seen insecure people become confident, sad marriages become happy ones. I have seen working mothers and fathers become their own bosses. I am no longer one person helping the few people around me, but I am part of a dream where thousands are helping thousands.

When I was threatening the miscarriage of our fourth son, John, and had to spend a lot of time in bed, Leo decided the time had come for him to become more active in the business. Since that time he has been shouldering an increasing share of the leadership.

Last year when we became Utah's first Amway Double Diamonds (when 12 of the people you have sponsored have become Directs), Leo announced that he was taking us to Crown (when 20 sponsorees go Direct). Most Amway businesses at the Crown level earn $300,000 to $500,000 a year. More exciting than the income, is watching Leo develop his full potential in running the business.

While our live-in houseboy takes care of our home, laundry and meals, the boys no longer have to do that but are able to enjoy the fruits of their labors with a full-time mother and a full-time dad. Our dream of total financial freedom has become a reality.

Today, my brother-in-law, Kent Greene, a tax attorney, oversees our money and investments. His wife Jan, my sister, who also felt the pangs of financial stress growing up, has also achieved security.

The man that used to call Terry "Soapy", became our bishop, and ever since our first meeting with him in tithing settlement (a yearly meeting where Mormons give an accounting of yearly church donations), he has ceased calling our son "Soapy." Amway really isn't a soap business any more. It's actually six businesses in one, rapidly developing into 10 major businesses on their way to a full-line, person to person department store.

For his eighteenth birthday, we gave Terry a new Amway starter kit during our annual Amway Grant Family Convention so he could start building his own business. I wondered how he would feel after almost six years of growing up with the business.

He said, "You can take away my silver 280Z. You can take away our home, my clothes, everything I have—but I will still become financially independent because my parents have taught me how!"

Terry's dream of saving enough money for a mission has been realized. On his nineteenth birthday, he accepted a call to serve the Lord as a missionary in Bristol, England. His younger brothers have now begun saving for their missions. Leo is running the business, and I am a full-time mother. What more could a woman ask?

Larry Haines—co-founder of Valtek Inc. of Springville, Utah, one of the world's leading manufacturers of automatic control valves, employing over 300 people.

Larry Haines

At the time of my birth in 1928, my parents were just moving from a very poor farming community in Nova Scotia, and were visiting Massachusetts to see if they wanted to move to the United States. My parents decided to stay in Massachusetts and my father found work as a house painter. One more child was born, a sister Ruth, who died of pneumonia at the age of five.

While I was growing up, my father had the opportunity to do some painting for Admiral Byrd, the famous polar explorer. When I was eight years old, my father got permission to take me down to the Boston docks to see the admiral's ship, the Bear, as it was being prepared for a trip to the South Pole. They were getting ready to load a huge snow vehicle which was supposed to be the ultimate in polar transportation. It had living quarters for a 15-man crew and huge wheels, 12 feet in diameter, each with its own engine. The vehicle had an airplane mounted on top, and many special extras which they felt might come in handy in the middle of the Antarctic waste.

When the Bear arrived at the Bay of Whales in Antarctica the huge vehicle was unloaded onto the bay ice, then driven up onto the barrier ice, about 100 feet above the water level. As the vehicle began its journey to Little America, the front wheels dropped into a crack in the ice.

Admiral Byrd and his men could not find a way to break it free, so it was abandoned before it was ever used.

When I was 12 years old, we lived in a three-story apartment house in suburban Boston. My bedroom was at the back of the apartment. I remember one night I couldn't sleep. I sat there by the bed staring out at the trees in the back yard, dreaming about my future, when a very strange thing happened. My mind drifted into the future, seeing things that were going to happen in my life. It's hard to describe, but I saw scenes, heard words and felt things which were to come. I crawled back into bed as the experience continued, a brilliant but somewhat confusing foretelling of the future.

I saw myself in a church, leading a group of people, as if I were the minister. This was a great surprise to me. I didn't belong to any church, nor was I much interested in religion. Even at an early age, my career ambitions were centered around engineering and science.

From that time on, I often felt a strong responsiblity to lead a clean, upright life. I didn't go out and look for a church, and I didn't change my ambition to become an engineer, but I tried to live a good life because I simply felt like that was what I was supposed to do.

After finishing high school, I joined the Navy. World War II was just ending. I had an opportunity as part of a Navy task force to go with Admiral Byrd on an expedition to Antarctica.

In addition to unloading ships and hauling supplies to the base, I was a photographer for the expedition. I remember finding the poles that marked the spot where the huge snow vehicle was abandoned more than ten years earlier. It was now under about 30 feet of ice, the result of the yearly snow falls packing into ice. Several of us dug a tunnel down to a hatch on the snow machine and went inside. We ate some of the food that had been there all those years and it was perfectly good. Admiral Byrd came down and found some tobacco and smoked it in his old corncob pipe.

My service in the Navy included a period of time working on the ships that were part of the first atomic bomb test at Bikini Atoll.

When I was released from the Navy, my burning

ambition was to go to college. None of our family's friends or relatives had ever gone to college but I wanted to do it so I could become an engineer. I enrolled at Northeastern University, which offered good engineering courses.

About the same time, I joined a youth group sponsored by a Congregational church in Boston. I still didn't belong to a church, but I was interested in meeting the young women in the group. I had always been somewhat shy and it was hard for me to mingle with other people. I would drive to Boston, about 15 miles, to attend the Sunday evening meetings. Sometimes if I was a little late and a lot of people were already gathered inside I would be hesitant to enter. Large groups of people terrified me. I remember standing around outside trying to muster the courage to go in. Once I spent the entire evening outside. Another time, I just sat in the car and then drove back home. It was in this group that I met my wife, Priscilla. We were married during the second year of school.

My school-related work experience was with Masoneilan one of the two largest manufacturers of automatic control valves in the world. After getting married I worked full time while continuing my education at Northeastern in the evenings. I started out at Masoneilan as a draftsman and enjoyed, most of all, the design work. I persisted in night school and eventually received my engineering degree.

Later, I was moved out of drafting and became a service engineer. This involved work on complicated control systems in various plants where our valves were installed. Part of the job required training plant personnel in matters related to the operation of the control systems. As long as I was training one on one with the production manager or an engineer, I could do a good job, but if it was necessary to call a group together, the engineering staff, or any group of three or more people, I felt embarrassed and awkward, and therefore became ineffective. I quickly came to the realization that if I was going to be successful as an engineer in business, I would have to overcome my fear of groups.

One day, I was discussing the problem with a close friend, the chief draftsman with the company. He was teaching an evening drafting and design course at Northeastern, and suggested that teaching a night class might help me overcome my fear of people.

With some serious reservations, I reluctantly submitted my application, to teach, and was accepted as an instructor. As the day of the first class neared, I would lie awake at night thinking there was no way I could get up in front of 40 students. These students weren't a bunch of easy-going college kids, but mostly World War II veterans, men with families, intent on learning a profession.

I prepared my first lesson well ahead of time, then attended the chief draftsman's class to see how he did it. I spent two more nights incorporating what he did, into my lesson plan. Seldom has a teacher been better prepared than I was for that first lesson.

The classroom was large, because of the many drawing tables. There was a raised podium for the teacher at the front of the room. A large blackboard extended the full length of the room.

I walked to the front knowing I was well prepared, but as I stepped onto the podium, the sweat began streaming over my forehead and into my eyes, causing the students to swim before me. I hadn't even begun to teach. When I looked down, my vision was so blurred that I could barely read my well-prepared notes. I was terrified.

At that point, my mind went blank, and to this day I cannot remember anything that happened during the remainder of that first class. I remember afterwards that I wasn't sure I had taught the lesson. I thumbed through my notes and discovered smears of dried sweat on some of the pages. I concluded that I had indeed taught the lesson, but I had no idea how well I had done, or how the students had reacted.

My fear of groups had not decreased at all. In fact, I was even more terrified as I prepared for the second lesson. Again, there were the sleepless nights, and the constant battle against the temptation to quit.

When I stepped onto the podium the second week, the backs of my hands began to sweat profusely. I remember looking down and marveling at how much sweat could come out of the back of a hand. Again my mind went blank, but part way through the lesson, my consciousness returned. At the end, I remember thinking that it wasn't all that bad, at least not the part I could recall.

It was a little easier each week, and I suppose it was

several months before I could maintain my composure during an entire lesson. Gradually over the course of that year, I got to where I could get up in front of the group without any problem. I knew the subject matter far better than any of the students, and even though they would embarrass me with an occasional question that I couldn't answer, the things I knew far outweighed what I didn't know, and my confidence continued to grow. This was a turning point in my career.

I soon became an application engineer, working primarily in the paper industry. When a company would call for a proposal on a particular system, I would visit their plant to see what they needed. Then I would return, designing a system for that particular application, then make a proposal. If the proposal was accepted, we would finish designing the system, manufacture it, including vessels, pumps, valves and instruments. Next we would install the system in the plant, start it up, then check back to make sure it was working properly. I was in on the entire job, from start to finish, and as a result, I began to develop a solid understanding of what the control valve business was all about.

It was during this period that I became close friends with one of our sales engineers, Charles Bates, who had also earned his degree at Northeastern University. We had a lot of success together. He would cultivate the initial contacts and pick up the inquiry. Together, we would design and sell the system, and I would put it in and start it up.

One time, we were selling to a paper mill up in Maine. When evening came, I suggested we go out and have a beer at a local bar. Charlie said he would go, but that he didn't want a drink. I asked why not, but he wouldn't say anything, except that he didn't want one. I felt strange, drinking alone that evening.

He didn't drink anymore after that, and he wouldn't tell me why. I later found out that he was getting ready to join the Church of Jesus Christ of Latter-day Saints, the Mormons. He quit drinking about a year before he joined, but he didn't tell me about it until he was ready to be baptized. I thought he had lost his mind—I just couldn't understand why a bright guy like Charlie could do such a dumb thing.

During that same period, Priscilla and I were looking for a piece of land where we could build a new home. As it turned out, we found just the right piece in the town where Charlie was living. After we built the home, Priscilla and Charlie's wife, Ellen, began spending a lot of time on the phone. I often found religious books and pamphlets by the telephone when I came home. The two would talk for hours discussing various scriptures dealing with Mormon doctrine.

One day, Priscilla told me that she wanted to join the Mormon Church. In addition, she asked if I would be willing to let two young missionaries come over and tell me about the Church. I told her I didn't want to listen to any such foolishness, but she gently persisted over a period of time until I finally gave in and agreed to let her invite two of the young men into our home.

At first, I just tried to argue with them, but they didn't argue back. At the end of the meeting, they asked if they could come back and talk some more. They kept coming back, week after week, taking my verbal abuse without complaint.

After five or six weeks, the thought occurred to me that if Charlie believed the doctrines of this church, maybe there was something to it. I decided to listen to the missionaries. The more I heard, the more sense it made to me. In fact, it paralleled very closely the things I already believed. It felt very comfortable to me.

I remember the expressions on the two missionaries' faces the night I asked to be baptized. They couldn't believe what I was saying. Their eyes grew big and one of them said, "What did you say?" I repeated my request to be baptized.

They told me I would have to stop smoking. I reached in my pocket and handed them my pack of cigarettes. I told them I was prepared to stop, and I have never smoked since that time.

Probably the most important thing the Church taught me in those early years was that it takes giving, listening, and patience to be happy with others. Learning these kinds of things helped improve my relationship with Priscilla and the children. Joining the Church was the greatest single thing that has happened in my life, and certainly has had a major influence, in many ways, on my endeavors in business.

One of the more difficult things about joining the Church was the law of tithing. Nobody ever talked very much to me about it before I was baptized. The subject came up once in one of the missionary discussions, but it was not discussed in detail. The idea was stuck in the back of my mind that there was no way I could ever pay 10 percent of my salary to the Church.

On the Sunday night following my baptism and confirmation, the branch president, Henry Isaksen, called me in and told me I was going to have to start paying tithing. I asked him what it was, exactly. He said it was 10 percent of my salary. I asked him if he meant after deductions. He said no, that it was 10 percent of my gross salary. I told him I couldn't do it, that I was already spending more than I was earning. I said there was just no way I could afford to do it.

He looked me straight in the eye, grinned, and said,

"I want to give you a piece of advice that a bishop gave me when I was a boy. It has worked for me and it will work for you. Just take 10 percent off the top, give it to the Lord, and he will take care of you."

I looked at him and said, "Well, that's hard to believe."

I went home and told Priscilla about the conversation. She said she had thought that I might be concerned about tithing.

"You're darned right!" I said. "We don't have enough money to pay it!"

"I know," was all she said.

She wouldn't argue with me, so I told her I was going to do exactly as Henry had recommended, take 10 percent off the top of every paycheck and put our trust in the Lord. We would just do it, and not worry about it anymore.

I was an application engineer at this time, and several days later my boss called me into his office. He said he needed to talk to me. He said he thought I needed a raise. I couldn't believe my ears. It was customary for the company to review salaries once a year, and this was in the middle of the year between salary reviews. I told him he wasn't allowed to do it in the middle of the year. He said he knew that, but he was going to do it anyway. He wasn't a Mormon, and didn't know about my tithing problem. I said that would be great. The raise amounted to 10 percent, exactly enough to pay the tithing.

The next time I saw the branch president I told him I didn't have any more questions about tithing. It was plain as day. When we give the Lord his ten percent, he opens the windows of heaven and pours out blessings, just as promised.

A little more than a year later, I was made the branch president. I was to be the religious leader for more than 300 people, and it seemed I hardly knew anything about the Church. I was brand new. I expressed these doubts to an older man who had been a branch president at one time. He promised me that after I was set apart, a mantle would fall on my shoulders and I would be able to do things beyond my present abilities. That is exactly what happened.

One day, I suddenly realized that the prophetic dream of my youth had been fulfilled. I was leading many people in a church, just as I had dreamed at that early age, joining and being active in the Church was like coming home. The things I learned and did seemed so natural, that they should have been a part of my life all along.

Once I joined the Church, Charlie and I became closer as friends. Occasionally we talked about going into business for ourselves. With me, there had always been a burning feeling, a need to be on my own. We didn't get very specific as to what exactly we would do and when we would do it.

The management of Masonelian sold our company to a large conglomerate, Worthington Corporation, and they in turn acquired a control valve company in California. Charlie was transferred out there to be the sales manager for the new company. Later, I became sales manager of Masoneian. The California company was assimilated into the mother company and the president of the California company became head of the entire control valve operation. When he came back to Massachusetts, he brought Charlie with him to become the general marketing manager and I became the general sales manager.

At the new combined company, Charlie and I became known as the gold dust twins. It seemed like everything we did turned out right. Worthington had expected control valve profits to drop off as the two companies merged, while the kinks were being worked out. Instead, profits improved.

We were the most profitable division in the entire company.

We did have some problems, however. Charlie and I knew the control valve business. We believed our product line could be simplified and improved, and therefore produced at lower cost. We recommended a product redesign that we felt would make our division much more profitable.

When the plan was presented to Worthington, we received a cold response. They explained that since we were already the most profitable division in the company, we shouldn't rock the boat by changing the product line. They were also worried about making the present manufacturing equipment obsolete. They refused to go along with what we knew to be a very sound course of action.

We had another problem bothering us, too. When we merged the two companies, we ended up with two representatives in each major city, one from one company and one from the other. One of the first things we had to do was go around to each city and decide which of the two representatives would remain with the company. This was a difficult job, but had to be done.

In Houston, Texas, we concluded that the longstanding Masoneilan representative was the one that must go, and we told him so. He wouldn't accept our decision, and went directly to the top management of Worthington, threatening an anti-trust suit against the company if his company was not retained as the representative in Houston. The owner was wealthy and had many influential friends. Top management from Worthington ordered Charlie and I to reverse our decision and let the more qualified representative go. We advised them that it was the wrong thing to do, but the troublemaker was reinstated as our representative in Houston.

Charlie and I were very disappointed when the company wouldn't let us call our own shots when it came to upgrading the product line and selecting personnel. It was about this time that a friend of Charlie's from California, Forest Anthony, bought a big camper and headed back to Massachusetts to see Charlie. Forest had lived in the same town in California where Charlie had lived during his stay there, and the two had developed a friendship. Forest was founder of Anthony Pools, a very successful swimming pool company.

Forest had decided he wanted to go into business with Charlie. He didn't know what business. He was tired of selling pool and thought Charlie would be a great partner for getting into something new.

Forest came directly to Charlie's offices. They talked for a long time. The door to my office was open. Finally, Charlie leaned back in his chair and looked through the door at me and said, "Forest wants to go into business." I said, "If you're going into business, then count me in." It all started that simply.

Next, we sat down to figure out what kind of business we wanted to get into. Forest didn't want anything more to do with swimming pools, so that was out. Charlie and I felt we knew the control valve business well, but we had never been in any other kind of business. It seemed only logical that we get into a business that we knew something about, so we decided we would design and build the new, simplified line of control valves that Worthington wouldn't let us develop.

Forest went back to California, and Charlie and I began making plans in my father's basement. My father lived in Norwood, Massachusetts, near Masoneilan headquarters.

During the fall months, we would go over there after work and plan our new company. We had an old calculator with a hand crank on the side, and we practically wore it out making financial projections. We projected income, expenses and cash flow every month for five years to see if our dream was practical. We projected sales, development costs, overhead. We went over our figures again and again, checking and double checking. We figured that somewhere, almost four years down the road, the company would become profitable. Unlike retail businesses, even the best beginning manufacturing companies often take a number of years to achieve profitability. We got help from an accountant in Boston to put the figures together. After all the projections were finished, it was clear to us that we should go ahead with the venture.

That winter, we held our national sales meeting in two parts. Half of the people were to go to Palm Springs, California, and the other half to San Juan, Puerto Rico. At these meetings, we discussed new products and our plans for the coming year. At the first meeting in California, in January, Charlie and I pulled the company president, Earl

Worner, to one side and told him we were leaving to start our own business. We had great respect for him and even invited him to join us. We told him we had made up our minds. We had been pushing numbers for several months and thought we knew what we were getting into.

When we returned to Massachusetts after the meeting, the president of Worthington Corporation came up to see us and tried to talk us out of leaving. As an incentive to stay, he told us about a new company that Worthington was buying, and intimated that if we stayed, "someone" would have to run the new company. He told us how it was started by a fellow who left another company a few years before. We asked how much Worthington was paying for the new company and he quoted a multi-million dollar figure. The fellow had built it up in a few years. That wasn't the kind of story to tell two guys who are thinking of going into their own business.

The president couldn't talk us into staying, but he did prevail on us to remain on board until the following April so they would have time to figure out what they were going to do to replace us. We agreed to do this.

We went to the other sales meeting in Puerto Rico. No one else knew we were leaving, except top management, so we had to go along with everything as if we were going to be around for a long time. Our departure wasn't announced until sometime in March, about a month before we left.

Since we were going to go into competition with Masoneilan, we tried very hard to be above board during those final months. Although we were constantly making financial projections, we didn't put a pen to paper to design a product until after we left. We didn't want anybody saying we designed our product in Masoneilan offices while on their payroll.

As soon as the word was out that we were going to start our own valve company, we received calls from many of our friends in the industry telling us we were out of our minds. They told us there was no way we could compete with major, well-established companies like Masoneilan and Fisher with plants and offices all over the world. They pointed out that only the big companies were making money, that the little ones were all struggling for survival. They said we were crazy.

Forest put up most of the money to get started, about $180,000. Charlie and I added, between us, about $50,000 more in start-up capital. We felt this was a pretty good chunk of money to start a business.

When we started looking for office space, I ran across a fellow with some offices, who wanted to develop and franchise a mobile car wash mounted on a little truck. He needed some help designing his mobile washer. I told him I would design him something with a lot of class—flashing lights, fancy buttons, gauges, dials, and a remote control system that would allow the man at the end of the hose to switch from wash to rinse without having to go back to the truck. I told him I would do all this for him in exchange for office space in his building. He agreed. I did his engineering and we had an office without rent.

I remember the first day as Charlie and I entered that small office and sat down at our table-top drawing board. We said to each other, "Well, here we are. What are we going to do?" We placed some blank paper onto the drawing board and began to design our first control valve. We had a lot of ideas, things we had wanted to do at Masoneilan, but had always been restricted by existing tooling and ways of doing things. Now we were free to design any kind of product we wanted. There were no previous commitments to restrict or hinder us. It was very exciting.

We made a list of the advantages and disadvantages of the existing valves on the market. We made sure that every advantage was designed into our product. Then we discussed each disadvantage, one at a time, until we figured out a way to design it out of our product. Since we were starting from scratch, we could do anything that seemed logical.

When we finished, we knew our valve would sell. It had so many advantages, we knew we could strike a responsive chord with most customers.

Knowing we were going to be a small company competing with big companies, we went the extra mile to design as much interchangeability as possible into our valves. For example, we designed a basic valve body that could be used for six applications from one casting. Our competitors needed three or four castings to do the same job.

About 90 percent of all control valves were designed for

six-inch or smaller pipe. We designed two actuators to cover all valves for pipe six inches and smaller. Our competitors had 10 or 12 actuators to cover the same range.

After designing our first valve, we designed some testing equipment so we would be able to test the new products as we built them.

At that point in time, we decided that probably the best place to have our business was California. We wanted to do machining on a subcontracted basis, and because of the aerospace industry on the West Coast, there were many excellent machine shops in California.

It was decided that I would go to California to find a plant. I checked out possible sites in San Jose, Santa Barbara, and all around the Los Angeles area without much success.

At the end of the first week I found myself in Los Angeles with nothing to do until the following Monday. I decided to fly up to Utah on Saturday morning and visit some of my Mormon friends. Because of the traffic, it took three hours to get to the Los Angeles airport, when it should have taken only 45 minutes. The smog was so bad that my eyes watered and burned all the way to the airport. I didn't like the idea of bringing my family to live in that environment.

When I arrived in Salt Lake City, the air was pristine. There were no traffic jams and the Wasatch Mountains were beautiful.

That night I arranged a three-way conference call with Charlie in Massachusetts and Forest in California. I opened the conversation, saying, "I've found a plant site."

There was a long pause. Charlie was the first to break the silence, asking, "Well, where are you?"

"I'm in Utah," I responded brightly.

There was another long pause. This time Forest, who was born and raised in California, broke the silence, saying, "I would rather live in Utah, anyway."

Charlie came out to join me. We looked over the machine shops in the area to see if they were good enough to handle our subcontract machine work. There weren't nearly as many to choose from as in California, but we figured we could probably get by. We looked at plant sites in Heber and Provo, and finally selected the Provo area to build our business.

We were back in Massachusetts getting ready for the move, when a fellow in the machine business dropped in to see us. We had worked with him at Masoneilan. He asked about our business and what we were going to do. We told him the whole story, and when we got to the part about our intentions to subcontract our machine work, he said, "You shouldn't do that!"

He told us that we should buy our own machinery. Not only would we make more money, but we would have better quality and production controls. To make a long story short, he convinced us that we should own our own machinery, and he sold us the machinery. Because of him, we changed our philosophy on subcontracting and went into the machining business. We bought the equipment, mostly used, in Massachusetts, then moved it to Utah. We were almost mad enough to move on to California when the state of Utah made us pay sales tax on the equipment.

Later, by owning our own machinery, we saw an opportunity to become more automated than any of our competitors. Numerically controlled (NC) machines provided automation possibilities that had not been available before. Today, about 70 percent of our parts are produced on NC machines. Even the design and engineering functions are now handled through computers—computers that give machining instructions to the NC machines. Our main plant in Springville is the most automated, and we feel the finest, automatic control valve plant in the world.

When it came time to move to Utah, Charlie's wife, Ellen, was about ready to deliver a new baby, so he stayed behind a few more months. As soon as I arrived in Utah, I set out to line up office space. In Massachusetts, we had traded design services for office space, and my goal was to work out a similar arrangement in Utah. We had to be very tight with our startup capital.

I ran into a fellow named Lionel Fairbanks who was part owner of an old, vacated Western Auto store in the center of Orem. The building was going to be torn down in a year or two to make room for a new shopping mall, but in the meantime, Lionel said we could use it, rent free. He didn't want anything in return. He did it out of the goodness of his heart to help us begin our business.

As we were getting started, we never really considered the possibility of failure. I suppose a lot of people who start new businesses do it because they get a bright idea, even though they may know very little about the business. This wasn't the case with Charlie and me. We knew the market, what valves were needed, and where to sell them. Before we ever started, we believed we knew what would work and what wouldn't work.

We were philosophical about the possibility of failure. Losing our investment capital was the worst thing that could happen. If the company didn't make it, we could always go to work for one of the major valve manufacturers making more money in salaries than we had at Masoneilan. We never felt threatened by the possibility of failure.

As soon as we were settled in our new Orem office we hired two draftsmen, Frank Brienholt and Ken Cluff, and finished designing and testing our first products.

We made appointments with valve users. We knew it would be tough for a brand new company without any kind of a track record to get orders. On the other hand, we knew we had a superior product, so all we needed was an opportunity to prove, through actual use, that our product was indeed better.

We prepared a series of sales cards, each picturing specific product features. I would take 20 or 30 of these cards with me when I called on a potential client. As I showed each card to the client I explained how that feature was engineered into our product. I would go through the cards, one at a time, until one of the features hit a hot button, and the client would say, "Gosh, I have wished someone would do something about that!" I would explain how our valve had handled the problem, and would ask him to try our valve.

Often the client would agree that our valves looked good, but would be hesitant to give an order to a brand new company in the fear that we might not be around a year or two down the road when the valve needed service or replacement parts.

This is a tough objection to overcome when you are brand new in the business. I would usually respond by telling the client that we would still be around a few years down the road because we had the best product on the market, and that we would like to prove it to him. I would ask him if he had a really tough valve application, a trouble spot where valves were wearing out every couple of years or where there were continual maintenance problems. I would ask him to give me that application so I could show him what our valves could do.

Once we got our foot in the door by taking on a tough application, and they saw how well our valves performed, we could begin selling them valves for more ordinary applications. Our valves had a remarkable string of successes in handling problem applications.

Asking for the tough applications helped get our foot in the door, but it also helped us get a reputation as the Rolls Royce of the industry. We had a hard time convincing some of the clients that we wanted all the applications, not just the difficult ones. We still have this problem after fifteen years of doing business. We had an excellent product and an excellent sales approach, and began making sales to small and medium-sized companies.

It became apparent, however, that if we were going to establish a solid footing in the business, we needed some large orders from the world's major valve users, companies like DuPont. At that time, DuPont was the largest purchaser of control valves in the chemical industry.

One day we received a call from a DuPont representative, saying they had heard about our products and were particularly interested in the actuation systems on our valves. They asked if we would be willing to have our valves undergo a series of tests to check some of the features they were interested in. We quickly agreed.

It was arranged for John Simonson, head of the mechanical engineering department at Brigham Young University (and later to become our Vice President of Engineering) to conduct the tests. He was a fluid dynamics expert.

We later found out from DuPont, that our products tested better in every measurable way than any valve DuPont had ever tested. As a result, DuPont began giving us big orders, and quickly became our biggest customer. They would build a new plant and order all the valves from us. It helped our sales pitch tremendously to be able to say to a potential client that DuPont was using our valves exclusively in some of the new plants. Frankly, DuPont's widespread use of our valves is one of the main reasons we were able to grow so quickly. They believed in our products, and that carried a lot of weight in the industry.

From the very beginning, one of the biggest sources of potential customers were names we picked up at conventions and trade shows. One of the first things they would always ask was where our plant was located. When we said Provo, Utah, they would respond by asking, "Where?" They would ask why in the world anyone would ever want to put a plant in Provo, Utah. We would explain that Utah was a great place to live and that our product had a high price to weight ratio, so shipping wasn't an important consideration. It didn't really matter where we were located. We usually pointed out that our major competitor was in the middle of the Iowa cornfields.

At first we were somewhat defensive about our Utah location, but we gradually began to realize that being in Utah was a big advantage for us. We didn't have the work ethnic problem common in major industrial areas. We felt we were getting a full day's work for a day's pay. I think that is one of our strongest advantages, even today. We have many excellent hard-working, employees. It's great to have a good product and willing customers, but unless you have the right people to build the product, you really don't have anything.

A few years after we began the business, we traded plant visits with Fisher, our major competitor. They wanted to see what we were doing, and we were interested in how they were doing some things. These trades don't involve the exchange of deep, dark secrets, but merely a chance to walk through each other's plant.

I remember going through our plant with the Fisher production manager. He would stop and ask how many parts were in a particular run. I would pick up the job sheet and tell him 1,000 or something like that. He would see a valve body and ask how many were in the run. I would pick up the card and say 300 or 400.

When we finished, he came into my office and closed the door. He said, "Do you realize that your runs are bigger than ours?" I said that I knew that.

He said, "Gee, I wish we could do that."

That visit made us feel pretty good. A brand new little company like ours had bigger production runs than the General Motors of our industry. Because we could build a wide range of valves from a few basic parts, we were able to keep our costs in line with the big volume companies.

Right from the beginning, we have insisted on neatness and cleanliness in our plant. Often when we hire a new machinist and take him back into the machine shop, his mouth drops open in amazement. He can't believe it is really a machine shop because it is so clean. We believe that quality begins in the employee's mind. If he works in a clean, well-organized environment, he builds a better product. Sweepers go through the shop two or three times each shift. We don't permit cigarette butts on the floor, or pictures of nude girls hanging near a man's work area. We provide air conditioning, good lighting, a nice lunchroom and other comforts. The result is that our people feel good about where they work. And compared to the rest of the industry, we have fewer quality control problems and lower employee turnover.

It is customary in our business to entertain clients by taking them out and getting them drunk. Charlie and I decided right in the beginning that we were not going to do this kind of entertaining at Valtek, even though it was the usual and often expected form of entertainment. As Mormons, we didn't believe in drinking, and we weren't going to help clients drink themselves senseless. We needed something else to encourage important clients to want to come and see us.

Utah's recreational opportunities provided that incentive. After a morning or a day at the plant, our visitors find themselves skiing Utah's powder snow, cruising the Canyonlands in a 4-wheeler, boating on Lake Powell, or just taking a leisurely drive with us around the Alpine Loop or Squaw Peak Trail in the scenic Wasatch mountains just east of our plant. We do things with our clients that they can't do at any other valve factory in the world, and they love it. Sometimes on the way to the airport, a departing guest will suddenly realize he hasn't had a drink in three or four days. He was so busy having a good time that he forgot all about the bottle.

We understood from the beginning that our ability to

succeed was dependent on our ability to successfully manage our cash flow. From our projections, we knew that the business would consume dollars for a number of years before it started to make money. We constantly reviewed and refined our financial projections. Occasionally, we brought in an expert to reassure us we were on the right track, or point out any possible difficulties unforeseen to us.

On one of these occasions, early in the first year, we invited John Schreiner, a financial analyst, to look over our projections. He is the son of former Mormon Tabernacle organist Alexander Schreiner. We met him in Massachusetts when he was working on a graduate degree. He came to Provo and carefully analyzed all our projections. He talked to us, asked a lot of questions—how much money we had, how we were spending it and those kinds of things. Finally he concluded, that as far as he could tell, it looked like we were going to make it. But just as he was getting ready to leave, he said something that we have since called, Schreiner's Law.

"There is just one thing I want you to remember," he said. "Everything will cost twice as much as you figure, and take twice as long."

We thought he was grossly exaggerating. We knew our projections wouldn't be exactly right, but twice as much and twice as long, that was ridiculous. But as time passed, we found Schreiner's Law to be true. When we considered a new project or product, we asked ourselves if it was still worth doing if it cost twice as much and took twice as long. If not, we didn't do it. Everyone starting a new business ought to be aware of Schreiner's Law.

Schreiner was right. Everything cost more than expected, and soon we needed more cash to keep things going. We knew from our projections that the business would not make any money for nearly four years, so we needed cash from outside sources to keep things going during those early years.

We had a hard time telling our story to the local bankers. They were familiar with loaning money to retail businesses and farmers who turned over their dollars every year. You either make a profit, or you don't. When we told them we wouldn't show any profit for four years, they would just look at us like we were kids, shake their heads and tell us

they didn't have any money for us. We visited a number of
banks in the Utah Valley area without any success. We
began thinking of getting the government to help, through
the Small Business Administration.

Finally, someone suggested that we contact Fay
Packard at Central Bank and Trust in Springville. He had a
reputation for helping new businesses. We set up an
appointment with him at the Sprinvgille Branch. His desk
was up front, right in the middle of things. He was a big,
burly fellow with a white shirt and tie, but no coat.

He asked us to sit in front of his desk, then asked what
he could do for us. We told him our whole story, how we
went into business, what our projections were for the
coming years, what our experience was in the industry, and
how much money we had. He asked several qustions about
our background.

He said, "You fellows seem to know quite a bit about
your business. Obviously, you have been in it all your lives,
and you have more money than most people have when
they start. If I give you a line of credit for...

He didn't speak the amount, but rather handed us a
piece of paper with $200,000 scratched on it. As I mentioned
earlier, we were seated in the busy section of the bank, and I
guess he didn't want anyone around us to hear how much
he was thinking of loaning us.

"If I loan you that much," he continued, "will you get
your money from me and not sell your souls to the
government?" We had told him, earlier, we were considering getting a government-backed small-business loan.

He told us he would loan us the money but that we
should understand right from the start that he was going to
insist that we make every penny squeak, every step to the
bank. We shook hands and he said he would have someone
draw up the papers right away. In my opinion that's the
way more American banking ought to be. He listened to our
story, believed in us and what we wanted to do, then agreed
to loan us the money right there on the spot, less than an
hour after he had met us for the first time.

We banked with Fay for a long time, and he really did
make every penny squeak. Whenever we needed money he
would ask all kinds of questions about our receivables and
payables and other matters related to cash flow. He would

make sure we took full advantage of the float at the bank, the time it takes for checks to clear. Finally, when we would get down to the very last penny, and had to have more money that very day, he would advance us another few thousand against our line of credit, which, with time, was extended beyond the $200,000 mark. Eventually, our cash demands became too big for the bank and we had to seek out other sources of cash. But during those early years, it was Fay's faith in us that provided the cash to keep going.

You hear a lot of talk today about how banks like to help business, but when you get right down to the heart of things, it is a matter of people trusting people. Personal traits like integrity and character mean a lot. It's pretty hard for a bank to help small business if it doesn't take stock in these basic virtues.

Another individual who played an early crucial role in providing financial direction was Talmage Jones. He was related, through marriage, to Forest. He was a CPA and active in investment matters. We invited him to come in and look over our books at a time when we desperately needed more cash.

After going over all the figures, he said that if we were going to get where we wanted to be, we would need more cash, a lot more. He said we couldn't grow without more cash. He said the problem with some people is that they want to keep everything to themselves and, as a result, their businesses can't grow, and if they can't grow, they die. He told us we needed to sell stock. At that time, Forest, Charlie and I were the only ones who held equity in the company.

"I want to leave you with one thing," said Talmage. "Don't be afraid to let other people get rich with you. Be generous and let people, who can put up some money, share in your success."

With that advice, and the fact that we desperately needed money, we decided to make the first of a number of private and public offerings of Valtek stock. That first block of shares sold for five cents each and are now worth about $10.00 each. Not a bad increase. The first offering was private. We approached a few individuals and organizations who reportedly had money to invest.

Later, it became necessary to make a major public offering, about $250,000 worth of stock. The stock company that was going to sell the stock for us was unable to do it. They could sell only about $50,000 worth.

I decided to go out and sell it myself. Our stock was just too good of a buy for people to pass up, and I knew I could sell it. I soon found out, however, that only registered securities dealers were permitted to sell stock. I signed up to take the test to become registered.

I bought the necessary books, but due to the pressure of business, when the day of the test came, I hadn't studied nearly as much as I should have, and flunked the test. One needed about a 70 percent score to pass and I got something like 60 percent. I signed up to take the test again the following month. During the month, things were really busy at work and when the day before the test arrived, I hadn't opened a book. I couldn't afford to flunk again so I began to cram, reading very carefully every word in the books and taking notes, then memorizing the main points in the notes. I studied all day and into the night. The next day, I passed the test with flying colors, receiving a score of about 90 percent, and became a registered stock dealer.

I went mostly to people we knew, especially to people we worked with, representatives and business people who believed in us. I sold much of the offering, myself, then at the end, another brokerage stepped in and helped finish it off. Selling the stock was fun, it really was. Most of those who bought, still hold the stock today, and they have done pretty well by it.

With the various public and private offerings through the years, we have sold about 70 percent of the company. Today, Charlie, Forest and I still own just under 30 percent. We believe we did the right thing in following Talmage's advice to let others get in on a good thing, too.

Our initial projections that we would hit a low point nearly four years out, proved to be correct. In spite of the bank loans and stock offerings in the beginning years, there was a period of about a year when the pickings were very slim. Somehow, we always managed to meet the payroll, but personal paychecks were small and occasionally infrequent, during that period. We didn't tell anyone about it, and the employees didn't know what was going on. At home, we lived on our food storage which the Church had encouraged us to accumulate during more prosperous years. More than once, I remember eating fried bread dough with a little honey for dinner. That was all, but it was really tasty and filling. We didn't buy new clothing, but patched and mended what we had. We didn't have enough money for the children to fully participate in school and scouts and those kinds of things, but we had a lot of pride as a family and the children were very careful not to let friends and neighbors know how tough things really were. The financial hardships of that year pulled our family closer together, and we now look back upon that time as one of the finest years of our lives.

I have said to myself that if I ever went into business again, there was no one I would rather have as partners than Charlie and Forest. Even when things were tough, there was never a cross word, never an argument, never any hard feelings between us. Whenever things became really tough, and I would begin to worry, Charlie would always find some humor in the situation. One of our favorite sayings during that low year was, "Damn the torpedos, full speed ahead."

There were those who said we were in trouble, that we might not make it. When Charlie, Forest and I would get together to see how far we had come and where we were headed, we knew we would make it. Even during hard times, it never occurred to us that we might fail.

Our unshakeable confidence was due, in large part, to our detailed planning and record keeping. We knew exactly where we had been, where we were, and where we were going. We began our business by planning everything we could think of, and we have continued that kind of meticulous planning. Success doesn't just happen, it has to be planned and charted. Businesses can't succeed without it.

Even today, our top executives meet twice a year to chart out our directions for the coming months. If we have money, we go away to a quiet, private place where we can work undisturbed. If we don't have a lot of money, we stay here to do our planning. We look at every single expense item and every source of revenue. We analyze new markets and industry developments. We, very painstakingly, maintain a month-by-month plan for two years in advance, taking into account all projected revenues and expenses. We evaluate our progress against our plan to see where we need to work harder. Occasionally, the plans need to be adjusted in light of unforeseen circumstances. Some people think we are planning fools, but that is the cornerstone of our business and certainly one of the primary ingredients of our success. For many of our 15 years, we were able to maintain a compounded growth rate of better than 30 to 40 percent a year. We are very proud of that growth rate and know we couldn't have done it without a lot of careful planning.

For the year ending April 30, 1981, our world-wide bookings were about $40 million. When we started in the business, about 75 percent of the automatic control valve market was in the United States, whereas now, only about 40 percent of the market is in the United States. As the business has become more international in scope, so has our company.

For example, we recently sold a million dollars worth of control valves to go into an offshore natural gas operation in the Persian Gulf. It was a joint venture between Qatar and Shell, headquartered in Holland. The engineering was done in Japan and the United States. We had to deal with people in Qatar, Holland, and Japan in putting the project together.

With the growth of sales into international markets we have expanded our manufacturing arm into Alberta, Canada, Brazil, England, Australia, Japan, New Zealand and Singapore.

How far we will go, I don't know. Presently, we are the number three control valve company in the United States, and we have grown at a faster rate than our major competitors.

If I had to sum up the main reasons for our success at Valtek, I would give the following:

1) The working relationship between Charlie, Forest and me. It is often said that one shouldn't go into business with close friends. We are the exception to that rule. Charlie and I were close friends before we started Valtek, and we are still close friends. Even though we have worked together as a team most of our working lives we do not exchange cross words or hard feelings. I don't believe one of us could have accomplished alone what we were able to do together.

2) We knew the business we were getting into. From our

experience at Masoneilan, we knew how valves were built, marketed and used. We knew what constituted a good valve and who our potential customers were. It is not enough for an entrepreneur to have a good idea, he must also know the business he is getting into.

3) We planned for success every step of the way. We established optimistic, but realistic goals and meticulously planned our progress towards those goals.

4) We were new in the business at a time when modern automation methods were just becoming available. Whereas our competitors were committed, through large investments, to obsolete machinery, we were free to take advantage of the latest developments in automation.

As I look back on our success at Valtek, it is not the money that gives me the most satisfaction. Of course, it is great to have sufficient money for the needs of my family. This is important, but I am certainly not interested in becoming a billionaire or accumulating huge amounts of wealth.

The greatest satisfaction to me is knowing that we have created a solid, basic company that will provide food, clothing, housing and other needs to hundreds of families for generations to come. Long after Charlie and I are gone, Valtek will continue providing useful employment to the people of this community and other communities where we build and sell products. That is a very satisfying thought and makes all the work and struggle worthwhile.

Paul Jewkes—developer of commercial and residential real estate in California and Utah.

Paul Jewkes

When I was 10 years old, my sister and I spent the summer on my Grandfather Jewkes' farm in Emery County in central Utah. My grandfather had retired to the farm after having been treasurer for the state of Utah and before that a schoolteacher. He was tall, long-legged and strong.

I remember him taking me along with him one morning to help with the irrigation. The dogs came, too. It was a great adventure for me. He didn't tell me that the water turn was for 24 hours. The water kept coming through the day and into the evening. Mostly, I would help by walking into the fields to see how far the water had gone. Sometimes he would let me pull out a dam, letting the backed up water surge down to the next dam.

Occasionally, I would ask Grandfather if we were going to get something to eat. He would respond with, "I guess you are a little hungry. We'll eventually get around to eating."

Several times during the night I sought out a dry spot on a ditch bank and took a 15 or 20-minute nap. I could have gone back to the house, but being permitted to work through the night with Grandfather was well worth the accompanying hunger and fatigue.

I remember how good I felt returning home the next morning at 6 a.m., having put in a 24-hour work day.

Grandma wasn't home, but my sister jumped out of bed, stoked up the old wood stove, and put on a pan of water. She dropped some eggs in the water and served them to grandfather and me. The eggs were totally raw. "That's just the way I like 'm," said Grandfather, as he swirled them around in his dish and slurped them down. That was a proud day for me, one I will never forget. In the years since, I have often thought back on one of Grandfather's favorite sayings, "Consistency, thou art a jewel!"

My father was a professional singer. When I was nine-months old, in 1925, we moved from Salt Lake City to Canada, then to Southern California in 1927. Dad worked for Warner Brothers and all the other movie companies, singing and performing short parts in the first sound movies. He was always on call from the studios, but never on the permanent payroll. I vividly remember what life was like during the Great Depression in the early 30's. Some- times there were weeks and even months when father didn't have any productive employment. He had to go on the road, as it is called in show business, on the old Orpheum Vaudeville circuit. Sometimes he would be gone for months. He sent home the money he earned, which sometimes wasn't very much, and once, a mail plane carrying a dearly needed check, crashed.

As the oldest boy among the five children, I had to be as productive as possible. We lived in Southgate, at that time a farming community. We raised as much food as possible in our own garden, and often I went into the neighboring fields after the crops had been harvested to glean beans, greens and celery. It was a joyful experience to come home to Mom with a bag of beans gathered from some field.

It never occurred to me to ask Mom or Dad for a nickel or a dime. There just wasn't enough money for luxuries such as allowances. If I needed money for myself, I had to find a way to earn it.

Being raised in such meager depression-inspired cir- cumstances pasted a stamp on me for life. Today, I have little tolerance for the ill-managed affluence and waste I often see around me. Sometimes I long for a return to more austere circumstances so my children and grandchildren can learn, firsthand, some of the lessons that I feel have been so valuable to me.

When I was about seven years old, my father brought home a New Zealand doe rabbit. I didn't know what Dad was talking about when he said it was bred, so he took the time to explain all about the birds and the bees, and how rabbits can multiply. He explained that if I went into the fields and gathered lucerne and grasses for my rabbits, I wouldn't have to buy expensive feeds. If I didn't have major expenses to meet, I would be able to keep all the females for breeding stock and could soon have a large number of rabbits. Dad helped me build the first few hutches, and when he came home from his singing trips we always held conferences in which I brought him up to date on my rabbit business.

It took a lot of daily chore time, gathering feed and caring for the rabbits, but they multiplied just as Dad had predicted. Soon I had a thriving business consisting of several hundred animals. I sold the meat to local customers and the pelts to fur processors.

By the time I was 10 or 11 I felt financially independent. I wasn't wealthy, by any standards, but if I wanted to go to a movie, buy a new baseball glove or a bike, I did it with my own money. At 16, I helped Dad pay for the family car.

I don't know if my success in the rabbit business had anything to do with Dad's decision to get into the chicken business. All I remember is that early one morning Dad and I went to work converting an old shack into a chicken coop. We had moved it onto the rear of the property. We worked all day, and when evening came, Dad kept working without a rest or break until we finally finished at 11 p.m. He was just like my grandfather, once he got started on something he wouldn't quit until it was finished. I have tried to follow that example.

It was the same way when Dad decided I was old enough to have my own room. We borrowed an old truck and salvaged large pieces of flat concrete from the ruins of buildings that had been destroyed in the earthquake of 1933. We leveled a place behind the garage, laid out the concrete slabs and filled in the cracks with wet cement. From the same ruined buildings, we salvaged windows, doors, lumber and roofing. We purchased some knotty pine for finishing the inside. We spent a total of $16 on the room. It was square, perfectly plummed, and as good a room as any boy ever had.

Just before my 12th birthday, my father's brother, Uncle Reid came to live with us. He shared my room with me. He had been a highly publicized athlete in college and loved all kinds of sports and fitness activities. He found in me a skinny, but eager student.

Physically, I was slow developing. In addition to that, I was skipped ahead a year in school. As a result I was the smallest and youngest kid in my class, and remained pretty much so, until the last year of high school when I grew nearly 10 inches in one year.

One of the first things Uncle Reid did was to challenge me to a chin-up contest. Not only did I not know what a chin-up was, but after he explained it, I couldn't even do one. Uncle Reid sensed my need for physical development. He became a great friend, and challenged me continually to excel with my body. We all need to be challenged by someone who is better at doing something than we are, someone who can show us the way.

It took about five weeks before I could do my first chin-up, and about three weeks after that before I could do a correct push-up. Uncle Reid and I were delighted at my progress. After that I progressed quickly, and it wasn't very many months until I was doing 50, 75 and even 100 push-ups in competition with Uncle Reid. It was a proud day for my uncle and the rest of the family when I earned my first varsity letter on the high school golf team and later co-captained the senior class intra-mural softball and basket-ball team.

Uncle Reid had come to live with us because he had messed up his life with a drinking problem, and needed a place to stay while he tried to get his life back in order. He never talked much about his problem, especially to me, but one afternoon when I was 14, he leveled with me.

Looking me straight in the eye, he said,

"Paul, I don't like to talk about this, but I want you to understand that drinking is a terrible thing, and there is only one solution to it, and I want you to remember this all the days of your life. Never take your first drink."

He asked if I understood. I said I did, and as my eyes were fixed on his, and as I recognized the torment in his face, his words sank deep into my heart. It was a great teaching moment for me and from that moment forward I have never even thought about drinking alcoholic beverages.

As a boy I didn't have any well-defined career aspirations. I was a boy scout and active in the Church. I loved sports, boxing, sandlot football, games in the street, playing tennis with Uncle Reid, and wrestling and boxing with the boys in the neighborhood.

When I was twelve my father taught me how to drive the car, a 1928 Buick. We had moved to West Los Angeles, a farming community at that time, with sometimes large distances between houses. When father was gone I drove the family to church on Sundays. I could barely see over the steering wheel, and my legs weren't long enough to comfortably reach the clutch and brake pedals, but I felt very proud knowing my parents trusted me to drive the car.

The day after high school graduation I went to work in the script department at MGM Studios. I was one of four who had been recommended by our high school vice-principal. I hadn't been there very many days when it was my turn to go down to what was called the "sweat shop," an old shack on the back of the lot where used movie scripts were destroyed. I had never been there before, but my boss explained that the instructions were on the door, and that I wasn't to return until I was finished with the day's allotment.

When I entered the building I discovered a huge paper cutter and a stack of scripts piled to one side. Behind the paper cutter was another larger pile of scripts, about 20 feet wide and 10 feet deep. The instructions were simply to destroy the scripts by cutting them twice.

This was the job nobody wanted, but to me it looked fun. The challenge was to see how fast I could make that paper cutter fly. I experimented some, cutting stacks of varying depths until I found what I thought to be the optimum size for cutting, then concentrated on doing it faster and faster. Soon the pile of scripts beside the cutter was gone, and I waded into the larger pile. I have to admit I worked up a good sweat, but I enjoyed working as hard and as fast as I could, especially on such a simple task that didn't require much thought.

I finished the job in three hours and returned to the

office, only to receive a tongue-lashing from my boss for returning too soon. I told her that the work was finished and went to the back of the office to run the mimeograph machines. About an hour later the boss called me into her office and apologized for the verbal abuse. She complimented me for a job well done.

I didn't find out until later in the day while talking with some of the other workers that the day's allotment of scripts for me to destroy had been the little pile by the cutter. The big pile represented the cut-up work for the rest of the week, and I had done it all in three hours.

I didn't realize the full consequences of that morning's work until six months later. The United States had just entered World War II and the supervisor of my department had enlisted in the service. They needed a new supervisor. At 17 years I was the youngest of the more than 30 employees in the department, men and women, and was more than a little surprised when I was called into the boss' office and offered the supervisor's job. There is no doubt that my speedy script cutting was the single most important factor causing my boss to want me for the supervisor's job. My hourly pay rate was increased from $.51 to $1.50.

Three months later I was drafted into the U.S. Army. Earlier I had tried to join the Army and Navy Air Corps, and in both instances was turned down because I was found to be color-blind.

I was sent to New Mexico for my infantry basic training, and ended up with a military escort guard duty assignment. I received the top trainee award and the first non-commissioned officer promotion of my group. As a result I was allowed to apply for a West Point appointment. I went through a battery of tests and oral board reviews with senior officers. A few days later the camp commander called me in and told me that my application was one of two that were being forwarded to West Point.

While waiting for my application to be processed and evaluated I was transferred to Brooke General Hospital for medical training. Two months later, on a Sunday morning, I was aroused by my first sergeant who said he wanted to personally see the only guy who had received a West Point appointment out of Fort Sam Houston, a command area consisting of about 185,000 troops.

I was sent to Amherst College in Amherst, Massachu-setts for a year of pre-West Point training. Army appointees were sent there in order to bring them up to par with the college students and graduates entering West Point.

While studying at Amherst one night, a small voice, somewhere deep within me, asked "What about a mission?" As a boy I had always wanted to become a missionary for the Mormon Church for the usual two years, but with war going on, and entering the service, I had more or less given up the idea. I tried to forget the small voice, but a week, or a month later I would hear it again.

I realized that if I went to West Point I would be committed to at least nine years of military service, and that would remove any chance of serving a mission. Again and again I heard that little voice, "What about a mission?"

At the end of the year I asked for reassignment in the Army and gave up the appointment to West Point. I was immediately transferred to an infantry unit and shipped overseas without a single day of field training. The captain of my new unit looked me up and down and asked how I had done in basic training. I told him I had done very well, that I had the top firing record, and it took him about ten seconds to decide to make me his personal bodyguard. I wasn't particularly impressive as a bodyguard at 145 pounds and five feet, ten inches tall, but I was in excellent shape as a result of my athletic involvement at Amherst. My greatest claim to fame was holding the top record in the obstacle course.

Our convoy was broken up by a submarine attack, but I finally arrived in England by way of South Hampton.

I crossed the English Channel late in the summer of 1944, and crawled out of a landing craft onto Utah Beach at Normandy, France, as part of a later contingent of men and equipment to reach shore.

Our senior officers had given us brand new combat boots the night before the crossing. I experienced firsthand, along with thousands of other men, the misery of walking 12 to 15 miles a day carrying a full combat pack with blisters the size of half dollars on my heels.

I found myself in a real shooting war, like in the movies, and hundreds of men went through our company as replacements for the dead and wounded.

My platoon sergeant was an "old" man about 36 years old, a seasoned career soldier from Kansas. We called him Potts. His speech was colorful, and his grammar sometimes shameful, but he had a great heart. He was eager to protect and preserve the lives of his men. He showed us how to keep a rifle clean, how to hang grenades on our combat jackets so the pins wouldn't inadvertently get pulled, and how to set a bayonette. When the supply lines were cut, he showed us how to find a bottle of cherry juice or peaches in a bombed out cellar, how to avoid the booby traps set on dead bodies with weapons.

The last time I saw Sergeant Potts was the darkest day of my life. He didn't get blown away with the usual burst of enemy fire. Because we were on the front lines and never knew when we would have to attack or retreat, it was easy to go day after day without removing ones boots. Our feet were wet and muddy all the time that fall, so we had many trenchfoot problems.

It was in the basement of a bombed-out German house that we had to cut away Sergeant Pott's boots and socks with a knife. The room was filled with the stench of decaying flesh. His feet were purple and rotten, and it was obvious that some amputation would be necessary. He was immediately carried off on a stretcher and I have never seen him since.

I had just turned 20 years old and had come to rely on Sergeant Potts for my day to day survival. He was my anchor. Now he was gone. It was at times like this that I had second thoughts about leaving West Point.

Feeling lost and depressed, I went back to another small room in the basement to think things out. Suddenly, there in front of me, was my buddy who had shot himself to get out of the war. My spiritual and mental reserves were already depleted, there was nothing more to draw upon. Every day during the previous weeks I had witnessed one, two, five, or ten of my companions killed or seriously wounded. I had lost weight until I was nothing but skin and bones. I sat down, not having enough strength to remain on my feet.

An officer came in and ordered me to stand guard duty. I didn't think I had the strength to stand, but somehow I managed to get to my assigned guard position. It seemed to me that I just didn't have any more strength to continue.

It was at this moment of deepest despondency, that I heard that small voice again, the same one I had heard at Amherst. This time it said, "You can pray." Like a breath of fresh air in a hot crowded room, I received that voice, and I began praying as I had never prayed before. It was an earnest and sincere prayer, right from the heart, and it didn't seem like very long until I was overwhelmed with a feeling of peace and strength that was as distinct and decisive as anything that has ever happened to me. The weight was removed from my body. The darkness was lifted from my mind and heart like a curtain opening on a stage. I saw the sun shining through.

When I left guard duty that day, there was a bounce in my step and a song in my heart. In the long weeks and months that followed I never again returned to that debilitating despondency, that spiritual and mental darkness that physically weakens a person. I had found a new and deeper faith in Jesus Christ and His great love and power.

Our company fought in the Limburg sector of Holland and the Geilenkirchen sector of the great German Siegfried line of concrete pillboxes until we were called up at the Battle of the Bulge, in the Ardennes in Belgium only hours after the German counteroffensive was mounted. On returning to the Siegfried line offensive, we fought our way to the Rhine River. Then I was with Task Force Church leading the Allied drive from the west to Berlin. Our unit crossed the Elbe River with a patrol and penetrated 27 miles to meet the Russian Army, then sat back with our hands tied watching the Russians take Berlin.

I left Germany in the middle of the winter of 1945 and arrived home to a sunny Southern California. My parents didn't know I was coming, and weren't expecting me. I climbed the back fence and walked unannounced into the family kitchen.

In addition to all the tears, my mother said, "Sonny, you look great. I didn't expect to see you look so good."

It was at that moment that I realized how marvelous it was that I arrived home in one piece. Shells had exploded within five or six feet of me. So many times I had had to bury my face in the mud as shrapnel and bullets hissed over me. I gratefully found my life spared.

I enrolled in school at U.C.L.A., and soon after that my good bishop asked me how I felt about going on a mission for the Church. I responded with a quick yes, and we sent in the necessary papers. I decided that all girlfriends had to be eliminated, I didn't want any binding ties of that nature. I received a call to serve in South Africa, but since there was a problem getting transportation to Africa at that time, I had to wait for further instructions as to when to enter the mission home in Salt Lake City.

Weeks passed as I waited for the phone call telling me to come to the mission home. One evening the bishop called and asked me to go with one of the other elders to administer to a sick person. I didn't recognize the name, but he gave me the address. I went to the home, knocked on the door, and found that the wife's younger sister, who was visiting from Utah, needed a blessing. The young woman was reclining on the sofa in the living room, and as I visited with her I discovered that she was recovering from undulant typhoid fever and was literally fighting back from death's doorstep. She had been in the hospital 27 times for numerous blood transfusions. She had come to California to stay with her sister in the hope that the warmer climate would aid her recovery and her effort to gain some stability from a hypersensitive balance center.

After administering to her, we chatted for about an hour. I was impressed enough with her to suggest to the young elder with me that if he was going to be around, he ought to get to know that young lady a lot better. Her name was Lorna Golding.

By the time the next day rolled around I thought better of my earlier decision and pursued her myself. I called for a date and we started seeing each other. Our friendship developed quickly and ten days later I drove Lorna and her sister with two children to Utah where I eventually entered the mission home, but not before I got her to promise to wait for me.

My missionary experience included temporary sevice in Texas and Louisiana until a freighter was located to take two of us to Africa's Gold Coast by way of Brazil. After two weeks of travel by rail we finally arrived in the Transvaal, a province in the northeastern part of the Union of South

Africa. Because of the war the area had not had missionaries for a number of years.

In addition to the usual tracting and teaching of the
white populace, we visited the compounds where the black
mine workers lived. Sometimes we put on basketball
demonstrations which were always popular. On one occasion we attempted to enter a black compound to attend a
birthday party at the home of a black family, and were
physically turned away by a big, burly white guard who
didn't like us associating with the blacks. The apartheid
policies made it almost impossible for us to teach the black
population.

My father had been to South Africa 32 years earlier, and
it was a thrill to meet some of his old friends. There is no
doubt that that two years of missionary experience was
more valuable to my personal development than my six
years of formal college education.

On one occasion I was transferred from Springs to Cape
Town, about 1,100 miles to the south. On the morning before
my departure I was familiarizing my replacement with the
territory, showing him the neighborhoods where we had
been working. As we were returning home for lunch, I
pointed out a house, a number of yards back from the road,
where we had not yet talked to anyone. Like many of the
yards in South Africa, this one was fenced to contain dogs,
and my new companion was reluctant to enter and suggested that we postpone the call. I felt an urgency to make one
more call to this home. I entered the gate alone and started
down the walk. When I could see that the coast was clear,
that no angry dogs were lurking in the bushes, I motioned
for my companion to follow.

We were greeted by Mrs. Hugo who invited us to have
lunch with the family. We returned that night and stayed
long past the "witching hour" explaining the message of
the restored Gospel. I had a good feeling about that family
as I headed south for Cape Town, never expecting to see
them again.

Thirty-three years later, during the fall general conference weekend of 1980, I met Shorty Hugo for the second
time. As he introduced me to some of his children and
thanked me for bringing the Gospel to him and his family, I
knew I had done the right thing in giving up the West Point

appointment.

Lorna waited for me and we were married 14 days after my return from the mission field. I wore a worn-out blue suit and a white shirt with a frayed collar. I had holes in my shoes and seven dollars in my pocket. I didn't have a car, apartment, or job prospects.

I found a part-time job working 20 to 30 hours a week and enrolled in school at the University of Southern California to study business management. Lorna was still somewhat frail from her sickness and not able to take on a job other than keeping up our little apartment and cooking for the two of us. She never complained about not having enough money to buy a new dress or any of the other items she wanted, but later worked at a telephone job producing some very welcome dollars for our slim budget.

After a year we transferred to Brigham Young University in Provo, Utah, where I graduated with a degree in business management. During the last semester we lived almost entirely on a tough, gamey venison someone had given us and several bushels of reject apples which we bought for fifty cents each. There was little else.

When I arrived at BYU, the one thing that impressed me more than anything else was the willingness of the teachers to take time out of their busy schedules to help me plan my future career. Great men like Hugh B. Brown, Weldon Taylor and Dean Edwards always seemed to have five minutes, or even an hour to help me figure out which direction I ought to go.

After finishing school, I went to work for one of the large retail chains in Southern California. They made a lot of promises about large salaries and big benefits for individuals who could handle responsibility. It wasn't long until I was made manager of one of their branches. They raised my salary from $216 to $266 a month, but as manager I didn't qualify for commissions because I wasn't supposed to sell ahead of the salespeople. Without the commissions, my take-home pay had actually decreased.

I had to work two nights a week and all day Saturdays, in addition to the five regular work days. To make matters worse, I had to spend a large portion of my meager salary on expensive suits, shoes, hats and topcoats, the expected apparel of store managers. I felt the company had misrepresented itself. The hours were longer, and the pay lower than had been promised in the initial interview. I began to look elsewhere for employment.

Next, I landed a job as the purchasing agent and office manager for an electronics company which I soon discovered was on its last legs, financially. I was the last employee on the payroll before it went under.

After that I went to work for a big paint company where they said I would have to learn the business from the ground up. I drove a delivery truck for several months delivering 55-gallon drums of paint to Southern California businesses. I soon discovered that my sinuses were highly sensitive to the acrid paint odors, and the situation became unbearable. I asked to be transferred to sales.

They put me into their sales training program and soon turned me loose to muster up some business. I made the mistake of being too successful. I made a favorable contact with a major processing firm that used a lot of lacquer and paint in finishing their products. They agreed to buy their paint supplies from me if I could meet certain reasonable product and price requirements. I was very excited because my commission from this one account would be over $1,000 a month.

As soon as my bosses found out what I was putting together, they started looking for ways to get the account away from me so they wouldn't have to pay such a big commission. They told me I wasn't knowledgeable enough to handle such an important account. I needed more experience. I told them that if I had enough experience to land the account, I ought to be able to maintain it. They didn't agree, however, so I concluded that they were greedy and dishonest in trying to take the account away from me. I resigned. They begged me to come back, but I felt it was a matter of principle and moved on.

My next job was with North American Aviation as a material procurement expediter and assistant buyer in their special purchases department. I worked in a large room with many other employees, most of whom smoked. I soon discovered that the tobacco smoke was more irritating to my sinuses than the toxic odors at the paint company. My eyes burned and watered through the entire work day. My wife's health was still fragile, and there were times when I needed to be with her. I longed for an outside job with more freedom, a job where I could breathe clean air.

One day a sympathetic friend told me that Los Angeles County was testing applicants to become real estate appraiser trainees for the county. He challenged me to take the test. I wasn't very excited about the job because I would be earning less money than at North American and therefore wouldn't be able to quit my part-time job selling shoes. But my friend was insistent, and I told him I would take the test.

On the Saturday morning when the test was to be administered I drove to the address my friend had given me and parked a few blocks away. As I approached the entrance to the Civil Service building, I discovered a line of hundreds of men coming out of the door and extending down the street. I walked into the lobby to pick up the papers for the exam and was told to go to the end of the long line. Apparently all those men wanted to be county real estate appraisers. I figured if that many guys wanted the job, there might be something to it, maybe I really would like it. I waited in line, took the four-hour exam, went home and forgot about it. Two weeks later I received a little card in the mail telling me I had received one of the top scores on the test, and that they had a job for me if I would come down and accept it. The job looked interesting, and would provide the freedom I had been looking for. Each week I would spend four days in the field and one day in the office.

I gladly resigned at North American and became a trainee real estate appraiser for Los Angeles County.

I worked up through the ranks until I found myself acting as a principal appraiser supervising a large geographical area of the county. I spent ten productive years with L.A. County. In addition to my appraisal work I was in charge of a training program for new appraisers. I received regular salary increases until I was earning a very substantial salary and things looked bright for us. I had a good job, security and freedom to organize and do my work as I thought best. There was very little supervision.

Eventually, pressures developed from certain people in our organization for me to make appraisal adjustments with significant tax consequences that went against my better judgment. After ten years on the job, one day I submitted my resignation rather than give in to the pressures.

The next week I removed my personal belongings from the office and joined the ranks of the unemployed. Everything had happened so suddenly. My wife asked what I would do. On the side I had been investing in real estate, and I had been spending my Saturdays building spec houses. I told her I was going to go into building and development.

I understood Los Angeles real estate values and trends and I was familiar with the building industry. It was 1963, and I was well prepared to jump into what was to become one of the hottest real estate development markets in the entire world.

The very next day I began work on a project that eventually became an 80-unit apartment complex, using my modest cash savings as startup capital.

Now that I was a full-time developer I began finding all kinds of projects to get involved in. Once I made up my mind as to what I would do, even without a lot of cash, I found plenty of ways to keep busy in building and development. I liked the business, everything from getting zoning clearances and lining up financing, to putting in streets and gutters and working with sub-contractors. I didn't mind putting in 12 and 15-hour work days, and often rolled up my sleeves to help with the cement, carpentry and other work.

My brother-in-law, Les Cantrell, was a machinery and equipment dealer with an interest in real estate developing. I often had lunch with him to discuss our common interests. On one occasion he told me about a piece of property that he had purchased some years before. He had a chance to sell it at a substantial profit, but there was a cloud on the title. He asked for my advice on how to clear up the problem. He said he had tried to talk with the lady involved, but had been unable to negotiate with her. I asked him to give me her name and address and I would see what I could do to obtain a settlement.

A few days later I called on the lady, only to discover that I already knew her. I had recently been involved with her in putting on a regional cultural arts festival for the Church. She invited me into her home and I explained my brother-in-law's real estate problem, assuring her Les was a reputable individual, and that he was only interested in doing what was fair and just for all the parties involved. I suggested she sign off her interest in the property in exchange for a reasonable payment from Les. She did so, and he was able to sell the property.

Les was delighted and I was more than happy to do a favor for a good friend.

A short time later Les asked me to appraise a large piece of commercial property, about 12 acres, that he was thinking of buying. I did the appraisal and advised him to buy it, that it was well worth the price. As we discussed the property, I mentioned that if the whole piece was too large for his needs, I might be interested in a small piece along the back.

A few days later I received a letter from Les offering me the piece along the back at exactly the same per acre price that he was paying for the entire parcel. I explained to him that the piece along the back was smaller and more workable, and therefore more valuable than the rest of the land. But this was his way to pay me back for favors I had done for him.

His letter arrived the day after I had sold some spec houses. My equity from the houses was $16,000 cash, in the bank. In fact, this money represented everything I had, except the equity in my home.

When Les told me that the down payment on the piece of property was $16,000, I told him we had a deal. As I studied my new acquisition I decided that the most profitable way to go was to develop an industrial park, but in order to do that I needed more land. Within two weeks I negotiated the purchase of a neighboring dairy. I was unable to raise the down payment, so I went to Les, explained my plans, and offered to make him a partner if he could come up with $12,000 for the down payment. He liked the idea and got the money.

I supervised the project and brought in some of the first industrial accounts that now make up the industrial city of Paramount, California. I went from building to building— constructing, selling and leasing. It wasn't but a few years until my equity in that one project was multiplied many times—wealth that came as a result of hard work, yes, but also from the help and favor of a friend. From this and similar experiences I have come to the conclusion that no matter how hard we try to give to others, like bread on the water, it often comes back multiplied.

Probably the most exciting and satisfying project was a 20-acre blend of apartments and office buildings in Camarillo, California. An attempt was made to make it first class all the way, aesthetically pleasing, a blending of artistic ideas—architecture, landscaping, pools and waterfalls into a unified whole. It is very satisfying to see dreams and concepts become reality.

I discovered an unexpected problem associated with wealth and success, a problem that has caused some heartache over the years. When a person achieves success, there are often people standing around who try to shoot him down. Among your business associates, in your neighborhood, and even in the Church, there are a few who don't have the capacity to live with other people's success. These are the fault-finders, the rumor starters who focus malicious gossip on the successful people around them. The full-blown lies don't hurt as deeply, or spread so far, as the half-truths springing from a business deal gone sour, or your refusal to invest in what you consider to be the ill-conceived dream of a mutual friend.

One time our LDS ward was anticipating a costly church building project. I donated my services in designing and supervising construction of a multi-unit apartment building for the ward. The idea was that everyone would help build the apartment, then the proceeds from the sale of the building would help for the new chapel. Even though I didn't receive any payment for supervising the project, including renting and maintaining of the units until sold, I started hearing rumors, fourth or fifth generation, that I was making a huge personal profit at the expense of the other ward members. By the time the building was finished I think half the people in the ward believed I was profiting on the project, all this the result of one or two loose tongues. It would have been very easy for me to have become bitter and withdrawn from that ward had not the bishop spoken strongly on my behalf at the time the new chapel was dedicated. He reminded the ward that over $30,000 went into the building fund as a result of the apartment project. Over the years I have tried to be less critical of other people in the hope that they would be less critical of me.

With time, the Los Angeles smog became increasingly irritating to my lungs, and the driving chores more burdensome. In 1973, we closed out most of our California projects and moved to Provo, Utah. We built a home in a nice neighborhood, and have enjoyed making new friends.

The fact remains that we all leave this world as naked as jaybirds, nobody has yet figured a way to take it with them, so I figure one might as well give it to a worthy cause. My wife and I can't think of a cause more worthy than Brigham Young University, and we are proud to be included among its many benefactors. I certainly don't want to spoil my children and grandchildren with large sums of money from our estate.

They need to learn that abundance does not justify waste. Even the most wealthy people can eat only one meal at a time, and wear only one suit at a time. How can we justify a whole closet full? Why drive a Rolls Royce when a Ford will provide adequate transportation? Why live in a house with a dozen unnecessary rooms, good for little else but to impress visitors?

My children and grandchildren need to learn, too, the lessons that can only be learned through hard work and struggle. They need to learn to work in spite of hunger, thirst and weariness—to have the discipline to keep working after others quit. True success cannot be achieved without the ability to roll up one's sleeves and work. These lessons are more valuable than any amount of money I could ever leave behind for my posterity.

Vic Cartwright—co-founder of Deseret Pharmaceutical, producer of medical devices for world markets. Sold to Werner Lambert Company in 1976 for $130 million.

Vic Cartwright

I graduated from North Cache High School, Richmond, Utah, in 1936. I was the youngest in a family of seven. Mother was very concerned that none of her children had graduated from college. I was her last hope.

We didn't have much in the way of material things. I don't think my father in all his life earned more than a hundred dollars a month. He worked at the milk plant. We had ten acres of ground on which we grew most of our food. We didn't go hungry, but we never had any cash.

During the summer after graduating from high school, my oldest brother, Bert, came home for a vacation. He worked for a steel company as an engineer in Granite City, Illinois, just across the Mississippi River from St. Louis. One day, Mother got Bert and me together and said,

"Now, I have prayed to the Lord as to what your brother Vic should do."

She looked directly at Bert, and continued, "And I am convinced you should take Vic back to St. Louis with you. He should study the pharmaceutical business."

Today, this may not sound like such a strange idea, but back in 1936 there weren't very many drugs on the market. This was before the days of penicillin. About all one had with which to treat illness was mustard plaster, and maybe a little aspirin or morphine for pain.

Mother didn't know if there was a pharmacy school in St. Louis, and neither did Bert. But she had prayed about it and knew beyond any doubt that I should go with Bert to study pharmacy. It was decided that that's what I would do.

Mother wasn't what many people would term a religious woman, in that she didn't hold a lot of positions in the Church. But if a neighbor needed help, or someone was sick in bed with the flu on Sunday, she'd go over and do their housework and prepare meals for them rather than go to church.

I gathered a few things together, I didn't have much, and went with Bert to St. Louis. Upon arriving, I discovered that St. Louis did have a pharmacy school, a good one, the St. Louis College of Pharmacy. It was still summer, so I set out to earn money so I could go to school in the fall, but there just weren't any jobs available. The depression had just ended and it was tough finding work. Mother had promised that she would work her fingers to the bone if I would attend pharmacy school. She sold eggs and sent the proceeds to me, a few dollars every week.

When fall came and it was time to register, I went over to the school and received the shock of my life. The tuition was approximately $150 a semester. In those days you could attend Utah State University an entire year for about $30. I had no idea where I would get that much money, but with mother's help, and what I scraped together, I managed to get through the first year. I worked part time in a pharmacy. At first I worked for free because I didn't have any experience, and working for free was the only way to get experience. The store owner gave me two packs of cigarettes every week. I told him I didn't smoke, but he gave them to me anyway. I sold them for 10 cents a pack.

Just as the year was finishing up, one Friday morning as classes were ending for the year, I received a notice to go immediately to my brother's house. When I arrived, he told me that our mother had died. This was a great shock to me. I bought a bus ticket and came home to Utah. That summer I worked on the farm.

The next fall some of my old high school friends talked me into going to Utah State University. I didn't have enough money to go back to the pharmacy school anyway. I didn't get very excited about my studies that year because I couldn't take any classes that had anything to do with pharmacy. Although my mother was dead, her dream about my future, continued to haunt me.

At the end of the school year I decided to return to the pharmacy school. About the first of July my brothers and sisters scraped up some money and clothes and I took a bus to St. Louis.

I was able to get a job in a pharmacy again, this time for money, 20 cents an hour. I found a room for $3.50 a week. For dinner each night I would buy three five-cent hamburgers and a piece of pie at the White Castle Cafe. The entire meal cost 20 cents. Afterwards I would go back to the pharmacy where I could eat all the ice cream I wanted for free. The school, realizing how destitute I was, loaned me the books I needed and let me pay the tuition in installments. I lived this way for two years.

In the summer of 1941 when the armed services began drafting heavily, I tried to get a one-year exemption to finish my schooling but was unable to do so, so I returned to Utah to wait for the draft to catch me. But a young lady, Fae Clark, caught me first, and we were married. I still hadn't been drafted by the end of 1941, so I decided to enlist.

While in the service I worked up to the rank of captain and was able to save some money. In 1946 when I was about to be discharged, I was stationed at Fort Sam Houston in San Antonio, Texas. Like everybody else I was anxious to get out and start earning a living as a civilian. By that time we had one child, a son.

I had a job interview with Upjohn Company. They had an opening for a medical service representative in the San Antonio area. It looked like an excellent opportunity, so I told them at the end of the interview that I would take the job. On the way home, however, I remembered my mother's dream and the promise she had given me.

When I walked in the door my wife asked how the interview had gone. I told her just great, but I had to make a phone call. I called the fellow who had interviewed me and told him I couldn't take the job, that I was returning to Utah.

Soon after our arrival in Utah I contacted the pharmacy school in St. Louis to see about finishing my degree. While I had been in the service the curriculum had changed somewhat and I needed one more class before I could begin my final year in the fall. They said I could take the course during the summer.

My wife stayed with her parents while I flew to St. Louis to take the course. With the G.I. bill and my savings, I was a lot better prepared to go to school than I had been before the war. The class was called pharmocognosy, and dealt with the identification of drugs. They gave me numerous packets of powders and I had to identify them through chemical tests. The professor said I could go as fast as I wanted to.

Before the war, I had really struggled in school, but now it came easy. I had never enjoyed such clearness of thought, or such an ease in learning. I often thought of my mother's promise. It was almost like I had a photographic memory. It may have had something to do with being older, more mature, more experienced. The summer course normally took six weeks. I was finished in 10 days.

I returned to Utah for my wife and child and began my final year of school in the fall. Learning had never been so easy. When a chemical formula was written on the blackboard, I could go home and write it in my notes from memory. Instead of the usual 16 credit hours, I took 20 hours including six labs. I would have lab experiments going on simultaneously on different floors and would have to run back and forth checking progress. I ended up the number one student in the graduating class.

I returned and opened a pharmacy in Orem. I was never very happy working in the retail store, so after about a year I sold it and went to work for Parke Davis as a medical service representative. My territory was all of southern Utah. Parke Davis had just come out with some new products and my quota was very low. I soon became what I considered to be very successful. I worked very hard, sometimes 14 to 16 hours a day at the beginning of the week enabling me to complete all my calls in four days, so I could be home with my family for a three-day weekend. Sometimes I would take the family with me and camp in Zions National Park, or the Grand Canyon.

In 1956, a good friend, Dale Ballard, and I began talking about starting our own drug company—buying bulk generic drugs and packaging them under our own label. It was a tough decision to make. I was making good money working on commission for Parke Davis. We had just finished a new home on Locust Street in Provo and my wife was due any day to deliver our fourth child. It didn't seem like a very good time to walk away from a steady job.

The more I talked to people about the situation, the more confused I became. Finally, one Sunday I really poured my soul out to the Lord, asking what I should do. I asked for some kind of sign that I was on the right track. Nothing happened immediately, but I'll never forget the next morning. When I woke up, all my fears and doubts had vanished. My enthusiasm for the new venture was free of any fear of failure. I knew my prayers had been answered.

I called the division manager of Parke Davis in Denver and told him I was quitting in order to start my own business. Next I called Dale Ballard, who was younger than I was, and told him we were in business. We sold stock to capitalize the new company. We called it Deseret Pharmaceutical.

Since we lived in the heart of the world's baby capital, some of our first products were prenatal vitamins and vitamin drops. Then we got into diet control drugs and many other products. We provided formulas to drug companies who manufactured the products to our specifications. Our only involvement in the manufacturing was labeling the products.

I covered the same geographical area I had covered with Parke Davis, and my partner went in the other direction. Since we were new, we were criticized a lot by our competitors, particularly from B.K. & S. Company in Salt Lake City. We liked to call them the party boys because they often took big breaks away from their sales efforts to vacation and party. Since we were working with other people's money, Dale and I felt obligated to work all the time.

When we went into a town, we called on the doctors, first. We told them about the products and got them to agree to prescribe our products. Next, we went to the drug stores and sold them the products the doctors had agreed to prescribe. We carried all the merchandise with us in our station wagons. Back home, we had three or four people handling the packaging.

When we tried to expand beyond the borders of Utah, we

ran into problems. People were suspicious of our name—
Deseret Pharmaceutical. Even as close as Elko, Nevada,
people would tell us that they would not buy our products
because our company was owned by the Mormon Church. It
took a lot of talking to convince them that that was not the
case. We ran into this problem everywhere we went, outside
Utah. With persistence, however, we were able to gradually
expand our market area.

Near the end of 1956, when most people were beginning
their Christmas vacations, Dale and I headed over to
Colorado in an effort to get a few more sales before the end
of the year. Upon arriving in Grand Junction, we attempted
to contact an old friend we had dealt with before, Dr. George
Dougherty, an old Irishman, an M.D. anethesiologist. I
didn't have any product left to sell him. He was just a good
friend, and I wanted to see him while I was in town. He
wasn't at the hospital, so we went to his home.

Good old George, as we called him, asked us in, offered
us a seat and a can of cold beer. We declined the beer but
gladly accepted the invitation to sit down and chat.

He showed us a little invention he was working on. It
was nothing more than a needle and a piece of plastic
tubing. He said it was a catheter that could be inserted in
the vein for blood transfusions, giving solutions, IV's and
that kind of thing. He showed how the plastic catheter could
be inserted into the vein through the needle, and then how
the needle could be removed, leaving the plastic tube in
place for making the transfusions. It seemed much better
than the old method of leaving a needle in someone's arm
for long periods of time.

The doctor said, 'If you young fellows can put something
like this together in a sterile, disposable package, easy to
use, you will sell millions of them."

He said that if we hadn't come along, or if we weren't
interested in the product, his intention was to send the idea
to Abbot Laboratories, a large Chicago-based manufacturer
of medical devices. He said he would prefer to deal with us
because Abbot had already beaten him out of another good
product. He had sent them an idea on an IV set, and they
had sent him back a bottle of vitamins saying thanks, but
one of their research and development men had had the
idea about three or four months before they received his

letter. They made a lot of money on the idea, and all good old George got was a bottle of vitamins.

He knew we didn't have any experience in manufacturing medical devices, but he liked and trusted us. We were young and energetic, and he thought we could do it. He challenged us to do it. After agreeing what George's royalty would be, we returned to Utah where we spent the remainder of the Christmas vacation working on the new product.

We found two little old ladies in Bountiful who had a plastic injection molding machine in their basement. It was one of those old-fashioned machines with a big wheel that had to be turned by hand. They helped us get the molds made, then we helped them crank out the parts. We poured little pieces of plastic into the hopper. From there they fell into the mold. Then we turned the big wheel and pressed out the parts. They were very crude with rough surfaces and lots of flashings around the edges.

After Christmas, we went back to work selling pharmaceuticals. It wasn't until October, 1957, ten months later that we did anything with the new device. We made six prototypes.

We scheduled a booth at the National Anesthesiology meeting in Los Angeles. George came over from Grand Junction and the three of us went to Los Angeles in my big old Lincoln. We drove up in front of the Statler Hotel, unloaded all our gear including the display table. We carried everything through the lobby and up to the mezzanine to the display area and set up our table in the assigned space.

We were about finished when a representative of the Teamsters Union showed up and threatened to throw us out into the street. Apparently we had violated union protocol. He explained the facts of convention life. He said that union trucks carried all displays to the convention center, that union men carried the materials to the display area, that union carpenters erected the displays, and that union electricians made the necessary connections. Not only would we be unwelcome, but unable to participate if we didn't follow the established procedure. Fortunately, we were able to convince the man that we had set up our booth in ignorance of union rules. He agreed to let us stay, only after we promised to use union people for all future displays.

We never set up our own displays in a union town again.

As soon as the show opened, a doctor walked by our booth, stopped, picked up one of the prototypes. We explained how it worked. He called over one of his friends, who in turn called to another doctor. Soon we had a large crowd of doctors enthusiastically discussing our prototypes. They had never seen anything like it before. Every one we talked to said he would use the catheter. One doctor told us to call our factory immediately and have several dozen put on a plane to his hospital in Chicago. I wonder what he would have thought if I had told him that our factory consisted of two little old ladies in Bountiful with an old-fashioned molding machine in their basement, and that they couldn't produce any more parts because they weren't strong enough to turn the big wheel without our help.

We drove back to Utah, knowing we had a winner, and that we had to get it on the market as soon as possible. The antiquated machine belonging to the little old ladies was too unreliable for steady production so we found a Mr. Rider who had a pretty good plastic injection system set up in his basement. He lived in Salt Lake City.

Next, we had to line up the needles. I remember meeting with Matt Rohr at the El Rancho Hotel in Las Vegas. Matt was from Connecticut and made the finest needles on the market, the sharpest needles anywhere, and that's what we needed to get the catheter into the vein.

At first, he didn't want to make the needles for us. When we showed him how we intended to use them, he said we were wasting our stockholders' money. He finally agreed to make them, though, but still felt we were making a big mistake. We made a deal wherein he would provide us with disposable needles for about 15 cents each, an outrageously low price in those days.

As soon as the product was in production, we began attending medical conventions all over the country. We attended a surgical convention in Chicago, an anethesiologist convention in Houston and a nurses meeting in New York City. The orders started pouring in faster than we could fill them. About that time we entered into a distribution agreement with C.R. Bard Company in New Jersey. We shipped everything we built directly to them. They warehoused the products and distributed them to the dealers.

I don't know how many millions of dollars we made on that first product, but good old George in Grand Junction received over a million dollars in royalties before we bought out his interest for a large sum in addition to the royalties.

With the success of the catheter, we began to think about making other medical devices, and began to drift away from the pharmaceutical business. Besides, the FDA was getting a lot more involved in pharmaceuticals, and with all the resulting red tape, it just wasn't very profitable for us. On the other hand there was very little control over the medical device market, and we could more or less do what we wanted as long as the doctors were happy with the products.

We called our first product the intracath, and even though it was selling well, there were several problems that bothered us. The needle had to be big enough for the plastic catheter to slide through it. As a result the needle made a very big hole. In addition, once the plastic catheter was in place in the vein the needle couldn't be removed from the catheter because there was a little hub at the back of the catheter, necessary for connecting up the IV set. As a result, when the catheter was in place, the needle was in the way because it couldn't be removed. Doctors usually taped it in place so it wouldn't move around.

One day I was reading in a medical journal and discovered an article by a doctor from the Mayo Clinic. It talked about a special needle he had developed that would work inside of a catheter, instead of on the outside. This seemed like a natural answer to our problems. With the needle on the inside the hole would be much smaller, making a tighter fit for the larger catheter. And once the catheter was in place the needle could be easily removed and discarded.

We immediately set to work developing what we called the angiocath. There weren't any patent problems because the doctor who had invented the needle, published all his findings in the medical journal before he had applied for a patent. The angiocath, with hundreds of variations in size and shape, became the main product of Deseret Pharmaceutical.

Since the information on the needle was public knowledge and not protected by patents, we tried to keep our

success as quiet as possible, so as not to encourage
competition. We bought needles from as many manufacturers as possible, so no one would know how many needles
we were using. We did the same with the plastic tubing,
using a number of suppliers.

We were able to keep the market pretty much to
ourselves until Matt Rohr, a needle supplier, sold his
company to a bigger needle company in St. Louis, A.S. Aloe
& Co. Bectin Dickinson, was also supplying us with needles
and tubing. When thse two companies saw how many
needles we were using, it didn't take them long to become
our major competitors.

About this time we decided to get more heavily involved
in production and purchased a mold-making company in
California, and injection molding machines for our main
plant in Utah.

But just when it looked like we had the world by the tail,
we almost spent ourselves into bankruptcy. Our first
product, the intracath, had cost us $3,300 to develop. That
was all, and most of it was spent at the convention in Los
Angeles, where we learned there was a ready market for the
product. We soon found out that every new product couldn't
be produced as easily, or as inexpensively.

It is interesting that our second major product also had
its beginnings in Grand Junction, Colorado. We were
visiting with a Dr. Marasco who told us we ought to develop
a better surgical mask. He said the ones on the market were
no good. We started nosing around and found most doctors
felt the same way.

We hired a microbiologist at the University of Utah to do
a study for us comparing different filtering media, taking
into consideration availability and price of raw materials.
The study showed fiberglass to be very effective, provided
that 20 percent of the fibers were smaller than one micron in
diameter, very small. Apparently an electrical charge is
generated in these small fibers which resulted in a strong
attraction to particulate matter.

We purchased some ordinary fiberglass from Owens
Corning Company and experimented with it and concluded
that it made a very effective filtering medium. By this time
we were very excited, figuring we would soon be capturing
the entire surgical mask market, and make a huge fortune

in the process. The fiberglass was very inexpensive.

The first thing we did was visit Owens Corning's fiberglass plant in Santa Clara, California. We told them some things about their product that they didn't know. They agreed to provide all the fiberglass we needed.

Next, we needed a machine that could make the masks. We contacted an engineering firm in Monterey, California. They said they had already built a machine for making Kotex pads, so making a machine for surgical masks would be easy, no problem. We signed an agreement with them wherein they would build our machine for $10,000. The raw materials would go in one end, and the finished masks would come out the other end. By this time we were really excited, figuring we would have finished masks on the market in just a few months.

It didn't work out that way. We soon found out that it isn't easy to get a machine to blow fiberglass onto gauze and still maintain the tolerances required for best filtration. This was just one of the problems, and everything else that could go wrong, did. I was flying to Monterey so often that one of the stewardesses on Pacific Airlines accused me of having a girlfriend in Monterey. After discussing the current problem with the engineers they would always ask for more money, another ten, twenty or even fifty thousand dollars. It wasn't long until we were into the project over $100,000, and the end was not in sight.

We were advised to stop throwing our money down a rat hole. In addition our company was in somewhat of a precarious financial position at that time, but there was about a six-month lag in our bookkeeping, so we were not aware of our difficult financial situation. We just kept spending money on that crazy machine. We were convinced there was a big market for that mask if we could make it.

By the time we passed the $300,000 mark, we were beginning to realize we were getting into financial difficulty, and still the machine didn't function properly. Finally we took it away from the engineers and brought it up to Utah. We hired a young mechanic to get it running. He didn't have an engineering degree, or even any certification as a mechanic, if I remember correctly, but he seemed to be a pretty good tinkerer, so we gave him the machine and told him to get it running. We didn't tell him about all those high-priced engineers who couldn't make it work.

The young man would twist one part and bend something else. It didn't take him long to conclude that the machine was too big, that it ought to be divided into two parts. He split it in half, and soon thousands of surgical masks, which hospitals could purchase for about 10 cents each, were pouring out of the machines. The demand for the new masks was so strong that we recovered our $400,000 development costs in about two years.

As we developed new products, the company continued to grow until we had twenty-seven injection molding machines working 24 hours a day, consuming fifty tons of polyethylene a month. Our stock went from the local exchange to the American Exchange to the New York Stock Exchange. Each time we made a change the security analysts would come by to look things over. Most of these guys were just young kids, Ivy League MBA's still wet behind the ears, thinking there wasn't anyone west of the Mississippi who knew anything about business.

They always wanted to know what our research and development (R&D) budget was. We told them we didn't have one because it was impossible to budget the cost of putting a new, unknown product on the market. They couldn't comprehend our reasoning. "Everybody" in the industry had an R&D budget. We tried to explain that when we discoverd a product that was needed in the market place, we spent whatever was necessary to develop that product—anything from several thousand to several hundred thousand dollars.

They couldn't grasp our reasoning so they would ask to see our R&D department. They were probably thinking they could plug the salaries of our research scientists into some formula to get a ball-park R&D figure. But when they discoverd that we didn't have a single PhD or engineer on the staff they became totally confused. We were one of the largest manufacturers of medical devices in the world, producing hundreds of highly technical medical devices and we didn't have a single PhD or engineer helping develop these products. Impossible, they thought.

The analysts didn't understand our business. They figured that PhD's in laboratories ought to know more than anyone else about what the doctors and nurses in the hospitals needed. That was an incorrect assumption. The doctors and nurses themselves knew a lot more what they wanted and needed than any PhD in an isolated laboratory.

We didn't have a big R&D department in our factory because we did our R&D in the field. We went out and met the people who used our products. We scrubbed with surgical teams, and put on the masks, caps and gowns to watch various surgical operations. We were always trying to improve our products by rubbing shoulders with the people who used them, and we were always looking for suggestions or ideas for new products.

One day we were eating lunch with a doctor who had just completed a bladder operation.

"If you guys could build catheters that looked like this," he said, as he began sketching on his napkin, "every doctor performing gall bladder operations would use them."

He sketched in detail how the catheter should be shaped and how it should function. We went home and built it.

One day we were chatting with Peg Butler, nurse at the little hospital in Payson, Utah. Peg doesn't have a PhD degree to qualify her as an R&D expert, but she spends a good portion of every working day supervising work in two operating rooms. When she suggested that we make a disposable scrubbing brush with built-in soap that could be activated with a little water, we knew it would sell, and went to work developing it. Today, we fabricate millions of scrub brushes every year. Thanks, Peg.

The stock analysts couldn't understand when we told them that our R&D department was every hospital that used our products, and that our R&D staff was made up of all the doctors and nurses in those hospitals. Our job was to keep open lines of communication with those people so they could tell us what they wanted.

At one time the man who was in charge of R&D at one of our biggest competitors, Abbott Laboratories, came to Salt Lake City and asked us to make a product for them. He said he had to come to us because Abbott wasn't getting anything out of its own R&D department. He said they had PhD's coming out of their ears, and every kind of engineer, spending millions of dollars every year, and nothing was coming out. Everybody busy, piles of papers shuffling from office to office, but no new products.

Thanks to the doctors and nurses in the hospitals, we maintained a steady stream of new products, and didn't have any of the high R&D overhead so common among our competitors.

While we were building the business, we had our share of the usual business problems—cash flow, personnel, accounting, receivables—and probably more than our share of governmental harassment or interference.

When we were first getting started in the late 50's, we were called back to Washington, D.C., to testify before a senate sub-committee investigating anti-trust violations. The party boys at BK&S in Salt Lake City had accused us of having a drug monopoly in the intermountain area. At that time our total business including pharmaceuticals and devices was less than $3 million a year, hardly a drop in the bucket compared to what the big companies were doing.

Senator Dirkson was a member of the committee. As soon as he saw how small we were he said the investigation was a total waste of the committee's time because it was obvious that a company doing only $3 million a year couldn't have a monopoly on anything. He got up and walked out. The rest of the committee agreed with him, and after a few questions we were dismissed with a clean slate.

A few hours later I received one of the shocks of my life. We were back at our hotel room watching the evening news. Suddenly across the TV screen appeared my partner and I walking out of the sub-committee hearing, looking like hoodlums. It was a combination of things that made us look bad—camera angle, five o'clock shadows, and of course the supporting commentary stating that we were Utah pharmaceutical executives guilty of anti-trust violations and forming a drug monopoly. Nothing was said about the size of our company and how the senators had laughed off the accusations and given us a clean slate. The same inaccurate story was picked up by *Time Magazine* and *Newsweek*. No attempt was made by either publication to get the truth. It was a sobering experience to realize firsthand how irresponsible and inaccurate the news media can be.

We had a much more serious run-in with the government in 1974. By that time our sales had grown to $35 million with sales in every state, Canada, Mexico and several other foreign countries. By this time we had totally eliminated pharmaceuticals and were dealing strictly in medical devices. We had about 1,300 people on the payroll and had just expanded our plant to 40,000 square feet.

One day several representatives of the FDA walked into my office and said that all of our catheters presently on the market were unsterile and would have to be recalled. This was a big shock to us. We had what we thought was a very tight quality control system which incorporated the best techniques and the most modern procedures. We just couldn't believe what they were saying. We asked for verification, where and how they had arived at their conclusions. They said that would come later, but first we had to make a choice. We could voluntarily recall all our catheters, or the government would do it for us.

We had no choice but to send out the recall notices and buy back 15 million catheters. Many of the dealers hadn't rotated inventories, so many of the returned catheters were several years old, obsolete, and good for nothing but the scrap pile. Another problem was that as we checked the incoming catheters, they were all sterile. We couldn't find any signs of unsterile packaging, the supposed reason for recall.

We went and hired the best bacteriological quality control man in the United States. Working with independent laboratories, he supervised an intense testing program for all of our products. We took samples from each lot in the storage area and sent them to the independent laboratories. Their results were the same as ours, that the products were sterile.

It was finally determined that the FDA had not used the approved method in testing our products. The electrostatic nature of plastics makes testing for sterility a very sensitive operation, and there are only a few laboratories approved for such testing in the entire country. The FDA didn't use these approved labs, or the approved methods. When it was all over and the costs were tabulated, the phony recall cost us $2 million dollars cash, to say nothing of the lost confidence on the part of our dealers.

When the recall problem was over I took Dale Beck, one of our most knowledgeable people and made a whirlwind trip to all of our major dealers throughout the world. The purpose of the trip was to eliminate any doubts generated by the recall and give the dealers additional training in the use of our products.

Up front, the recall cost us $2 million dollars, but in the long run it probably did us more good than harm. It made us a stronger company. When the employees saw what could happen to a good company seemingly overnight they seemed to appreciate their jobs more. People worked together better, with more cooperation. There was a better attitude in the plant. Productivity went up, profits went up, sales increased to over $50 million. There were bigger bonuses and more fringe benefits. The adversity made us a better company.

As we continued to grow, our relationship with C.R. Bard, our New Jersey distributor, became strained. They became concerned that our products comprised about 40 percent of their business. It was a case of the tail wagging the dog. They decided that they were going to buy us out, or drop our product line. We went back to New Jersey to talk with them and it was soon apparent that if we didn't agree to sell out, that we would have to build our own sales force because they weren't going to handle our products anymore.

After a day of meetings we returned to our motel rooms thinking that it would be best to sell out. I remember praying earnestly to the Lord that night so I would know what to do. When I woke up the next morning, I was filled with that familiar, quiet confidence, knowing exactly what I wanted to do. I told my partner that we ought to go ahead and terminate the agreement with Bard, head straight home and start building a sales force and a distribution network. That's what we did.

We bought a fleet of trucks and started delivering 90 percent of our products. We were real believers in service. If a dealer from New York called in an order on a Wednesday, the truck would leave Thursday and would be parked at the dealer's door Monday morning when they opened for business. Instead of coming home empty, the trucks would bring back needles, plastic pellets, tubing, fiberglass and foam for our brushes. At one time we had 20 trailers and 14 tractors on the road all the time.

Because our profits were usually very high, there was often a big jump in our stock when we announced periodic profits. Once, a big profit announcement made the trading so furious that the exchange stopped all trading on our stock in order to let it cool off.

As our high profits continued, big companies began to take notice and approach us about the possibility of selling out. We narrowed the prospects down to a few and began earnest negotiations. In 1976, after almost 20 years of business, we agreed to sell Deseret Pharmaceutical to Werner Lambert Company for $130 million. That was one of the few times in the history of the company when I felt a few regrets about having gone public. That would have been a pretty big chunk of money for two partners to divide up. As it was, many people made a lot of money in Deseret Pharmaceutical.

Werner Lambert wanted me to stay on for a while, but it was tough trying to conform to their big-company organization after having been free for so many years, so I left to do other things. They still retain me as a consultant, so I won't compete with them, but they never consult me about anything.

I have started a new family business called Cartwright Enterprises which includes a furniture store, a trucking company and a pharmacy where I fill prescriptions two days each week. My children do most of the work in Cartwright Enterprises, allowing me plenty of free time for fishing, church work and golf.

Sometimes when I'm alone with a fishing rod or a golf club in hand I think back on mother's dream and regret that she never lived to see her dream realized. Then I think that even though her body is in the ground, perhaps her spirit has been able to look over my shoulder and see the dream come true. I sure hope so.

Dave Halls—president and owner of Halls Industries (manufacturer of the Heat King wood stove), and American Steel Works, a steel fabricating plant. Both companies are based in Manti, Utah.

David Halls

I was born in 1943 and raised on a remote 160-acre ranch near Ouray, Colorado. The only heat in our home came from two wood-burning stoves—a cookstove in the kitchen, and an upright model in the living room. One of my responsibilities as a boy was keeping the two stoves supplied with wood and coal. Some of my earliest memories were of a team of horses dragging cottonwood logs out of the river bottom, and of my father and I cutting up the logs and splitting them for use in our wood stoves. Our stoves were not as efficient, or as well built as the models on the market, today, but they kept our home warm and comfortable—and they helped me gain invaluable experience in the operation and maintenance of a wood-heating system. I didn't think anything about it at the time, but I was learning principles that someday would help me achieve a dramatic business success.

When I was about eight years old, my father recognized my interest in building things with my hands and gave me an old chicken coop to be my own personal shop. He built a workbench with a vise, and I collected all the old tools I could find, oiled them and hung them on the wall of my shop. Much of my childhood time was spent in that shop, building such things as downhill coasters, and boats for the ditch.

About half of our land was tillable and the other half was in grazing. At first, my father raised sheep, but while I was still small he sold the sheep and got into cattle, beef at first, but eventually, mostly dairy cattle. As I grew up, we had 15 to 20 milk cows, most of the time.

The dairy operation could never entirely support our family, so father would frequently have to go away to work. When he was gone, it was my responsibility to take care of the cows. Sometimes he would work in the gold, silver, zinc and copper mills. In the spring he would work on the nearby ranches shearing sheep. That's when most of the cows had their calves, and when new heifers had to be trained to the milking process. When I was old enough to start helping with the cows my two younger brothers were still in diapers, so I was left to do the work alone when father was gone. In addition to taking care of the cows, there was the usual farm work, planting and harvesting crops, irrigating, repairing machinery and fences.

When I was nine years old my mother died of cancer, a big tumor on her brain. When the news reached me that she had died in that Denver hospital, the grief was sufficient to turn me away from my childish ways and thoughts, and I grew up overnight. After that, when I associated with my peers at school and church, it seemed I was a lot older than them. Besides, I was doing a man's work on the farm. I didn't think of myself as a child any longer.

I wasn't very interested in school and my grades were mostly average. Father would get after me in an effort to make me try harder, but I just wasn't interested in doing more than just the minimum to get by, at least not until my senior year. That's when I started thinking about what I wanted to become, and decided I wanted to go to college. I began to study very hard in an effort to win a scholarship, and earned a perfect report card, except for one B during the final semester. The scholarship had already been given to someone else by the time the report cards came out. I learned that one semester of super effort can't totally overcome 11 years of mediocrity.

After finishing high school, I went to work for a local contractor involved in cement work and steel buildings. I started out as a laborer and 18 months later I was running a carpenter crew, and discussing with the owner the possibility of becoming a partner with him.

That is when I decided it was time to go to college. I moved to Grand Junction, Colorado, found a part-time job in a laundry called American Linen Supply, and enrolled as a freshman at Mesa College.

It wasn't long until I met Flo McQuilkin, who was to become my wife. She grew up in Olathe, Colorado, only 60 miles from my home, but we had never met. She was not a member of the Church and I hadn't been a regular attender myself for several years, but the Church is all we talked about on the first date. In fact, we stayed out all night until 6:30 a.m., talking about religion. I immediately began attending meetings again, taking her with me. We were married a few months later, and she was baptized six weeks after our wedding.

When school was finished in the spring, we returned to Ouray to live rent-free in a little house belonging to my grandmother. I immediately found a job in a small silver mine with two other fellows and put in my application at one of the large mines. Two months later, they gave me a job.

I started out as a nipper, running a little hoist, hauling supplies up and down the shaft. Next, I was a trammer, hauling ore out of the mine. Finally, I ended up doing what I liked best, a mechanic, keeping the machinery in good running condition.

The continual blasting kept the air in the mine saturated with powdered rock and carbon monoxide. Breathing that stuff all day gave me tremendous headaches. I noticed that some of the men, who had worked in the mine for many years, and appeared to be 60 or 70 years old, were actually only 30 or 40. I decided to look for something different.

Flo had a brother in California who was a sheet metal worker. We called him one night and asked what my chances were of getting into an apprentice training program. He checked it out with his union and discovered that the waiting list wasn't very long, but that in order to get on the list, I had to live in California. He said we could stay with him if we wanted to move to California and get on the union's list.

I quit the job at the mine. We loaded everything we had into the back of our car, and with $150, we headed for

California.

After getting my name on the list, I landed an interim job in a dairy, processing milk. We lived with Flo's brother about a month until we had enough money to rent a place of our own.

After about six months my name was called up to enter the apprentice program. I quit the job at the dairy and became a sheet metal worker.

I worked days and attended apprentice classes two nights a week. I had an interest in becoming an industrial arts teacher, so I enrolled in college and attended night classes three nights each week.

After several years, I had earned enough college credit to receive a degree in English with an industrial arts minor. All I lacked were some general education courses. As I began to look more closely at the industrial arts profession, I realized that if I were to teach, my earnings would be about half what I was earning as a sheet metal worker. It seemed to me at the time that college was training me to go out and earn about $3.00 an hour, unless I wanted to go on for an advanced degree. Then, I would still earn less than what I was making as a sheet metal worker.

Sometimes, at the beginning of a new semester, I would get very excited as I read course descriptions, only to find out when I attended the class that the teacher had no business teaching it. In my industrial arts classes, more often than not, I knew more about the subject than the teacher, and often became the tacher's assistant. I lost interest in college and dropped out a few hours short of graduation.

During the seven years I worked in the sheet metal trade in California, I worked for 11 different employers. When I learned everything that a particular shop was doing, I would get bored and start looking for another shop that did things that I had not yet learned. Sometimes I would arrive home and tell Flo I had quit my job. She would get a long face and begin to worry until I told her that I had found another one on the way home. Construction was booming in California and there were plenty of sheet metal business. I did a lot of work on ventilating systems in aircraft plants. I worked on kitchen equipment, air conditioning systems and all kinds of industrial sheet metal work, as well as various types of welding.

As I became more experienced in the business, I began to see more and more what I felt to be errors on the part of my employers. I yearned to have my own sheet metal shop so I could do things my way. I began picking up used pieces of equipment here and there in preparation for the day when I would have my own shop.

I didn't know if I wanted to open a business in the Los Angeles area, though. We were becoming increasingly tired of the smog and congestion. We were worried about the negative influences on our kids in the Los Angeles school system.

On the Mothers' Day weekend of 1971, we drove back to Colorado looking for a sheet metal job that would enable us to move back. The very first place I walked into, offered me a job and wanted me to start the next day. I told them I had to go back to sell my home and get my tools. They said the job would be waiting for me when I returned.

After selling the house, we returned to Colorado. We felt like we were coming home at last. This time we were going to sink in our roots and stay. I thought often about going into business for myself, but was in no great hurry.

The sheet metal business had some drawbacks. The best jobs usually went to the company with the lowest bid, and sometimes the competition for work was intense, meaning that the company with the low bid sometimes didn't make any profit. And when a job was finished, you had to start all over by going out and finding a new job. I started to think that it would be more desirable to manufacture a product, a quality product that could be protected by patent laws.

After we had been in Colorado about one year, we bought an old schoolhouse not far from Durango, out in the country. It had been partially remodeled by two previous owners. We paid $13,000 for the building and four acres of ground.

Our plan was to finish remodeling the school, then sell it. The profit from the sale would get me started in a business of my own. I still wasn't sure what kind of business I wanted to start.

The old school was a mess, and a big step down from the nice home we had been renting in town, but Flo was willing to make the move, realizing it was a way for us to get ahead.

I went through the schoolhouse with a note pad and made a five-page list of improvements that I felt needed to be made. I gave the list to a friend who was a real estate appraiser and asked him to do an appraisal on what the place would be worth after the improvements were comp- leted.

After he completed his figuring, he said it would be worth $34,000, after the improvements were completed. We had paid $13,000 for the property, and I figured the improvement should run about $7,000, leaving a $14,000 profit to use as starting capital for a new business. The local savings and loan company gave me an 80 percent loan based on the appraised value, enabling me to go ahead and start on the improvements. I worked days at the sheet metal shop, and evenings on the house.

One of the first things I wanted to do was install a wood- burning stove in the family room. I went down to the local hardware store to order a Ben Franklin stove, only to find out there was an eight-month wait. This was during the 1973 energy crisis and everyone was buying wood stoves.

I didn't want to wait eight months for a Ben Franklin, so I decided to build one from scratch. Because of my experience with wood stoves as a boy, I was familiar with how they worked. I liked the low profile look of the Franklin. I began working on my first stove, after hours at the sheet metal shop.

When the stove was finished it looked very similar to today's 48-inch Heat King stoves—made from heavy black steel with clean lines and decorated with solid brass trim. Even before I loaded it in my truck to take it home, several people who saw it in the shop, asked me to make them one, too. It seemed everyone who saw my stove, liked it.

I was so busy working on the house that I didn't have time to build stoves for the people who wanted them, but I got to thinking that here was a product I could build and sell when I went into business for myself. The more we talked about it, the better we liked the idea. We decided that as soon as the house was finished, we would sell it and use the proceeds to go into the wood stove business.

We finished the house, put it up for sale, then started looking for a place to start the new business. We had $4,000 left over from the construction loan which could keep us going until the house sold. We didn't want to start the business in Durango because it was too far from major markets and materials suppliers. It was an eight-hour drive to Denver.

We established several guidelines for selecting the right place to begin our business. We wanted to be close to a major market area where we could sell products and buy supplies. At the same time, we wanted to be out in the country, so we could raise our children in a small-town environment. We wanted a small town that offered the full Church program. We didn't want to drive long distances to attend meetings or the temple.

We had been over to Manti, Utah, several times to visit the Mormon temple and decided to check out Manti as a possible place to start the business. The town seemed to have everything we were looking for and it was just a couple of hours south of the big Salt Lake area markets and suppliers.

We drove over to Manti and located an old shop that had been used by sheep ranchers to store wool. The price was $7,600 with easy terms. We couldn't find any homes for sale in our price range, but we located a dumpy apartment building priced at $29,000. We felt pretty good about the situation in Manti, but neither one of us wanted to live in the apartment house, but we figured we could do it for a while while the business was getting started. Flo didn't complain.

We returned to Durango and carefully considered our alternatives. We made the decision to start the new business in Manti, then we presented the decision to the Lord in fasting and prayer. I had never been in business on my own before and felt I needed a confirmation from God in order to take such a bold step. Flo and I received the confirmation that the move to Manti was the right thing to do.

With that confidence, I returned to Manti and put down a $1,000 deposit on the shop and another $1,000 on the apartment building. I used the remaining $2,000 to pay for our move and buy enough materials to build our first stoves. We moved to Manti in August, 1974. Our renovated schoolhouse in Durango was still for sale.

As we were getting settled in our apartment, a lady by the name of Lydia Sorenson noticed our wood stove and asked me to build one for her. We had our first customer.

I started building stoves and sold the first five or six Heat Kings quickly to our new neighbors and friends. I was beginning to think there would be a never-ending line of customers at the door. But this illusion didn't last long. Soon, I had an inventory of five or six finished units and no prospective buyers in sight.

By November we were out of money. Our house in Durango still hadn't sold and we had run out of friends and neighbors who wanted stoves. Flo had been in the Navy before we were married and was going to Snow College in nearby Ephraim to learn bookkeeping so she could handle that end of the business. (She has been taking classes ever since that time, and will soon receive a bachelor's degree in business and finance from Brigham Young University.) She received $390 a month on the G.I. Bill and that's all we had to live on. I had purchased some materials on credit and I had no money to pay the bills that were coming due. We were sick and more than a little scared.

Again, we made our situation a matter of earnest fasting and prayer. We asked the Lord to help us sell our house right away because we urgently needed the money. Again we received that undeniable confirmation that all was well and that we didn't need to worry.

Three or four days later we received a cash offer on the house. A widow whose husband had been killed by lightning wanted to buy the renovated schoolhouse with insurance money. After paying off our obligations, we had $11,000 to help get the new business going.

We realized that our biggest problem was getting exposure for the stoves. We didn't think we could afford expensive advertising, but we had to find a way to let people know our stoves were available.

We became aware of food and hobby shows being held in the malls in the more populous areas of Utah, and thought these shows might be a good way to get exposure for our products. We rented a booth at a food show at the Valley Fair Mall in Granger, just west of Salt Lake City. Because some of our first customers had requested a smaller stove, I had developed a 36-inch model to accompany our 48-inch model. I took two 36-inch models and one 48-inch model to this first show. Flo accompanied me and in the course of the show we sold all three stoves and had an order for one more. I figured I had died and gone to heaven. I hadn't dared hope that we would be so successful.

During the next year, we attended about 30 shows where we did the vast majority of our selling. I didn't set up retail stores as dealers because they wanted a 40 percent markup, and I felt that that big of a markup would make the stoves so expensive that nobody would buy them.

My goal was to sell five stoves a week. I had it all figured out that if I could do that consistently, I would earn over $2,000 a month, be my own boss, and everything would be great.

At the shows, I began to recruit salespeople among our customers by offering approximately a 20 percent commission on any orders they brought in. Someone could pay for his or her stove by selling five more to friends and neighbors. These owner-salesmen sold a lot of stoves for us for several years. Some of them are still selling for us.

I remember a fellow from Riverton, Wyoming. He bought a stove and didn't install it until several years later, after he had moved to Idaho. When he finally started using it, he got so excited that he quit his job and started selling stoves out of his home, full time. Next, he rented some sales,space in a downtown store, then built his own store. Last year he netted over $60,000 on his Heat King sales, alone. There are several people around with similar stories.

Most of our original owner-salesmen have died on the vine, and we have gradually replaced them with regular retail dealers. When we first got into the business there was very little competition, and prices were relatively low. But as more and more competitors have introduced wood stoves, the prices have been pushed higher. Generally, one would expect competition to push prices down, but the opposite happened in the wood stove business. The only logical explanation is that the old prices were too low and the companies who sold at the low prices couldn't afford to stay in business. Only those companies who could get a fair price for their products were able to survive.

Right from the beginning, I had no intentions of mass producing the cheapest stove on the market. I felt I was a craftsman, an artisan with metal as my medium of expression. In the terminology of the car industry, I wanted to build a Mercedes Benz, not a Ford Pinto. This may sound old-fashioned, but I really believed that I could earn an honest living by producing a quality product at a fair price. We have tried to maintain that philosophy, and even though our stoves are priced higher than most of the competing products, they still sell well because they are better built than any of the competing stoves. We don't sell to the people who shop around for the lowest price. Our customers are those who shop around for the best stove. We build our stoves to last for a lifetime, and offer a ten-year warranty.

Of course you have to hire the right management personnel if you are going to be successful in building a quality product. After we were in business about a year, I hired Lynn Nuffer, who is now our production manager. He is honest and capable, and a natural leader, and certainly shares in the responsibility for our success.

By attending shows at the malls, we eventually built a sales force consisting of about 30 owner-salesmen and were building about 60 stoves a month, more than twice as many as I had hoped to sell when I started the business. As I became more knowledgeable about the market, however, I could see that my competition was selling an ever-increasing number of stoves through retail stores. I began to realize, that even though I was doing well, I was only scratching the surface of a vast wood stove market.

I understood, too, that if I stayed small while my competition grew, that eventually the economies of long-production runs enjoyed by the competition would make it increasingly difficult for me to compete. We concluded that we would lose ground if we didn't grow along with the other successful companies, and go after as big a share of the market as possible.

The first thing I did was hire a sales manager with 17 years of selling experience. Vern Chadwick had been a machine tool salesman and after a year of friendly persuasion I finally convinced him that he ought to join our company. Together, we re-structured our pricing formula to allow adequate markups for dealers. With the help of a professional advertising agency, we prepared some first-class product brochures.

Vern hit the road, setting up dealers throughout the

western states. I bought some new equipment and expanded our production capability to meet the anticipated increase in demand.

Vern was very careful in setting up protected dealer territories. We didn't set up two dealers in the same market area. We didn't want two of our dealers competing against each other for the same customer. Prospective dealers appreciated this consideration, and they also liked our 10-year warranty, and our policies for servicing customers with warranty problems. Our general policy was that we would cheerfully fix anything that went wrong (except for paint scratches) even if it meant bringing the stove all the way back to the factory.

Eventually, Vern was able to set up about 130 dealers in 14 western states. Our production increased from 60 to over 200 stoves a month. Our operation became so big that we had to build new buildings.

Of course, there were plenty of problems along the way, some more serious than others. One of our owner-salesman started depositing checks he had received for stoves into his own personal checking account while telling us the payments hadn't been collected. He took advantage of my trusting nature to the tune of about $10,000 before I caught on to his scheme and cut him off. To this day, I haven't been able to collect any of the money.

When I first got into the business, I was unaware of all the government regulations concerning solid fuel burning appliances. At first it was very annoying to discover that our stoves didn't meet government specifications in all areas. Redesigning for compliance was costly and time-consuming. We had to set up our own testing program, and send stoves to independent laboratories. In the end, all this trouble helped us sell more stoves. The official stamp of government approval on the back of the stove helps the potential customer have confidence in the product.

At the time, we were growing so quickly we were hiring new people in large numbers, and weren't always able to provide adequate training. As a result, some defective stoves got into the marketplace and had to be recalled. It was expensive, time-consuming and a terrible blow to our public relations and product image. Only time and in-creased efforts at quality control, correct those kinds of problems.

The wood stove business is very cyclical, with 70 percent of our yearly sales coming in October, November and December. It takes tremendous amounts of cash to build and store inventory during late spring and summer, when very few orders are coming in. If you can't get the cash to be able to stockpile during the summer, you won't be able to fill all the orders in the fall. The ideal situation is to have all the warehouses full by mid-September and have every single unit delivered, and inventories down to zero by mid-December. To accomplish that, one must be a good planner and a little lucky.

One year, our accountant recommended that we postpone a large number of our scheduled December deliveries until after the first of the new year so we wouldn't have to report the revenue on our tax reports until the following year. It looked like a great way to postpone the payment of some tax dollars, so we held back a large number of deliveries. Unfortunately, when we called the dealers in January to confirm orders prior to making deliveries, most of the orders were cancelled because Christmas was past and spring was on the way. It was the wrong time of year to load up on wood stoves. That two or three-week delay made all the difference in the world and we had to go into spring with our inventories much higher than we wanted them to be.

It is helpful when dealers can shoulder some of the financial responsibility by loading themselves up in the late summer and early fall. The high and erratic interest rates in recent years have made this increasingly difficult for dealers to do.

Many wood stove companies take on other products to complement their wood stove business, products that sell at a different time of the year. The philosophy is that if you have wood stoves to sell in the fall, and roto tillers or patio furniture to sell in the spring, your employees are busy and you have money coming in during the entire year.

To relieve the seasonal nature of our business, we produce products for the mining and petroleum industries, as well as bidding on many government steel fabricating contracts. This diversification gives us a broader, more stable base.

We have found adequate opportunities to be innovative and creative. We had fun developing accessories for our wood stoves. Some of our most popular accessories include an attach-on oven, a swing-out pot hook and barbecue grill. In addition to three sizes of stoves, we have developed a popular fireplace inset.

I am a firm believer in sharing profits with employees. Every employee gets a bonus at the end of the year. Four digit bonuses are common. Some of our employees received bonuses of several thousand dollars last year. We also have a profit-sharing plan available to all employees. I think someone who shares in the profits, cares more about product quality. I think this is one of the main reasons for our success in an industry where literally hundreds of businesses have come and gone in the seven years we have been in the business. Many of the big name companies are having serious financial difficulties and are literally dying on the vine.

I see some changes ahead for the wood stove industry. With increasing energy costs for petroleum related heating fuels there will be steady demand for wood stoves, but as the supply of available wood is diminished faster than it can replenish itself, particularly in highly populated areas, people will have to look more and more to coal as a source of heat. In order to burn most efficiently, coal requires somewhat different ventilation and grating systems. It also burns hotter than wood and can quickly burn out the cheap stoves. There are a couple of good coal stoves on the market, and one of my immediate goals is to design a Heat King stove engineered specifically for coal.

There's been some talk about the undesirability of coal smoke, but recent development of pollution-control devices for chimneys should take care of this problem.

Coal is going to be around a long time, and wood is renewable, so as the prices of petroleum-based fuels continue to go up, more and more homes will convert to wood and coal heat. This business has a bright future.

Although there have been many times that we have felt extreme pressure, usually financial in nature, I am thankful that Flo and I made the commitment to start our own business. Even though we have paid the price of success, we realize that success is fragile and must be kept in the right perspective.

As our business has grown stronger over the years, we have worked diligently to make sure that our marriage has grown stronger, too. Building a solid business requires the same skills and an understanding of the same principles required in building a solid family.

I always try to emphasize the positive traits in people and build upon them, helping the people to realize potential beyond present capabilities. One of my greatest talents has been my ability to surround myself with quality personnel. I believe in giving them plenty of responsibility, allow them to perform, then reward them generously when they succeed. These principles certainly are not original with Dave Halls, they are eternal, but I am proud I have been able to apply them in my business and family.

As a boy on our ranch in Colorado, I sometimes felt we were behind the times and more than a little old-fashioned because we heated our home with a wood stove. Today, I look at it differently. We were progressive, 20 years ahead of our time. I never dreamed that someday my boyhood experiences with wood stoves would lead me into a business that would help many thousands of people keep their homes warm and comfortable by burning wood and coal.

George Murdock—Under the umbrella corporation Murdock International, George and his brother Ken own Rainy Day Fods, Natures Way (herbal products) and 12 other companies.

George Murdock

As a child in my Phoenix, Arizona, home, I can't ever remember seeing white sugar. Sometimes there was brown sugar, but sweets were rare in our home. On the occasion when we had homemade ice cream, it was sweetened with honey.

I never ate white bread until I went away to college. Several times each month Mom baked her own whole wheat bread. We ate cracked wheat cereal every morning, never the packaged cold cereals sold in stores, which we dubbed "concentrated air." We ate very little meat, and no junk food!

Even though Mom graduated from Brigham Young University with a degree in traditional nutrition, she picked up most of her nutrition philosophy on her own, using the scriptures as her guide. She was a health food "nut" long before it became a fad. She firmly believed that diet is an effective form of preventive medicine. She believed that most modern medical practitioners were so taken up with the magic of prescribing drugs to alleviate symptoms, that they pretty much ignored the problems that caused the symptoms. We were a very healthy family, with no major ailments that I can recall. I have never had a tooth cavity in my entire life.

After graduating from high school in 1961, I attended

Brigham Young University for two years. I supported myself, working for BYU food services, earning $1.10 an hour. I went to work at 3 a.m. every morning and made hundreds of sandwiches for the campus vending machines.

After two years of schooling, the LDS Church called me to serve a mission in the Samoan Islands. While there, I served as a mission translator and assistant to the president and wrote a handbook on the Samoan language which is still used as a training manual for missionaries. I liked the missionary work and decided that when I returned home I would study to become a seminary or institute teacher for the Church.

While assigned to a small island called Manu'a, I had a companion who was an excellent speed reader. He had a fantastic memory and a system to go with it. His father, a college professor, taught speed reading throughout the United States. My companion taught me some of his techniques, and I became so enthusiastic about what I was learning that I contacted his father at the end of my mission and applied for a summer job helping him with his speed reading courses in California.

I worked as his assistant until I was ready to teach my own classes. In the very first class I taught, there was a pretty, young Mormon girl named Marilyn "Mimi" Miller. Her beautiful blue eyes won my immediate affections.

She was eighteen, single, and in no hurry to make any marriage commitments. We began dating, and the more she tried to remain aloof and unattached, the harder I courted. Two years later we were married.

During our courtship, I was deeply influenced by her family. Her father was very successful in the honey business in Southern California. His company, called Miller's Honey Company, was founded in 1896. He had a second home in the mountains at Lake Arrowhead, a large boat and all the trimmings associated with a profitable, well-managed business. Mimi's mother was a Skousen, a family of high achievers—writers, lawyers, educators, and intellectuals. Yet in spite of the wealth and success, Mimi's mother was the best example of generosity I had ever seen. She supported missionaries, some of them not knowing where the money was coming from. She bought tuition and books for students who couldn't otherwise afford to go to college. She was generous in every sense of the word, and it was mainly through her example that I concluded that the Gospel of Jesus Christ could be compatible with financial success.

My dream to become a seminary teacher began to fade as my horizons expanded through contact with Mimi's family. I liked their lifestyle, but I knew it was out of reach on the salary of a seminary teacher. I still wasn't sure what I wanted to become, but I decided to develop strong public speaking and communicative skills by completing my undergraduate degree in speech and English, skills which I thought would be useful in graduate school. I returned to Brigham Young University.

It was necessary for me to pay my own way, but rather than take a conventional student job earning the going wage which was now up to $1.30 an hour, I bought a big Polaroid camera and started taking pictures of couples at school dances. The film cost approximately $.50 an exposure and I charged $1.50 for the print. At the preference ball during my junior year, I netted over $1,000, not bad for one night's work.

After graduating from Brigham Young University, I enrolled in the University of Utah law school. During the summer, I earned money by operating a water ski, canoe and food concession business at Lake Powell.

I hated law school, quickly surmising that lawyers are glorified librarians. After two years and one quarter, I dropped out and entered the MBA program at Brigham Young University. This was more to my liking, but I was restless, chomping at the bit to get out of school and do something. It seemed like I had been in school forever. Mimi was expecting our first child and had just finished her degree in drama and English.

One day, Mimi's dad called and offered me the job as sales manager. I knew that even with an MBA degree, I couldn't hope to start out in a better job than the one being offered me. Besides, I was weary of graduate school and needed the money. We accepted the offer and began making arrangements to move to Colton, California.

About this time, I discovered a book titled, *Count to Four*. It contained a very simple philosophy on setting and reaching goals. As I read it, it sounded familiar, like I had come home. The book showed the importance of being very detailed and meticulous in selecting priorities, establishing goals, making exact plans for obtaining objectives, and in visualizing yourself already in possession of your goals. The book discussed the subconscious mind, and how one's only limitations are in the mind, that the sky is the limit.

At first, my goals were very simple, generally dealing with the obtaining of material things, like watches, cars and stereos. With cars, for example, at first it was a Thunderbird. I cut out a picture of the T-Bird I wanted, then outlined a detailed plan for obtaining the car. I imagined myself already in possession of it. One day, it was really mine. After the Thunderbird, it was a Lincoln Continental, and after that a Mercedes Benz. I set deadlines and usually reached my goals before the time was up.

Then one day the thought occurred to me, that if these goal-achieving techniques worked so well for material things, they ought to work just as well for helping me achieve more meaningful, long-range goals. I began using the goal-stringing techniques in *Count to Four* to chart out my entire future, where I wanted to go and what I wanted to become. I decided that I would be a millionaire, an achiever. I would be involved in things that could help other people. I would be free with my time to let my enthusiastic nature grow and experiment down any path I decided to follow. I even described in detail the dream home I wanted to own someday.

I began to set and go after many different kinds of goals. I earned a private pilot's license in 30 days. I became a certified scuba diver. I developed my singing voice until I eventually qualified to sing tenor in the Mormon Tabernacle Choir. I learned to play dozens of songs on the guitar in just a few months. I trained and ran in numerous marathons, including the Deseret News Marathon in Salt Lake City, 26.2 miles! The first year of running, I lost 30 pounds and averaged 40 miles a week training.

I became a scoutmaster, and in one month, my 13 boy scouts earned 128 merit badges.

I don't say these things to boast, but to give the reader just a glimpse of some of the things that are possible when one learns how to properly and realistically set and work towards goals.

When I first set the goal to become financially independent, I wasn't sure what my vehicle would be. I was in a good position to move into the top management of Miller's Honey, especially since my father-in-law owned the company.

But, as it turned out, my business fortunes led me in a very different direction, in a direction I had never thought possible.

During the late 1960's while I was still in school, my mother was diagnosed as having breast cancer. She underwent major surgery. She took the usual drugs and treatments, but after everything had been done, the malignancy continued to grow and spread throughout her body. We feared it was terminal.

My father, Tom, heard about a man who reportedly had had success combating cancer with chaparral tea, a cleansing herb. Very little had been written about the herb, but an article in *Arizona Highways* Magazine, titled the "Deseret Drugstore" caught my father's interest. He decided to get my mother to take the tea.

The purpose of a cleansing herb is to help the body eliminate toxins or chemical irritants. There are a number of herbs that help do this, but chaparral is one of the most powerful ones. Also called greasewood or creosote, it grows abundantly in the Southwest.

Chaparral tea is extremely bitter, so my father sought a way to prepare it in a more palatable form. He gathered a plentiful supply of leaves, dried them, then took off to California with barrels of leaves in the back of his car. He borrowed a friend's milling and tableting machinery to grind the dry leaves into a powder and then press the powder into tablets.

My mother was able to take the tablets since they didn't have the unpleasant taste of the tea. She also started on a stringent regimen of healthy and fresh foods coupled with daily exercise. In only a short time, her strength began to improve. She looked and felt much better. The doctors soon noticed the improvement and wondered what she was doing. Naturally, she was reluctant to tell the medical doctors of her herb, health food and exercise cure.

At that time, Dad was in the water softener business. He is an excellent salesman, and recognized that he had a good product in the chaparral tablets. He started selling them to doctors (chiropractors, naturopaths, and osteopaths) and health food stores. Soon he had a good little business going and sold about $50,000 worth of tablets the first year. It was a very profitable business. The chaparral leaves were free for the picking. At first he picked the leaves himself and air dried them in the shade.

Herbs are considered foods, not drugs by the Food and Drug Administration (FDA), so Dad didn't have to go through any of the usual red tape. It usually takes a number of years, and millions of dollars to get a drug approved by the FDA.

My mother continued to get stronger, and the cancer went into recession. She took over the secretarial duties for the new business, and my sister, Madilyn, kept the books. Mom and Dad worked out of their home.

Then one day Dad caught his hand in the milling machine, and almost lost it. He was unable to make tablets to fill orders, so he called my brother, Ken, who was studying economics at BYU. Ken is two years younger than me.

Together they manufactured and sold over a hundred thousand dollars worth of the tablets the next year. They bought an old cannery from the Church and moved the business out of the home.

By then Dad and Ken could see that they really had something exciting, so they called and asked me to join them as a third partner, each of us owning one-third of the business. Mimi and I moved from Colton to Phoenix.

That year, 1971, we manufactured and sold a few hundred thousand dollars worth of tablets, and started to look for other products, mostly herbs, that could be made into tablets or capsules. We looked for natural products that were beneficial to health. We called the company Nature's Way.

We attribute much of that early success to being in the right place at the right time. The health food business was becoming a nation-wide trend. People were getting tired of chemicals, synthetics and drugs. They were losing faith in the orthodox medical profession. They were concerned with the environment and what they were taking into their bodies. More people wanted to do things the natural way, they were open-minded about natural products. This trend is commonly called the back to nature, or back to basics movement.

One of the biggest frustrations for us, then and now, was not being able to say something about the medicinal qualities of our products on the labels. As far as the FDA is concerned, our herbs are foods, not drugs. According to the FDA, only drugs can cure sickness. If we offer medicinal information on our labels we are guilty of 1) prescribing medicine without a license, and 2) selling a medicine which hasn't been approved as a drug by the FDA. Our labels are only allowed to say what the product is. In order for us to be legal, we have to consider our products as supplements or foods, which can be taken into the body without side effects.

As a result, our advertising and promotion has had to be very general, or institutional in nature. We can tell what our products are, but we can't tell how to use them. We must depend on the doctors, and magazine and book publishers to do that.

The health food industry holds a very low opinion in the eyes of the orthodox medical profession, including the American Medical Association (AMA) and the drug industry. We are at great odds with these people all the time. They hate and harass us. In the beginning we had frequent visits from the FDA. They tried desperately to find something wrong in what we were doing. Their visits were so frequent, and their tactics so shoddy, that I don't hesitate to classify the visits as harassment. We managed to keep out of trouble, using very good legal counsel, and being very careful not to violate the law.

As we began to buy and sell products outside the United States, we discovered that natural foods and herbs are much more readily accepted in the rest of the world. It is estimated that 90 percent of the people in the world have herbs as their main source of medication. Most people can't afford expensive synthesized drugs so they have no choice but to use natural herbs, which are often free for the picking. In many European and Oriental countries, more store shelf space is devoted to health foods than to conventional drugs. In China they actually have a toothpaste that cures colds. An entrepreneur, noticing how Americans put flouride in toothpaste, figured out a way to put China's most popular cold-curing herb into toothpaste. It is a very popular product there, but it will be many years, if ever, before such a product could be sold in the United States.

As we got into the herb business we began to seek out experts in the field—people who had written books on herbs, or held degrees in herbology. Many of them were osteopaths, chiropractors or naturopaths. There were very few M.D.'s who were knowledgeable about herbs, but today there are a lot more.

Right in the beginning we began to work with Dr. John R. Christopher who is probably the leading expert on herbs in the entire United States, and perhaps the world. He has authored numerous books on herbs, including the *Book of Natural Healing*, a 600-page volume which is considered to be the "Bible" on herbs. He formulated many of our products, consulted with us and worked for us on an exclusive contractual basis. Today we have additional people on our staff with degrees in herbal medicine, chemistry, pharmacy and microbiology.

Our second major product was concentrated alfalfa tablets, called Alfa-Con. We discovered that alfalfa products were becoming very popular in health food circles because of the numerous vitamins in high concentration in alfalfa. In fact alfalfa is one of the most complete natural sources of vitamins and minerals known to man. A cow can live on alfalfa from weaning until death and never lack in any of its nutritional needs. Humans can't do this, however, because alfalfa is partially indigestible to humans. A cow, with its multiple stomach cavities, has more digestive power than man.

We found we could produce a digestible alfalfa tablet by liquifying green alfalfa and removing the indigestible cellulose. It takes a ton of green alfalfa to produce 80 pounds of our concentrate. After the indigestible ingredients are removed, leaving only the oil and water-soluble nutrients, the concentrate is dried and pressed into tablets. The Alfa-Con has never sold as well as the chaparral but it has been a steady product over the years.

We felt very much at home in the health food business, right from the beginning. We were raised on natural foods, with whole wheat bread and cereal as the foundation of our diet. We were a healthy, energetic family, and now we were helping other people develop healthier, more natural life styles, too. Mom and Dad often said that they felt the Lord led us into the business so we could help other people lead healthier lives. We have received hundreds of testimonial letters from people who have improved their health through the use of our products.

As our business began to grow we soon realized that we needed cash to finance our growth. We were able to finance the purchase of a building when we moved the business out of Dad's home, but we couldn't get a bank to loan us money for operating capital. Many times we applied for small loans, about $10,000 or so, and we were always turned down. It seemed that the banks were telling us that they wouldn't loan us any money until we could prove through our financial statement that we didn't need it. We just didn't have enough equity and assets to warrant a loan for operating capital. An alternative was to raise money by selling stock in the company, but we were determined to keep it a family business. We had no choice but to plow everything back into the business. We only took home what was absolutely necessary for survival. For a while I was taking home about $500 a month, and my house payment alone was $300. Ken was taking less than me because he didn't have a family yet. And Dad sometimes didn't take anything. It was a very unselfish relationship which brought us very close together. We didn't have computers or other expensive overhead items. Our bookkeeping was very simple and inexpensive. We plowed every extra nickel back into the business and our equity grew at a steady pace.

Dad's work was without doubt the foundation of our early success. He is a very flamboyant, gregarious, outgoing person, an excellent salesman. He is worth about a thousand dollars an hour on the phone, and he has never heard of an eight-hour day. In fact an 18 or 20-hour day is more to his liking. Without eating or sleeping he just plunges tirelessly ahead. Ken and I organized and managed things while Dad built up huge piles of sales orders.

At first, our ignorance of business got us into trouble again and again as we had to learn the hard way. For example, when we first introduced Alfa-Con, our second product, we placed some ads to test what the demand might be. The orders started pouring in at an unbelievable rate. We didn't have enough money to install the equipment needed for packaging Alfa-Con or to build inventories. We didn't even have the labels designed and printed. Even with the pile of orders, the banks wouldn't loan us money, but eventually through our pinching, saving and hard work we were able to get the Alfa-Con into production. But even though we had immediate sales for the product, the margins were so small that it seemed forever before we began to realize any real profits. By 1973 our sales were over $1,000,000 a year and the cash flow was catching up to the point where we could take home enough money to allow us to live like other people.

In February, 1973, I was asked to give a talk in the Mesa 10th Ward of the LDS Church. At that time the national economy was in a recession and I was very concerned about my personal food storage situation, so I decided to talk about food storage. In preparation for the talk I started looking for a quote, supposedly from Brigham Young, that someday a bushel of wheat would be worth a bushel of gold. I couldn't find it anywhere, so I spent a hundred dollars to buy a complete set of the *Journal of Discourses* containing Brigham Young's speeches. Eventually, I found the famous quote, and many others on the importance of food storage.

I was well prepared when it came time to deliver the speech. I remember asking the audience to show by raised hands how many had a year's supply of food. I was surprised when just a few hands went up. After the talk a lot of people began asking me questions about food storage— questions about what to store, how to store it, and how much to store. I decided to get into the food storage business, in a small way, so I could help the people get the food items they needed, and get my own too, at wholesale prices.

The first thing I did was write to all the major suppliers of storable food. To my amazement, most of the companies didn't even bother to answer my inquiries. I figured business must be pretty good if they didn't have time to answer an inquiry from a guy who wanted to buy a truckload of food. Eventually I found a company in California that would sell me dehydrated food without labels. I printed my own labels in Arizona.

I ordered a truckload of food and sent a young friend to California to pick it up. As he was leaving Los Angeles to return home, he was hit by another truck. Our young friend lost his life. It was a very sad thing, and to make matters worse, most of the food was destroyed in the accident and the insurance wouldn't pay for all of it.

As Dad, Ken and I analyzed the food storage industry, we decided that it was a good business to get involved in. We just couldn't get over the fact that most of my inquiries to buy food had not been answered. We were beginning to see some of the problems of the health food industry, the persecution by the FDA, and the fact that we couldn't make any claims for our herbal products. It seemed like a good idea to diversify, to not have all our eggs in one basket. We decided that we would get into the food storage business in a big way.

Mimi and I moved back to California to build Rainy Day Foods. Her father let me use one of his empty honey warehouses for a future rent payment, which I think I paid with dehydrated food. I bought packaging machinery, hired some people, and purchased dehydrated foods in bulk containers. We re-packaged the food in N10 cans with an inert nitrogen atmosphere for extended shelf life, and attached the Rainy Day labels.

In exploring marketing outlets, I quickly became involved with Mimi's uncle, W. Cleon Skousen. He was building the Freemen Institute and needed a non-profit fund-raising project to finance his lectures and seminars on the U.S. Constitution. He began to sell Rainy Day foods through Freemen Family Foods and quickly became my biggest customer. He bought a truckload a week, for many months.

His organization had a large following in Utah. Therefore large quantities of Rainy Day foods were being shipped there. I was on a business trip to Utah in the summer of 1973, when one of the salesmen asked when the company was going to move to Utah. I thought he was joking. I had never even thought about moving to Utah, but now that he had suggested the idea, I couldn't get the thought out of my mind. The next day I started looking for a business facility and a new home. I found the home right away, in a small community south of Provo. It wasn't until my next trip that

I found some buildings suitable for the business.

In November of 1973, just three months after the salesman asked about moving to Provo, we loaded up truckloads of products and machinery and moved to Utah. Some of our key employees came with us.

This was at the peak of the recession. There were reports in the newspapers about shortages, grocery stores running out of various food items, toilet paper and other necessities. More and more people were beginning to think about getting food storage. Our business was good, especially our sales through Skousen's Freemen organization.

One day I was reading the *Wall Street Journal* and began to wonder if maybe we were just scratching the surface of a huge, nation-wide food storage market. I wondered how many *Wall Street Journal* readers would be interested in food storage.

I checked the advertising prices and found I could place a single 4 x 6-inch ad for about $600. We placed the ad in the commodites section where people find financial information on gold, silver and food commodities. The headline was "Food Insurance," and the body copy told how to protect against shortages by storing food. The response to the ad was immediate. There were days when we received thousands of inquiries in the mail. Many of the inquiries were from individuals who wanted to become dealers for us. Our sales organization expanded nation-wide and even into a few foreign countries. We ran the ad again and again. Our sales skyrocketed, approaching $1,000,000 for one of the months immediately following the placement of the first advertisement.

The *Wall Street Journal* editorial department got wind of the fantastic results we were getting from our advertising. They did a major feature article on Rainy Day Foods that appeared right in the middle of the front page. *Money Magazine, Time* and *True* followed the lead with articles of their own. Even *Playboy* wrote about us in an article on countercyclical businesses—those that prosper most when the rest of the economy is struggling. Other countercyclical businesses included wood stove manufacturers, and companies dealing in survival and self-sufficiency products and services.

The magazine articles produced even more inquiries,

many addressed simply to Rainy Day, Provo, Utah. We almost had more business than we could handle, but I determined never to get too busy to respond to inquiries from potential customers, as the other companies had done to me when I first looked into the business.

There seemed to be no end to the ways we could sell food storage. We bought the mailing list for the *Inflation Survival Newsletter,* 70,000 names and addresses of people supposedly concerned about future economic trends. Only about one percent of the recipients responded, but the average food order was about $500. We netted hundreds of thousands of dollars on that one mailing. Since then we have tried many different mailing lists, and many have been as successful as that one.

In March of 1974 I convinced Ken and Dad that Nature's Way should move to Provo, too, and share facilities with Rainy Day Foods, which was rapidly becoming the tail that wagged the dog. Because of the exciting things happening with Rainy Day Foods that's where most of our attention was focused. It wasn't long until Rainy Day had over 100 employees working three shifts, and through lack of attention, Nature's Way sales declined and the production staff gradually dropped back to three or four employees.

Rainy Day didn't have the same cash flow problems that we had experienced with Nature's Way. Much of the Rainy Day business was done through the mail where we received cash with orders. The up-front revenue financed our growth so we didn't have to beg and borrow.

Rainy Day had its problems, though, and in the beginning, we made some very costly mistakes. Because we were a countercyclical business, our sales decreased as the national economy got stronger. We miscalculated the economic indicators more than once and were caught with huge inventories we couldn't sell. There were several times when we were forced, through our lack of foresight or forecasting ability, to lay off large numbers of employees almost overnight and sell inventories at or below cost in order to pay our bills.

After a few years we became more proficient at predicting the ups and downs in the national economy and calculating our sales in relation to national trends.

About the time we thought we knew all there was to

know about predicting food storage trends, Vaughn Featherstone, a general authority in the Mormon Church, gave a speech in the general conference of the Church, the fall of 1976, I believe, challenging every family in the Church to have a year's supply of food by the following April.

Many people interpreted Elder Featherstone's challenge as a subtle prophetic warning, that after April it would be too late to get food. There would be a famine, natural disaster, war or something else to interrupt and deplete normal food supplies.

Mormons started buying food storage items as never before. Many were buying thousands of dollars worth of food at a time. We experienced dramatic sales increases each month as the April deadline neared. We anticipated a steady build-up until April, then a gradual decline afterwards.

In April conference, nothing further was said about food storage. Rather than the gradual decline we had predicted, there was a sudden halt in sales to Mormons, and we were caught with a huge inventory which had to be liquidated at a considerable loss.

At that time we decided that even though food storage was a very profitable business, it was just too risky to be our primary source of income. We decided to diversify into something more stable, hopefully something on the other side of the economic cycle.

We considered many different businesses, but finally decided to try an idea related to our food storage business. We determined that there was a huge recreation market out there, individuals and families that go away for the weekend in motor homes, campers, boats and so on. We figured this week-ender market was concerned with weight and bulk because of limited space and carrying capacities of the recreational vehicles. We developed a compact, light-weight meal-in-a-can product. We called it the Weekender. The can contained little packets of dehydrated foods that could be cooked up into a meal for two. We developed labels, menus, cooking instructions—and spent a lot of money putting our new product on the market. It failed miserably. The consumers wouldn't buy dehydrated meals in a can. We swallowed our pride, liquidated our Weekenders at below cost and started looking for something else.

We took a closer look at Nature's way and the health food business, and suddenly realized that while we had been busy in the food storage business, we had neglected to note the dramatic changes occurring in the health food industry. When we first started selling herbs in Arizona in the late sixties, only two or three percent of the population was buying natural products. Now, in 1976, it was estimated that between 10 and 12 percent of the population was buying health foods. We noticed that some of the little backyard companies that had started out like we had, were now multi-million-dollar corporations. We had missed out on this growth potential by not paying attention to what was happening in the health food industry.

We didn't waste any time feeling bad about our lack of attention to Nature's Way. We decided to make up for lost time. The market was ripe and we sensed it was time to act—and fast. We understood the need for a large sum of operating capital to develop new health food products, and put them on the market. Thanks to Rainy Day, we had invested in some large buildings and had built up a nice equity in our buildings and land, so we had a valuable asset to use in raising operating capital. This time the lack of operating capital wouldn't hold us back.

We let the word out in Salt Lake City and Utah Valley that we were looking for a party to buy our buildings and lease them back to us. We met Doug Snarr, also featured in this book. Doug was an answer to prayer. His financial expertise was just what we needed at that time. Everything fit into place and he helped us put together a package deal with the Small Business Administration and Walker Bank for about a million dollars in cash to fund our plunge back into the health food business.

One of the first things we did with the money was to buy out Dad's interest in the business. He was approaching retirement age and felt ready to step down to pursue other interests. We learned a lot about entrepreneuring from Dad. He liked to run things by the seat of his pants. His philosophy was to work hard and take advantage of the breaks as they came. His optimism was endless.

We had already begun hiring more sophisticated managers for our various departments in an effort to upgrade our management expertise. Our success in attracting and keeping top key executives has been a major ingredient to our success. Hugo Boren is a prime example. He was an old high school friend in Mesa. We sang in a quartet together. He has an engineering and MBA degree and is our financial vice-president. I don't know how he could be more honest or loyal.

While we were busy with Rainy Day Foods, our product line in Nature's Way had gradually dropped to just 12 items, bringing in about $25,000 a month. After carefully analyzing the market, surveying health food stores, doctors and trade press writers to find out what products were selling, and in what approximate quantities, we decided that we would expand our product line to include several hundred items, and in the process increase our sales volume to several hundred thousand dollars a month.

After deciding where we wanted to go, we worked out a detailed plan for reaching our objectives. First, we contracted with some of the herb experts, including Dr. Christopher, to start developing new products. With the help of Keith Eddington, an artist referred to us by Doug Snarr, we redesigned all our labels and logos to give our company and products a more professional look. We leased about $500,000 worth of new equipment so we would be able to produce enough product as we reached our sales goals.

It might seem to an outsider that we were risking a lot of money when we hadn't yet proven that we could be a major manufacturer in the health food industry. We felt we had done our homework, though, and after six years of manufacturing herbal products we felt we had enough experience to predict the outcome of our efforts. We had established accounts with stores, we knew what they were selling and in what quantities, and we had enough experience in the business to know that we could produce what the public would buy. We were confident that we really had this one pegged right, that the health food business was blossoming, and that we were going to get a big piece of it. Once the decision was made, we pulled out all the stops and plunged in with both feet and a million dollars cash.

One of the first major changes we made was in distribution. Instead of selling directly to thousands of stores (about seven thousand health food stores in the

United States), we arranged to sell through major jobbers and brokers. This made our products immediately available to all the stores while decreasing our distribution and marketing overhead. The distributors take a 25 percent cut on everything they sell, but the increased sales volume more than makes up for the discount.

As soon as we had our new products packaged and into the distribution pipeline, we focused on an aggressive advertising campaign featuring display advertising in most of the major health food publications. We attended every major health food convention and sponsored retailer seminars.

Our most successful promotion, that helped get our large line of products into the stores, was introduced at a convention for retailers in Las Vegas in 1977. Earlier, when we realized that we just weren't getting enough shelf space in stores, we decided to develop a revolving display rack.

I flew to Southern California where I searched through the yellow pages for manufacturers of display racks. After many dead-end calls I finally found a company which had developed a razor blade display for Schick, and a record display for Disneyland. Those seemed like excellent credentials. I visited the factory and checked out their sample display racks. I spotted a brake shoe rack that was just the right size, and structurally sound enough to support and hold bottled herbs, with a few modifications. The changes were made on a prototype and we issued the purchase order for our first hundred Nature's Way Herb Center racks.

We displayed the new rack for the first time at the Las Vegas convention. Loaded with our products, the rack sold for about $500. To generate interest in the display, each of us wore a $100 bill on our lapel. We gave one of the $100 bills to each retailer who ordered a rack loaded with our products. The bills were the perfect come-on, and we sold over a hundred racks at that one convention. The campaign was off and running and sales boomed! We did the same thing again in 1978, 1979 and 1980. The $50 or $100 bill on the lapel was to become our trademark. Today the retailers come looking for us at the conventions to see how they can get one of the bills.

Our commitment paid off. In just one year we became the largest supplier of herb products to health food stores in the world. In the process we established our own advertising company, a multi-level direct sales company, and a separate line of herbal products for doctors. Today, we have a dozen companies, most of them related to the health food or food storage industries. Our latest acquisitions include a health food store in San Francisco and a line of herb teas.

Our diversification has made us stable. If one company slumps, another picks up the slack. If the whole economy dives into a slump, then the Rainy Day business booms. People talk about no-win situations. We feel like we are in a no-lose situation.

Ken and I are both very competitive. My earliest memories involve competing with Ken in various sporting events. We were always together, like twins. In fact, we both received our Eagle Scout awards on the same night. Today we play raquetball, run marathons and scuba dive together. We do not compete against each other in the running of the business, however, because we are both on the same team. My responsibilities fall mostly in the area of sales, marketing and administration, whereas Ken handles the more technical aspects of the business—production, legal matters, and liasons with trade organizations and associations. Of our four largest companies, I am president of Nature's Way and Rainy Day, and he's president of Naturalife and Health Products International.

We now are building a new 90,000 square-foot plant in the new Springville, Utah, industrial park. Our holding company is called Murdock International. We have hundreds of employees and sell products all over the world. Our manufacturing facility makes products under numerous labels including private labels for major national health food companies.

When it comes to problem solving, Ken is the methodical, perceptive, analytical type. I am more impulsive and optimistic, always wanting to push for a quick decision. I am generally more enthusiastic, less reserved, and more egotistical.

We are very frank and open with each other, and both of us are always in agreement when major decisions are made. If we can't agree, we don't do it. Both of us have learned to give and take. When I was first beginning my family and Ken was still single, I took more out of the business than he did. Later, when he married and needed more to get his family established, I reciprocated and let him get set up.

We get along so well that we have become partners in many non-business acquisitions—the motor home, the boat, the plane, the cabin and income property. We drive the same kind of car. If we weren't Mormons, we'd probably drink the same brand of beer.

Most important, both of us are goal-oriented individuals. We understand the importance of planning and sacrifice in reaching goals. There is no doubt in my mind, that if this company were taken from us, and we were left with nothing, that Ken and I could build an equally profitable company from scratch in just a few years—thanks to our mutual ability to set and achieve goals. I really believe that.

Wilburn McDougal—Salt Lake area real estate developer with over 40 successful subdivisions to his credit. Owner of McDougal Real Estate, one of Salt Lake City's largest real estate firms.

Wilburn McDougal

I was one of three Mormon boys in my first-grade class. The other children were told not to play with us because we were Mormons. My father was in the logging business at Three Lakes, northern Wisconsin. I was the oldest child, and as time passed, my parents had four more boys and two girls.

One day, my father and the three other partners in the company came home from work early and announced that they had sold the logging business and that we were moving to Utah. Within a few days, we were all ready to go. We sold our homes and most of our belongings. Between us we had four cars, one truck and 13 children. Everything we couldn't bring with us was sold, given away or just left behind. Our car was the oldest, a 1929 Model A Ford.

When we arrived in Utah, the families scattered in different directions, looking for work. My father couldn't find a job at first so my mother and the children went to Alberta, Canada, to stay with my mother's parents until my father found something to do.

My father finally found a job pumping gas at the Covey Gas and Oil Company in North Salt Lake. He purchased a home at approximately 900 South and 300 West and sent for us. I remember the bus ride back to Utah. There was a man smoking a cigar, and the smoke made me very sick. The bus had to stop a number of times to let me out to relieve my sickness. Since that time I have never had even the most remote desire to smoke.

The next summer my father purchased a slaughter house in Nephi, Utah, and we moved there. I started the second grade in Nephi.

That fall, 1946, there was a nation-wide polio epidemic. One afternoon while I was playing football and tag with my new friends, I began to experience a terrible pain throughout my entire body. My parents called the doctor, and the next day, when the pain didn't go away, it was determined that I might have polio. I remember how concerned my parents were. My father laid his hands on my head and administered to me. They drove me to the LDS Hospital in Salt Lake City. From there they sent me to the old General Hospital where it was confirmed that I indeed had polio. They told my parents that I would never walk again, and probably never be able to lead a normal life. The polio worsened, and soon I was almost totally paralyzed from the neck down. When my parents returned home, the entire family was quarantined for two full weeks.

Every Sunday my parents would come to visit me. I didn't have any other visitors. Often, my father would bring someone with him to help give me a blessing. The blessings always promised me that I would become whole and be able to live a normal, successful life.

I was still in the hospital at Christmas. My main present that season was an old electric train that my grandparents had given to one of my uncles when he was little. My parents fixed it up so it looked almost new and would run around a little circle of track. I loved that little train and spent many hours watching it go around and around.

During the afternoons, I listened to the radio. My favorite program was Uncle Remus telling Brer Rabbit stories. During the mornings, I received therapy.

After I had been in the hospital six months, the doctors said my polio was no longer contagious and that there was nothing else they could do for me. By this time I could use all the muscles in my body except those in the right leg. They fitted my leg in a full-length brace, gave me two crutches and sent me home.

My parents had sold the slaughter house and leased a

dairy farm in Murray, Utah. I loved to go out to the barn and watch my father work with the animals. Often he would let me ride on the equipment when he worked in the fields.

When school started, my parents met with the principal of the school to discuss my situation. It was decided that I should take the second grade over again. I think this was a blessing for me because it allowed me to begin the year a step ahead instead of a step behind the students in my class.

My classroom was on the second floor so I had to negotiate the staircase for recess, lunch and everything else. At one time they tried to switch me to a classroom on the main floor so I wouldn't have to use the stairs, but I insisted on staying with my class. I wanted to be like the other kids, and if they could handle the stairs, I was determined to do it, too.

One of my first goals was to be able to use one crutch instead of two. We lived about half a block from the school and on the way to and from school, I practiced using one crutch until I was able to throw the second one away. In the third grade I outgrew my crutch and my parents had to buy a new one.

During the early spring, my father let me ride on the leveler while he prepared the fields for planting. As I sat there watching the soft, plowed earth pass under me, I couldn't resist the temptation to push the end of my crutch between the leveler braces and into the loose soil. I guess I wanted to make my own little furrow. I pushed it in too far, the earth jerked it away from me and the leveler mangled it beyond repair. The crutch was never replaced.

With the passing of time, my father paid less and less attention to my disability. I was expected to milk cows, haul hay, pull weeds and do other chores the same as my brothers. I didn't receive any special consideration. I couldn't use my leg as an excuse to get out of work.

While I was in the third grade, my father purchased a farm in West Jordan, and over the years, built up a large dairy. Working side by side with my father, I grew very close to him. He was a religious man and worked very hard. By the time I was 12, I knew how to put in a full day's work.

My missionary fund, started by my Grandmother

McDougal, the day I was born, grew and grew as more pennies, nickels and dimes were added. There was never any question but that I would go on a mission for the Church as soon as I was old enough.

Our family was a missionary family. My father was one of the presidents of the Seventy's priesthood quorum in our stake. The quorum had a farm where crops were raised every year to help support part- and full-time missionaries.

I remember one spring how all the families gathered together on the farm early one Sunday morning just after the seed potatoes had been planted. As the sun peeked above the Wasatch Mountains, we blessed the soil and the crops so we would have a bounteous harvest for the missionary work. The entire family was involved in the project—planting, hoeing, watering and harvesting.

During the third grade, I became active in 4-H. My first project was a Duroc Jersey pig. I remember getting it ready for the fair, washing it in the old washtub, assisted by other family members. The next year, I entered a dairy project and continued with cows every year after that.

The 4-H participation taught me many valuable lessons—setting goals, record keeping, public speaking, demonstrating, dedication and followup. The 4-H motto was "Make the best better."

I had the opportunity to go to a 4-H congress in Chicago. Some of my friends brought cockleburrs along, which we traded and sold as porcupine eggs. I was also active in FFA and Boys State where I was elected a senator to represent Utah at Boys Nation in Washington, D.C. There, I had the opportunity to debate in the old Supreme Court room at the Capitol Building. After that experience my ambition was to become a lawyer with involvement in politics.

When I finished high school, I immediately enrolled in summer school at Brigham Young University, taking general education courses, anticipating that I would soon be ready to go on a mission.

When I was finally old enough to serve a mission, my father was bishop of our ward. I'll never forget the interview prior to sending the papers into Church headquarters. We had been working together in the barns and when it was time for the interview, we went into the house and changed into our suits, white shirts and ties. My father felt we needed to be appropriately dressed for such a special experience. We filled out the papers and my father asked many questions. It was the most thorough interview I have ever received, before or since.

After my father finished with me, I was interviewed by a general authority, Carl W. Buehner, who was in the Presiding Bishopric.

I waited for a week, expecting the official missionary call to come any day. It didn't come and I waited another week. It still didn't come, so my father called the missionary department to see what had happened. They told him they were not going to call me on a mission. It was my leg. They had had problems with other handicapped missionaries and didn't think I was suited for the rigorous activity of missionary work.

I discussed the situation with my father. It had never occurred to either one of us that I wouldn't be able to go on a mission. My grandmother had saved her nickels and dimes for so many years. How would she feel? If I could work side by side with my father and brothers—bucking bales of hay, shoveling manure, milking cows—wasn't I strong enough to do the Lord's work? Certainly missionary work couldn't be more physically demanding than farm work, or was it? We discussed these questions at length and finally decided that I ought to go back and talk to more of the general authorities of the Church.

First, I met with Alvin R. Dyer, who told me about some difficulties he had had with handicapped missionaries in the Central States Mission. Next, I met with Elder Delbert L. Stapley, who talked about the same kinds of things. Finally, I ended up with Elder Henry D. Moyle. After listening to what the other two general authorities had to say about me, President Moyle, asked me to walk across the room. I did so, trying to minimize my limp as much as possible. After watching me carefully, he said, "He can go."

After the meeting with President Moyle they consulted each other and decided that anyone as determined to serve the Lord as I was, ought to have the opportunity to do it.

One of them told me I ought to buy a cane to help me get around. Another suggested that if I was unable to keep up with the regular missionaries, I could probably be useful in the mission home—keeping books, answering the phone and those kinds of things.

I went home and waited for the call. Nothing came the first week, or the second week. I was beginning to worry that they had changed their minds. Finally, after about three weeks, I received a call to the Northwestern States Mission, the Oregon and Washington areas.

Whereas most young men are asked by the Church to serve missions, I had to beg for permission. I was determined not to disappoint any of those general authorities who reluctantly decided to let me go.

When I arrived in the field, I asked the mission president, Douglas Driggs, to let me be a proselyting missionary. I told him I didn't want to work in the mission home. He agreed to give me a chance. I had purchased a cane as the general authority had suggested, and faithfully tried to use it for three or four months. It was continually in the way, tripping me up, so I finally threw it away.

I spent the entire two years as a proselyting missionary, without having to work in the mission home a single day. Towards the end, I had the opportunity to serve as a supervising or traveling elder. Those were the days when the Northwestern States Mission was leading the Church in missionary converts. We had a lot of success as a mission, first under Douglas Driggs, then Franklin D. Richards, then Don Wood.

It was while working under President Richards that I decided on a career in real estate. He had a real estate background, and I admired him so much that I thought I would like to get into the same business.

At the very end of my mission, I was sent to Hood River, Oregon, to open that city for missionary work. We had closed the area earlier, and at first, I didn't think it was a very good area to re-open.

At the end of my first day in Hood River, I attended the local LDS ward M.I.A. meeting for the young people. We wanted to meet some of the members and see about getting a few referrals. I was sitting on the stand, waiting for the meeting to begin, when I noticed a young woman entering at the rear of the hall. She was talking to several of the girls, probably her students. There was something very special about her, and I suspected very strongly from that first moment, that she would become my future mate.

Later that night when we were visiting at the relief society president's home, the same young woman stopped by with some of the M.I.A. kids to say goodby to the relief society president's daughter, who was leaving for B.Y.U. the next day. I was introduced to Charlotte Kofford. She was single and was the Oregon State University extension agent, stationed in Hood River. She was on the faculty of the home economics department at the University.

The next Sunday, I met her again at another member's home where we were invited to dinner. After dinner, we had a chance to talk to each other. I was convinced that she was the one for me, and I think she felt the same way.

The following Tuesday, I flew home to Salt Lake City, my mission completed. A week later, she came down to general conference, and our courtship began.

Upon arriving home, I immediately enrolled at Brigham Young University and changed my major to business with an emphasis in finance and banking. I attended school during the summer, wanting to get through as soon as possible so I could afford to marry.

While in school, I decided to get a real estate license and get a head start in the business by selling a few properties. I studied the book, passed the test and became a part-time agent for Stan Katz Realty.

On the first day I worked for Stan, I obtained a listing to sell a home, then came back to the office and showed it to Stan. He told me of someone who might be interested. I called the party and was able to write up the sale that same day. I soon found out that listing and selling real estate is seldom that easy, but I have always been very proud that I was able to list and sell a piece of property my first day in the business.

During the next two years, I carried a full load in school, while selling real estate on the side. Charlotte remained in Oregon, so most of our courtship transpired through the mail. Whenever I had a three-day weekend, I would go up to Oregon to see her.

I remember the first time. As I left Provo and was driving towards Orem in my old Corvair, I began to figure the amount of gasoline I would need to get there and back home again. I quickly concluded that I didn't have enough money to buy the amount of gas needed. I pulled off to the side of State Street in Orem, locked the car, started hitchhiking, and was fortunate to get a ride almost immediately.

The Orem police noticed my car parked beside the road for a longer than normal period of time. They checked out the registration and called my parents, who became very concerned when they couldn't reach me. They had no idea why I might have left the car there. They were very relieved when I called from Oregon.

Other than the misunderstanding with the Orem police and my parents, the hitchhiking worked so well for me that I did it again and again, thumbing my way to Hood River and back at least a dozen times over the next two years.

Charlotte and I decided to get married at the end of my second year at Brigham Young University. Including the credit hours I had earned before my mission and during the summers, I was only nine hours short of graduation. We figured I could finish up after we were married.

In early May of 1963, just before school was out for the summer, my mother received a telephone call from Franklin D. Richards, my former mission president. He wanted to talk to me. When mother gave me the message, I became very excited, thinking he had heard that I had a real estate license and wanted to list one or two properties with me.

I called him the next morning. He asked if I could come to his office. I was there by 10 a.m., but instead of listing a piece of property, he offered me a job with the Richards-Woodbury Mortgage Corporation. He said he would like to teach me the mortgage business and help me make it a part of my life. We talked about it for several hours, then I went home and called Charlotte to see what she thought about it.

I accepted the job and started working part time while finishing out the school year. I went to school in the mornings and worked in the afternoons. I didn't like the idea of quitting college just a few hours short of graduation, but I figured I could pick up the remaining nine credit hours in correspondence or night school.

The starting salary wasn't very impressive, only $400 a month, but President Richards took me into the business like a son, teaching me everything he could. When Charlotte and I were married on June 6th, one month later, I received a full week of paid vacation so we could go on a honeymoon.

Charlotte and I didn't have any money when we were married. I had been unable to save because I had been going to school. I owed more on the old Corvair than it was worth. Charlotte had been earning about $800 a month as an extension agent, but her savings was mostly used for the wedding and moving to Utah. I remember asking my father for a $100 loan so we could go on the honeymoon. My grandparents and parents each gave us a $100 wedding gift which helped get us into our first apartment.

Upon returning home from the honeymoon, I became an assistant loan officer at the company. After a month, they made me a full-fledged loan officer with full responsibility for making loans. I made some mistakes, but they backed me up and continued to give me additional responsibilities, not only in residential financing, but in construction and land development. On evenings and weekends, I continued to use my real estate license, listing and selling an occasional piece of property.

After we had been married for six months, we decided to try to purchase our first home. I remember going in to sign the mortgage. We were borrowing $15,300 for 30 years. Our monthly payment was $116. I was really concerned as to whether or not we could make that large of a payment from my $400 a month salary, but we boldly went ahead and signed the note. We furnished the home with what we had, and hung sheets on the windows for a long time.

I became very close to my former mission president, and I would be ungrateful if I didn't attribute much of my later financial success to the lessons learned from Elder Richards. He ran his business exactly like he ran his mission. There was no double standard. In business and church work, the same standards applied. His motto was "Plan, simplify, and be strong."

After I had been with Richards-Woodbury about a year, I remember taking a Napoleon Hill course. There was one phrase that sank deep into my heart, one that I have never forgotten. It goes something like this, "Whatever the mind of man can conceive and believe, it can achieve."

The more I thought about that statement, and compared it with many of the things I had learned in the scriptures, the more I began to believe that I really could make it big in real estate. I wasn't exactly sure how I would do it yet, but I had that quiet assurance that if I was patient and learned all I could, someday I would be very successful.

Charlotte and I began buying old, run-down homes and fixing them up. We usually bought on contract with very low down payments. When the painting and repairing were completed, we put the homes back on the market at a higher price to reflect the improvements.

After I had been at Richards-Woodbury about three years, I decided to broaden my experience by accepting a job with American Savings in their loan department. I continued to list and sell property on the side and was beginning to build a good clientele.

One day, I was looking through a magazine and was attracted by an advertisement featuring a beautiful gold Cadillac. I wanted to have that car, but knew there was no way I could afford it. I was a firm believer in setting goals, however, so I cut out the picture of the Cadillac, mounted it in a frame and placed it on my desk at American Savings. The employees kidded me when I told them why the picture was on my desk. They knew as well as I did that I could never afford such a car on my salary.

Charlotte and I continued to fix up old houses. We didn't have any children so Charlotte was able to do a lot of the work. We wanted children right from the beginning, but Charlotte was unable to get pregnant. We spent several thousand dollars in doctor fees trying to correct the situation, but without any success.

On one occasion, we purchased an old run-down home near Liberty Park in Salt Lake City. One room was completely full of old newspapers. Another was full of nuts and bolts and old motorcycle and car parts. There was a dirt floor in the kitchen. The place was filthy.

We worked together in the evenings, and Charlotte did what she could during the day between substitute teaching assignments in the Jordan School District. One day she discovered that the kitchen really didn't have a dirt floor after all. Under four or five inches of filth, she discovered linoleum!

Suddenly, Charlotte became very ill. We thought she had picked up some germs at the old house, but the doctor diagnosed the problem as morning sickness. She was finally pregnant with our first child.

It is interesting to note, that as long as she was at home trying to become pregnant, it never happened. But as soon as she gave up on the idea and started working and teaching, it happened. Maybe it had something to do with being more relaxed. I don't know.

By this time, we had fixed up about a dozen old houses. We made a profit on all but one. It was after completing the single losing transaction, that I went down to the local Cadillac dealership and wrote out a check, in full, for the gold Cadillac. I was feeling a little discouraged, and buying that car, realizing my goal, made me feel a lot better. It was the best car I ever owned. No one teased me when I removed the picture from my desk.

As a loan officer, I was entitled to one personal loan. I decided to go for a big one, one that would get me started as a land developer. I located 30 acres in the South Jordan area that seemed ideal for developing into one-acre lots.

I didn't have any cash. All of our equity was tied up in the little house we were fixing up. Because of our weak cash position, I knew I would have to put together some very creative financing to make the thing work. I felt more than a little uneasy about tackling such a big project on my own.

I went to my father to see what he thought about the idea. He said, and I can still remember his exact words,

"Well, young man, you have prepared yourself. You feel good about it. What do you have to lose? You have a bright future, and if this doesn't work you can always begin again. You are not so far down the road that you can't start over. Go for it!"

With Charlotte's blessing and encouragement, I went back to American Savings and borrowed all they would allow on the property, then using the equity in our home, I arranged for some second and third mortgage money and was able to finance all of the purchase price.

I remember having mixed feelings that first day as the bulldozers began cutting the roads. It was a beautiful pasture. Having been raised on a farm, it was easier for me to visualize grazing cows than rows of new homes on the land. But our home was going to be there, too, and that made it easier.

Selling the lots was a positive experience. Since we were

going to be living there, we were selling to our future neighbors and friends. Of course, this also put a lot of pressure on us to do things right. We couldn't walk away from any mistakes. If we did something wrong, all our neighbors would know about it. Being close to it, you can't buy time for people to cool off and forget. You have to be very careful and call it like it is. We developed some good habits for future projects.

We had to watch the cash flow very carefully for the first two or three years. I became very good at juggling second, third and even sixth mortgage money in order to maintain a good credit rating and meet development expenses.

I learned that the Lord's counsel to Oliver Cowdery in the ninth section of the Doctrine and Covenants applies to business matters as well as to personal and religious matters. It reads as follows:

"...you must study it out in your mind; then you must ask me if it be right, and if it is right I will cause that your bosom shall burn within you; therefore you shall feel that it is right." (Doctrine & Covenants 9:8)

Whenever we found ourselves in a financial bind, or had a tough decision to make, we carefully explored all the alternatives, gathering all the available facts. We would make a decision, then go to the Lord in earnest prayer until we had a good, warm feeling about what we should do. It wasn't always easy, but it worked. Even though we had our backs against the wall, from time to time, we always knew we would be successful in the end.

When you develop land, you are changing the status quo. You are changing what people have become accustomed to. As a result there are plenty of critics who try to shoot you down—government agencies, neighboring land owners, news media and your competitors. A land developer has to have a cast-iron self-image, and a well-prepared game plan. He must be better prepared than all of his critics put together. Land developing, with its many rewards, is not a good business for those with timid spirits, faltering hearts or weak stomachs.

It is also important for the successful developer to have a brave spouse. When a big sale falls through, the typical reaction of the spouse is, "I knew you shouldn't have gotten into this. You can't make a living in real estate." These kinds of comments can be devastating.

Charlotte always had a different reaction when a big sale fell through, especially in those early years when every sale was so important. When I told her the bad news, she would respond with, "It's too bad it didn't work out, but look at all the good sales you have been able to hold together. You'll get another one soon. I'm not worried, we'll survive."

After this first subdivision was off and going well, I decided that it was about time I went back to school to pick up the nine hours I needed for graduation. I wanted to earn a law degree, too. It was early in the summer of 1967. I gave American Savings two weeks notice, telling them I was going to work in real estate during the summer, then return to school in the fall.

By the time classes started I had purchased and begun development of an 80-acre parcel in the West Jordan area, and just couldn't see my way clear to return to school. I developed 110 lots on that piece over the next seven or eight years, selling nearly all of them to the same builder. To date, our company has developed 30 or 40 pieces of land.

As I began developing land, occasionally a real estate person would like the way I worked and wanted to join me. With time, the listing and selling of property replaced development as our main business.

In the beginning, I worked out of our home, but as more and more people began to work with me, it became apparent that we needed an office. In 1969, we opened a big office up town, just like everybody else. It gave us a high-class image, and prestige in the community. Soon, we had about 20 salesmen working out of the office.

There was only one thing wrong. We weren't making any money. With Charlotte's encouragement, I swallowed my pride, admitted a big mistake, closed the big office and returned to a trailer house parked on the 80-acre development in West Jordan. Three of the salesmen came with me. We began to rebuild the organization, this time with more care and deliberation. Instead of placing an ad in the paper and hiring nearly everyone who responded, we focused our attention on sound individuals, some without previous real estate experience, who had good attitudes of success, and invited them to join us. Over the years, we have developed a sales force of about 70 individuals who sell enough property to make us one of the largest real estate companies in Utah in dollar volume. There are a number of companies with more agents, but not very many who do more business.

As head of the company, I try to be a catalyst to see that the work gets done. I firmly believe that the individual who does the work should get the credit or recognition. I don't think a real estate company, or any organization for that matter, can be very productive if recognition isn't freely given to those who deserve it. It is amazing how much you can accomplish when you're not reluctant to give credit where credit is due.

I try to surround myself with people who know more than I do about their particular area of responsibility. For example, Van Nielson manages the brokerage and Cyryl Simmons handles our land development. I know that when Si comes to me with a project with the accompanying facts and figures, that he has done his homework. He knows more about it than I do, and I trust his judgment, completely. He makes recommendations and I give him the OK to go ahead. I take pride in being able to make quick, bold decisions that don't have to be changed later. I credit the ability to do this to knowledgeable assistants who do their homework and make sound recommendations. Seldom do we have to reverse a decision.

In January of 1978, I began thinking again about the nine credit hours I lacked to graduate from college, and decided to return to BYU. Over the years, the graduation requirements had changed, and I now needed 21 credit hours to graduate. I changed my major to political science and signed up for a full-time study load.

I graduated on my birthday, 1978. As I stepped forward to receive my diploma, without the use of crutches or cane, I remembered my father's earnest blessings when I was stricken with polio—his promise that I would have a normal, successful life. His blessing had been realized beyond my greatest expectations.

Dave Campbell—inventor and manufacturer of the first widely used automatic potato sorter. President and owner of Cambelt International Corporation, a Salt Lake City-based firm specializing in materials handling and oil well support systems.

Dave Campbell

For as long as I can remember, I have been fascinated by machines. While my brother sat behind the old Monarch stove reading books, I was out in the garage building a miniature threshing machine or a water wheel.

My younger years were spent on a small farm outside the town of Rupert, Idaho. We had lived in the town, but our father felt a farm was a better place to raise his family. It provided us with plenty of work and kept us "off the street." Dad's work ethic was very basic: Work first, play later. If there was a Saturday afternoon Tarzan movie we wanted to see, we would spend Saturday morning cleaning the corral, weeding the garden, or cleaning ditches. Every reward came through the proper amount of effort. As I look back, I appreciate that early training.

Our father owned and managed a wholesale produce business which included warehouses throughout southern Idaho. We sorted, packaged and shipped potatoes, beans, and onions, purchased from local farmers.

Clancy (my brother) and I had a little produce business of our own. When the vegetables we had grown were ready, we would wash, sort and package them. Then Dad would take us to town and we would put the vegetables in our little wagon and sell them door to door.

As a teenager, I worked for my father on afternoons and

Saturdays. He was a firm believer in learning the business from the ground up. I started out sweeping floors, cleaning bags and other odd jobs. Eventually I was given experience in every phase of the business. I loved working for my father and had every expectation of spending my life in that business.

After high school, I attended Utah State University in Logan for two years. I took business courses that helped prepare me for my work in the produce industry.

After two years of college, the LDS Church called me to serve a mission in Great Britain. Some of my ancestors came from Scotland, and I was fortunate to be able to serve most of my mission there. I also had the opportunity of belonging to a singing group known as the Millenial Chorus, which performed before audiences in every major city in the British Isles. This was a thrilling experience.

Near the end of my mission, I received some disconcerting news from home. Someone sent me a newspaper clipping announcing the sale of my father's business to his brother. My father hadn't told me of the proposed sale and since the produce business had been my first love, news of the sale was difficult to take. I could understand my father's reasons for selling—he was getting on in years and the produce business was very demanding. After selling the company, he started a retail furniture business in Rupert.

When I returned home from my mission, I worked for a short while for my uncle. This kept me close to the produce business. One of the more fascinating aspects of the business for me was the amount of equipment involved in the sorting, cleaning, and packaging of the produce. One part of the business that my father had developed was the sizing and marketing of Idaho baking potatoes. The sizing was handled by crews of women who examined each potato individually and divided them into two-ounce weight variations (8 oz., 10 oz., 12 oz., etc.). This process was very slow and expensive.

I felt there should be a way to do this mechanically. I began toying with some ideas and was soon working on my first machine.

Working for my uncle was not the same as working with my father and I soon joined Dad in the furniture business. However, I continued to work on the automatic potato sizer.

While this was going on, I courted and married a beautiful, talented young lady by the name of Mary Elizabeth (Betsy) May. She was to become my friend, support, and counselor in the somewhat trying years ahead. Shortly after our marriage, I came home one evening, excited about a part of the sizing machine I had been working on. It was about the size of a mousetrap. I held it up to her and asked, "Isn't it beautiful?"

She asked what it was and I explained that it was the new balance beam for the automatic sizing machine I was building. This small part was to perform the crucial function of weighing each potato as it moved through the machine. It determined which electronic plunger would be activated to direct the potato into its proper bag. With the balance beams perfected, the rest of the machine could now be developed into what later became known as the "potato pinball machine." There was still much development to be done. Much of this work was done late at night after other responsibilities were taken care of. During this time, I served as a stake missionary, in the stake mission presidency and as a member of the stake sunday school superintendency. Time was at a premium.

I continued working with my father in the furniture business and enjoyed it very much. One thing bothered both of us. It seemed that many of the more successful furniture dealers were using what appeared to us to be unethical advertising and pricing policies. Unreasonable trade-in allowances were being made on used furniture without even examining it. This meant that the new furniture had to be priced too high to begin with. Mattress manufacturers would print any price you desired on their labels, regardless of the quality of the mattress, to make it look like you were giving bargain buys on bedroom sets, etc. This seemed dishonest to us. My father and I didn't like to do business this way. After talking it over for sometime, we decided to sell the company. Dad would retire and I would go back to school and study engineering with the intention of starting a manufacturing firm. This would get me back to my childhood dream of building machines.

It was a difficult move. Betsy and I had three children and expecting our fourth. We had very little financial support and a future full of many unknowns. We packed all of our belongings into a truck and headed for Salt Lake City and the University of Utah. I remember us singing on the way "The future's not ours to see, what will be, will be," a song made popular at the time by Doris Day.

We rented a home just below the University and I began my studies. I continued working on the sizing machine in the only room big enough—our living room. I worked at a furniture store after school. The money I received from that, along with money I had coming from the sale of some property in Idaho, was just enough to keep me in school and feed the family. It was difficult to find money enough to continue work on the sizing machine. My wife, recognizing my frustration, gave me four flange bearings for Christmas that year. She knew I needed them for the machine. As I unwrapped the package on Christmas morning, nothing could have made me happier. That was a memorable Christmas.

I had a brother-in-law living in Salt Lake City. His name was Doyle Green. He was the editor of the Church magazine, *The Improvement Era.* He was a wonderful man and seemed to have faith in my project. With his financial help I purchased a drill press, a vise, and some hand tools which were a great help to me.

I continued at the University of Utah for two years, taking the classes I felt I would need to help me in my chosen field. One of my favorite professors at the University was Dr. Jenikie. One day I invited him to our home to see my machine. His response was, "Goodness, you have your thesis for your doctorate right here and you're only a sophomore!" After seeing what work I had done and knowing what my plans were. Dr. Jenikie advised me to get what classes I needed, get out of school and get established in business.

After two years at the University, we purchased a new home in Taylorsville (southwest of Salt Lake) and I began to build the first full-size model of the automatic potato sizer. I worked on it in the basement of our home. It was necessary to use bolted construction since I couldn't have taken it out of the basement without disassembling it. While still developing the full-scale model, I received word that someone else had introduced a machine to size potatoes by weight, and that their first unit was already installed and operating in the little town of Morland, Idaho. Upon hearing this news I felt more than a little sick to think I had worked over eight years on this project only to have someone else beat me into the marketplace. Along with the disappointment, I felt very curious about this "intruder." I wondered how the man who had designed it had overcome all the problems that had challenged me for so long. I drove to Idaho, picked up my father and my brother Clancy, and drove to Morland to see this new innovation. To my amazement, I discovered that my machine, though not yet completed, was already superior to what we saw. I drove back to Salt Lake City intent on finishing the sizer and getting it on the market as soon as possible. Clancy, having tired of a dairy operation he had developed, offered to sell out and join me.

When the first unit was finished, we convinced the J.R. Simplot Company (Idaho's largest potato packer) to lease the unit on a trial basis. They were also trying the one we saw in Morland, Idaho, and were about to make a decision on which one they wanted to buy. After disassembling the unit, taking it out of the basement and re-assembling it at the J.R. Simplot Plant in Heyburn, Idaho, the test period began. After several weeks of great anxiety, we were informed that our machine had been selected. We received a check for $450.00 for the first month's lease. After eight years, that was the first money to be realized from our efforts. I still have the stub of that check.

That winter, we built and sold ten Camweigh Sizers (the name we had selected for our new product) all going into southern Idaho. We didn't have any financing for our manufacturing endeavor, so we asked for one-third of the money down before we would begin work on a machine. That down payment was enough to buy all the materials. We asked for another third when the machine was finished. That covered most of our labor and delivery costs. We received the final third after the machine was installed and working properly.

I trembled whenever the phone rang, especially if it rang in the middle of the night. More often than not it was some irate potato processor wanting to know what was the matter with his machine, and how soon I could come up to fix it. I spent many nights on the road going up to Idaho to work out the bugs in those first machines.

One night, I was working on a problem machine, adjusting one thing and fixing something else, when the young man who was looking over my shoulder suggested that they ought to make the guys who design the machines come up and fix them. I smiled in agreement, but didn't say anything.

Clancy became the sales manager, and I handled production and engineering. We drove all over Idaho, Washington, Oregon and even back east, selling Camweigh Sizers. We had a station wagon. One of us drove while the other slept. We drove at night and sold during the day. In four or five years we had saturated the market with our machine. They were without doubt the best on the market and every major potato processor wanted one. But soon everybody that needed one, had one, and we had to start looking for something else to do.

We had rented a building on Redwood Road west of Salt Lake City, hired some employees, and if we were going to be able to maintain our overhead, we had to find something else to manufacture. I started a research and development program investigating various product alternatives.

One day a fellow came in and explained some of the problems he was having conveying prilled fertilizer. He said that he, and everyone else in the fertilizer industry, desperately needed conveyor systems with steeper inclines and larger carrying capacities.

I didn't have any idea how we would do it, but I told him I thought we could develop a better conveyor for him. I immediately went to work building prototypes and testing them on fertilizer products. After several weeks and much testing, I began to realize that I had taken on a tough problem for which there didn't seem to be an easy solution.

Then one Friday night as I was driving back from a fertilizer plant in Idaho where I had been testing one of our unsuccessful prototypes, I got to thinking that if there was just some way to hold the fertilizer onto the belt on high inclines, our problem would be solved. I remembered a material called scrubber rubber which we wrapped on rollers in the hopper of the potato sizing machine. It was a four-inch-wide rubber belt covered with numerous half inch nubs. It allowed the potatoes to roll around very gently without getting bruised.

I thought that if that material was attached to a high incline conveyor belt, perhaps it would prevent fertilizer from falling back. By the time I got home, I was very excited about the idea.

The next morning, Saturday, I went down to the shop and built a little conveyor system about two feet high, and used scrubber rubber as the belt. In order to save time I put a hand crank instead of a motor on it. I built a little bin at the bottom and dumped in some fertilizer. Just as I had hoped, the nubs held the fertilizer in the belt as it moved up the high incline.

On the following Monday I demonstrated my new idea to the rest of the organization. They agreed that the principle was sound. It was all so simple, and was the beginning of what was to become known as the CamBelt Conveyor. We laminated the scrubber rubber onto a 12-inch belt and installed it onto the back of a fertilizer truck. It worked beautifully.

It wasn't long until Clancy was on the road calling on potential customers for our new product. Our biggest problem was getting the scrubber rubber to stick to the conveyor belts. After experimenting with every possible laminating technique, we decided to design our own belt with the nubs built right into it. There would be no gluing or laminating. It was expensive and took a long time to make the molds, but the end product was worth it. We were fortunate to get a very tight patent on our new product.

We sold the system all over the intermountain area, not just to fertilizer plants, but to all kinds of businesses handling pelleted or powdered materials. The Link-Belt Corporation, the General Motors of the material handling industry, heard what we were doing and invited us back to Chicago to discuss the idea of selling our patent to them for a sizable down payment and future royalties on CamBelt sales. At first the idea sounded good to us, but as we thought about it, we became worried that a big company like that, carrying competing products, might shelve our product and we would never see any royalties. We decided not to sell to them.

About the same time, we gave our conveyor presentation to a company by the name of Eimco, who had expressed interest in buying a number of conveyors. At the end of the meeting I asked the engineer, who had invited us, who the fellow in the back corner was, the one who had asked all the bright questions. He said that was Mr. Shepman, the president of the company. We received an invitation to meet Mr. Shepman in his office the following week.

When we entered his office, he came right to the point and said he didn't just want to buy a few conveyors. He wanted to buy worldwide manufacturing rights for our conveyor system.

After about six months of negotiating, we entered into an agreement with Eimco. They gave us a cash down payment and agreed to pay us a royalty on all our conveyor systems that they would sell throughout the world. We thought we had the world by the tail. It was 1965.

We continued to manufacture conveyor systems for Eimco for several months until they were tooled up to do it themselves. Rather than shut our plant down, we started doing job shop work. We also built conventional conveyor systems, but it was hard to make a profit because of the intense competition.

I decided to develop a new product. I had a hunch that powdered, pelletized or pulverized materials, if moved along a system fast enough, could be handled as a dry fluid material. If my hunch was correct, it would be possible to develop a high-speed conveyor system with high capacity and the ability to carry material vertically. Such a system could also be patented and the market would be tremendous.

In 1969, four years later, I had developed the basis for the new system. There was nothing like it on the market. I felt it was bound to revolutionize the high-volume conveyor market.

In the meantime, Eimco had done very little with my earlier product. The royalty checks had been very small. They knew it was a good product, but they just didn't have the materials handling know-how to get it going.

I called the president of Eimco and told him I was going to come out with a competing conveyor system.

The first thing I knew, Eimco was trying to buy the rights to the new patent. I wasn't interested in selling, considering their poor performance with the first one. But, this time they added a new twist. They wanted my staff and me to take over the manufacturing of both products. That didn't sound so bad, and we soon reached an agreement wherein Eimco purchased the assets of Campbell Manufacturing, Inc. (my company) and we took over the management of the CamBelt Division of Eimco.

We immediately launched a crash program to complete the new system and work the bugs out of the old system. Within six months, we were selling enough conveyor systems to put the division in the black, and profits continued to grow. Everybody seemed happy with the agreement.

Five years later, in 1974, Envirotech, the company that owned Eimco, suffered a serious financial crunch. They were growing rapidly and were having difficulty raising operating capital. They decided to sell all divisions outside their regular line of filtration equipment, including Cam-Belt, in order to generate immediate cash flow. I tried to discourage them from selling the CamBelt Division, knowing the great potential we had. However, they felt the decision had been made, and they had no other choice.

I exercised a clause in our contract giving us first rights at buying the division, and bought it back. We named it Cambelt International Corporation. That was in 1975, and we have been growing at an average yearly rate of about 75% per year since that time.

Since forming Cambelt International Corp., we have developed several new product lines. Not all of these developments have been in the area of materials handling. We are now heavily involved in oil well support equipment. Our market area has also been extended. Our products can now be found throughout the western hemisphere as well as in Europe. The most satisfying accomplishment for me is the organization we have developed. It is the finest I have ever been associated with. I like to think we are a people-oriented company. The best products in the world will not make you successful without good people to sell, engineer and build them.

Even though I enjoyed working for Eimco, I am glad that we broke away. We now have a lot more flexibility, not just in business matters, but in personal matters as they relate to the business. I believe in God and believe he can help determine the outcome of business endeavors. Whenever we have board meetings, or employee meetings, we pray for guidance and help. Only those employees or board members who have expressed a willingness to do so, are called on to voice the prayers.

Tied in with my faith in God, is a strong commitment to the family. I have discouraged overtime and Saturday work. Those are times to be spent with the family, rather than on business. I am especially adamant about not working on Sunday. If someone feels they must work on Sunday, they have to look for employment elsewhere.

I suppose there are those who would accuse me of trying to force my religion on my employees. That is not my intention. Some of our best employees have religious beliefs different than mine. On the other hand, I believe that the Lord does not want his children working on Sundays, and as long as I am responsible for the work that is done in my business, I will see that that work is not done on Sunday. One of the advantages of owning your own busines, I suppose, is being able to establish policies in accordance with your own convictions.

I enjoy my work, the challenge it gives, and the associations I have because of it. Our philosophy has been to build on the strength of new ideas. We have been fairly successful in doing this. Because of this approach, I have had many people come to me with ideas of their own. Typically, they say, "I have a good idea and someday I'm going to do something about it." Quite often the idea is a good one, but "someday" never comes. Most people don't have the faith, the determination or the vision to roll up their sleeves, go to work, and do what is necessary to make the idea a reality.

I suppose fear of failure is the big thing holding most people back. One of the best ways to overcome fear is through preparation, finding out everything possible about the product, competing products, markets, etc. Thorough preparation can overcome fear.

As I look back on the past, knowing what I know now, I wonder if I would have the courage to try it again. It wasn't easy and there were times of great disappointment and doubt. Yet these were the times that made the successes so enjoyable. The lessons my father taught me still hold true. First comes the effort, then the reward. There is much to be done in our industry. New ideas to be developed, new machines to be designed, and new markets to be found. The challenge is more exciting than the reward.

Jim Burr—founder and owner of Rocky Mountain Helicopter, third largest helicopter flying service in the United States.

Jim Burr

I grew up in Moab in the southeastern desert of Utah, one of the few communities in Utah where Mormons are in the minority, during the uranium boom of the 1950's. As the rough and ready element associated with uranium prospecting moved in, I became fascinated with the airplanes they brought with them. By the hour, I watched them take off and land, and developed a burning desire to someday learn to fly.

While participating in high school sports, I developed another ambition, to play football for Brigham Young University. My older brother had played for BYU, and I wanted to follow in his footsteps. The BYU coaches didn't recruit me, however, so I accepted a football scholarship at the University of Utah in Salt Lake City. I wasn't very happy there, especially after wanting to go to BYU for so many years. The U just didn't seem like the right place for me. After the first year, I dropped out and went to work in California as a salesman for a printing and publishing company.

One year later, in 1959, I enrolled at Brigham Young University to study business management, having reluctantly given up my ambition to be a college football player. With the little extra money I managed to save from a part-time job, I began taking flying lessons—an hour here and an hour there, whenever I could break away from my studies and had enough money to rent the Cessna 120 at the Provo airport. The rental price was $11.00 per hour.

During the course of my business management studies, I took a marketing class from Dr. Clinton Oaks. One of the assignments was to complete a marketing research project. Because of my intense interest in aviation, I decided to research the need for an additional helicopter service in the intermountain states. I recruited several classmates to work with me on the project.

We identified what we thought would be all the potential users of a helicopter service—mining companies, oil exploration firms, government agencies, and utility companies. We sent out detailed questionnaires asking them what their anticipated future demands for helicopter services were, how they used helicopter services, what they paid for the service, their criteria in selecting a helicopter service, etc.

We tabulated the results, ran them through a computer, entered in the element of bias and other considerations that could color the results of such a survey. I thought we did a pretty good job, but when Dr. Oaks saw how one-sided the results were in showing a need for an additional helicopter service, he figured we had somehow biased the conclusions. I went back over our qestionnaire, double-checked the tabulations, and couldn't see where we had done anything to bias the conclusions. I concluded that there was indeed a healthy and immediate demand for additional helicopter services in the intermountain area. I decided I was going to get into the helicopter business.

At that point, I had never been close to a helicopter, except for a brief ride over the San Francisco Bay when I toured the Hiller helicopter factory during the year I worked in California. I didn't know the first thing about flying or servicing helicopters. But I knew they were magnificent machines with a lot of potential. In addition to forward flight, they could fly up, down, backwards, sideways, and hover motionless in flight. They could lift heavy loads, and carry men and supplies to seemingly inaccessible areas where conventional aircraft could not land. I knew that a large portion of this country's undeveloped mineral wealth was in the intermountain area, and, to a large degree, in areas inaccessible by roads.

I convinced my older brother, Bob, to be my partner in the helicopter venture. He had a successful repair shop in Moab where he serviced trucks and mining equipment. He caught the vision of what I wanted to do. He sold his business and moved to Provo, bringing with him, $20,000 from the sale of his business, and a pickup truck.

I borrowed $15,000 against my wife's life insurance policy to bring our total investment capital to $35,000. We went to Los Angeles and made a down payment on a used helicopter.

We had a tough time financing the machine. I spent two weeks visiting Utah banks, making presentations, explaining the need for a helicopter service. It is not easy to borrow money when you need it, when you have to have it. But worst of all, none of the Utah banks I talked to, believed in "hee-locopters."

Finally, I contacted the manager of one of the Bank of America branches in Santa Monica, California. He was a member of the LDS ward I had attended while living and working there a year earlier. I explained that we were putting up a substantial down payment, that the aircraft was insured, that the helicopter itself would be the collateral for the loan. I showed him the results of my study, indicating a need for an additional helicopter service.

After listening to everything I had to say, he told me how he had once taken a chance on a fellow by the name of Bill Lear, and how Lear Industries, over the years, had been one of the bank's best customers. He said he was going to take a chance on me, too, that he would give me the money for the helicopter. I promised him he wouldn't regret his decision.

Bob and I didn't know the first thing about our helicopter, we couldn't fly it or fix it. We loaded it on a truck and brought it back to Provo and parked it at the airport. I began contacting the people who had responded to the survey. It didn't take long until I had put together a contract with the National Park Service in Zion's National Park. They had a problem with sheep encroaching from the east, across the park boundary. They wanted to build a fence to keep the sheep out. The area was inaccessible by road, so they needed a helicopter to haul in the fencing materials.

The first thing we needed was a pilot. I called the fellow
who had sold us the helicopter and asked him who we could
get to fly for us. Back in those days there were not many
helicopter pilots around. The Vietnam war was still in the
future, and the Korean war had been over for a number of
years. He said he knew one guy who might be available. I
asked for the man's qualifications. He said, "Well, he writes
real neat." I'm serious, that's all he could say about the
pilot.

I couldn't find any other pilots, so I called the "neat
writer" and he agreed to come out and do the flying for us at
Zion's National Park. We arranged to meet the pilot and the
Park Service people with their fencing materials at
Hurricane, Utah. I was still in school, so Bob agreed to take
the machine to Hurricane. We loaded it back on the trailer.
The helicopter had wheels under the landing skids, making
it relatively easy for us to push it up the ramp onto the
trailer.

About two hours after Bob had left, I noticed that we had
forgotten to load the ramp. I hoped Bob would be able to
find a suitable replacement in Hurricane so he wouldn't
have to come all the way back to Provo.

When Bob arrived at the job site and it was discovered
that the ramp was missing, everybody started trying to
figure out how to get the helicopter off the trailer.

"No problem," said the pilot. "You don't need a ramp. I
can fly it off."

They put the blades on, gassed it up, and got it ready to
fly. The pilot climbed in and started the engine. Just as he
was starting to lift off, one of the skids hooked on a bolt in
the trailer bed. The helicopter flipped on its side. Bob ran
over and pulled the pilot out as the machine started to burn.
The pilot escaped without a scratch, but the helicopter was
reduced to a heap of smoldering ashes.

Bob went to the nearest phone and called me, saying,
"Jim, you have just experienced the shortest existence of a
helicopter company you'll ever see in your life. We just
crashed."

My whole world crashed, too. I couldn't have been more
shocked, disappointed, or hurt. The agony was unreal.

Fortunately we had purchased insurance. Even though
the insurance company was based in California, the

adjuster happened to be in Page, Arizona, at the time. He was at the crash site within a few hours of the accident.

That afternoon, I received a call from the purchasing agent for the Park Service. He said he was terribly sorry about the accident, but wanted to know what we were going to do about our contract to haul their fencing materials.

We called the insurance company, who in the meantime had received verification from the adjuster that the aircraft was totaled, and they informed us we could pick up the insurance check, Monday morning.

Needless to say, our California banker was shocked when we walked into his office the next Monday to pay off the helicopter note. We told him what had happened, and that we wanted him to loan us the money to buy a second helicopter. He agreed to do it, and within a few days we were back in business.

We trucked the new helicopter to Hurricane, and using the same pilot, finished the fencing job for the Park Service. While Bob stayed with the helicopter to make sure it was serviced, and that the work was completed, I went to work trying to round up more business.

We landed contracts with the Idaho Fish and Game Department to count elk and deer, the U.S. Forest Service to scout forest fires and haul in men and equipment, Mountain Bell, Kennecott Copper, Utah Power and Light, mining exploration companies, and even department stores who hired us to haul in Santa Clauses for special promotions. We would do almost anything to keep our helicopter flying.

I made countless presentations, telling people what our machine could do, how it could save them time and money. When they complained about the hourly charge, I told them they had no idea what a helicopter could accomplish in an hour.

With time, our incessant selling paid off, and we were able to keep busy during the summer and fall months. To keep us busy in the spring, we developed a program to spray sagebrush, mostly for large ranchers. Sagebrush and grass don't grow together, so by killing the sagebrush, we could help the ranchers grow more grass for their livestock. Helicopters were excellent for this purpose because the downward thrust of air from the rotor blades pushed the spray down into the brush instead of just laying it on top like conventional crop-dusting airplanes. In addition, a helicopter could come right to the job site to load and mix the spray. Sometimes, airstrips were as far as 50 miles away, making dusting with airplanes impractical.

After the sagebrush work finished in May, we were usually booked through June and July with forest fire contracts. I remember Junes when it rained 25 or more days. When it rained, there was no fire danger, so we didn't fly, and didn't make any money.

Sometimes, our financial situation was almost bad enough to pull us under. I remember driving to Ogden one afternoon with my wife, to a bid opening. Our bid was sitting on the seat between us. We desperately needed the contract if we were to remain in business. There were 15 or 20 companies competing for the job. The lowest bid would get the contract.

As we were driving along, my wife said, "I really feel strongly that we should change the bid." I had been very careful in preparing it and didn't figure we could go any lower, but we stopped in at a little restaurant for a hamburger, went through the figures one more time, and lowered the hourly helicopter rate, $1.30. I initialed the change and put it back in the envelope. When the bids were all tabulated, we were the successful bidder by 10¢!

There are those, I suppose, who would credit such a fortunate break to luck. I am convinced it was an answer to prayers, that the Lord had heard our earnest prayers and was giving us a hand when we really needed it.

It seemed we were having continual problems with pilots. They were generally an itinerate bunch of people. There was a lot of turnover, and frequently, there were differences of opinion as to what a helicopter could and could not do. It was pretty hard for me to win an argument with a pilot when I had never flown, myself. I was tired of pilots telling me they couldn't or wouldn't do something. I always wondered if they were giving me the straight story, or just pulling my leg.

I decided the only solution to the problem was to learn to fly, myself. I hired a pilot with an instructor's license and began to take lessons. After I had logged 25 hours of dual instruction flight, the pilot quit. Before we could find a replacement, Utah Power and Light called with an urgent request for us to set some power poles for them in rugged Price Canyon, about 50 miles east of Provo.

We decided to give it a try, with me flying and Bob walking from hole to hole, guiding the poles into the holes. It's impossible for anyone besides a helicopter pilot to appreciate the skill, timing and precision flying required to complete such a task, and me with only 25 hours of flying time! It is comparable to someone attempting brain surgery after completing a Red Cross first aid course. It is nothing short of a miracle that we accomplished the job without an accident.

I continued flying on other jobs until I could do all the kinds of flying required of helicopter pilots. I was the pilot and Bob was the mechanic. We were on the road continually, sleeping in Forest Service fire camps and motels. I remember one year, when I was figuring expenses, that I had accumulated 310 hotel receipts for the year.

By 1962, our business was solid and growing. We bought another helicopter and hired a pilot. Soon we had more helicopters, pilots and mechanics. All the work, education, begging and pleading was beginning to pay off.

I found a lot of satisfaction in the business. I remember flying out of Stanley, Idaho, one stormy night to rescue the survivor of a plane crash and bring him back to civilization. It really felt good to know I was helping to save a life.

In 1964 we bought Provo Flying Service. We bought and sold airplanes, provided service and gasoline, and offered flight instruction. It was great to have our own hangar at last, where we could work on our machines and store parts. Eventually, we were running about 10 helicopters and a dozen airplanes. We expanded to the Salt Lake airport, buying Thompson Flying Service. We became a large retailer of aviation fuel.

We arranged a line of credit with Walker Bank in Salt Lake City, paid off the Bank of America in California. Next, we expanded into a little community airline, called Air Utah. We flew out of Salt Lake City into Jackson Hole, Sun Valley and other locations in neighboring states. We expanded our helicopter and airplane services with fixed-base operations in Jackson Hole, West Yellowstone, Durango (Colorado), and even Alaska.

We called the company, Interwest Corporation. It included Mountainwest Helicopters, Skychoppers, Thompson Flying Service, Air Utah, Jackson Hole Aviation, Big Sky Aviation, and Tundracopters.

We gradually realized that our company was growing faster than our cash flow. We were in desperate need of additional operating capital. We found some investors who were willing to put money into the business in exchange for part ownership.

By the time the investment deal was put together and finalized, in 1969, Bob and I ended up with less than 50 percent. Suddenly, I found I didn't have any more say in the company I had worked so hard to buld. In less than a year, I was on the outside. They fired me!

I had $600 in the bank, a large mortgage on my home, and my Bank Americard. That's all I had after working hard for ten years to build the business.

That Thanksgiving as I contemplated my future, I figured there were two options open to me. I could forget about aviation and do something else, or I could pick up the pieces and start over. I knew more about helicopters than anything else, and I liked the idea of being a thorn in the side of the people who had taken away my company. I figured I still knew more about the helicopter business than they did, and I liked the idea of competing with them, taking business away from them, making them fight for every contract. Yes, I would start all over again in the helicopter business. And I was determined that this time I wouldn't take in investors—not ever!

I couldn't afford an airplane ticket, so I drove my Volkswagon to Los Angeles to find a helicopter. I located an old friend, Bob Shultz, a wealthy fellow who was in the business of buying, selling, leasing and trading helicopters. It was kind of a hobby with him.

I explained my situation, that I didn't have any money, but that if he would let me take a helicopter, I would drum up some business and start making payments. I had dealt with Bob a number of times over the years, and he trusted me. He agreed to give it to me on my word.

I immediately went to Idaho and landed a contract with the Idaho Fish and Game Department counting deer and elk. Within a short time I was making payments on the machine. Later, in the spring, my brother Bob joined up with me again. We rented a shed at the mouth of Provo Canyon, just behind where Osmond Studios are located today. That was our base of operations, where we stored and serviced the helicopter. I flew and Bob serviced, just like in the early days with the other company. This time we were determined not to get involved in anything other than helicopters. It was 1970 and we called the new company Rocky Mountain Helicopters.

Today we operate 65 helicopters and employ about 300 people with an annual payroll of $5 million on gross receipts of $25 million. We're the fourth largest helicopter company in the United States. We've been in Peru, Costa Rica, Libya, Saudi Arabia, and the Sudan. We have hospital-based contracts from Florida to California. We are the largest company in the world for providing emergency helicopter service for medical facilities. We handle more seismic operations than anyone in the world, carrying men and equipment to remote areas for oil and mineral exploration. Much of that work is in the overthrust belt here in Utah, Wyoming and Idaho.

In 1978 we had the satisfaction of buying back our first helicopter business from the people who had taken it away from us. We like to think the competition from Rocky Mountain Helicopters was too tough for them.

If I had to list the reasons for our success, I would list an undeniable determination to succeed, a lot of hard work, including long hours and much travel, giving more than a fair share of service for the monies received, a little bit of luck and the help of a loving Father in Heaven.

I think one of the key ingredients for any man to succeed, is to have the support of his wife and family. Any man who denies that, is either a liar, or too dumb to recognize the truth. A man needs that castle where he is loved, not threatened. With that base firmly in place, he can venture forth to battle the dragons, knowing all is well at home. Over the years, especially when times were hard, my wife never faltered in believing in me and my helicopters.

Today, as I travel around the Intermountain West, there is hardly a valley I pass through where we haven't sprayed to make it more productive. It is rare that I pass a mountain peak where we haven't helped build a relay station or put out a forest fire. When I see the lights of a city at night, I know that we helped with the power lines that provide the electricity. I see hospitals that have been able to save more lives because of the rapid emergency service provided by our helicopters. I see oil wells and silver mines that were located with the help of our helicopters. I watch movies that were made with the help of our helicopters. And when I read the threatening headlines about the instability of the Middle East oil-producing countries, I feel good knowing my helicopters are helping develop petroleum resources in the Intermountain area.

For the future, I see an increased demand in nearly every area of our business, especially on the international scene where third-world countries are beginning to develop their natural resources.

I never succeeded in my ambition to play football for Brigham Young University, but my ambition to fly has been realized far beyond my childhood dreams and expectations.